Islam and Christian Theology

A Study of the Interpretation of Theological Ideas in the Two Religions

Part One – Volume I

Preparatory Historical Survey of the Early Period

J. Windrow Sweetman

©
James Clarke & Co., Ltd
Cambridge

Published by
James Clarke Co., Ltd
P.O. Box 60
Cambridge
CB1 2NT
England

e-mail: **publishing@jamesclarke.co.uk**
website: **http://www.jamesclarke.co.uk**

ISBN 0 227 17198 5 hardback
ISBN 0 227 17197 7 paperback

British Library Cataloguing in Publication Data:
A catalogue record is available from the British Library.

First published 1945 by The Lutterworth Press
Reprinted 2002

DEDICATED

IN AFFECTION AND ESTEEM

TO

CHARLES PHILLIPS CAPE

WHO INSPIRED MY FIRST
VENTURES IN THIS TASK

FOREWORD

Why add another book on the subject of Comparative Religion? Is it any use setting Christianity in comparison with other religions? Religion as an anthropological phenomenon is not accepted by the author of this book as the criterion of judgment. To one who conceives that a Word of God has been uttered in speech and act, whereby religion may become true worship and not a soul-destroying opiate, it may seem useless to embark on any comparative study such as we present here. Why compare light and darkness?

Such objections we readily admit, but still persist in offering this thesis. We would point out in the first place that our title is "Islam and Christian Theology". In this we have used the word theology in its strictest sense as the Word of God, though from time to time in the course of this work it will be impossible to avoid using it in its secondary signification as systematic doctrine. Christianity has the human custody of the Word of God. Within itself the essential nature of that Word has been subjected to the profoundest and most fruitful scrutiny. It has had to exercise an interpretative function, and has done so under the ever-present guidance of the Spirit of Truth. But outside Christianity, if we exclude the Jews, who have not yet entered into the fullness of their own heritage, there is presented in Islam a counter-interpretation which is significant for Christian theology. This cannot be ignored by any one, much less by those who believe that God is speaking His Word in Christ to every follower of Islam. The Muslim thinks that the Christian holds many superstitions. He does not know how the Christian thinks the message of Islam affects the fundamental Word of God to man. If his point of view is presented in a serious way, and shown in parallel to the progress of the human exposition within the Christian fold, the Muslim may perchance find the final statement more intelligible to him and relevant to the needs of his heart and soul when it cries out for the Living God. It is in the hope that the evangel may become the power of God unto salvation to the Muslim that this book has been written.

The present position is, that in hardly a single book written by a Muslim have we seen a correct appreciation of the theological position of the Christian. The gravest philosophers attack as Christian doctrine beliefs which Christians themselves repudiate. Sometimes a Muslim writer will confess himself puzzled, and say, as an able Lucknow scholar said after revealing a complete misunderstanding of the Incarnation, "If Christians mean something different from what I have stated, let them put it before us in an intelligible manner, so that we may be able to form a correct judgment on it". This also points to the inadequacy of the statement of Christian doctrine in languages spoken by Muslims. We have been great writers of tracts, but where are the standard works on Christian doctrine ? Even in the translation of the Scripture into Arabic and Urdu, in spite of the general excellence of the work done, mistakes are to be found which must be a stumbling block and which could have been avoided with a deeper knowledge of Islamic theological usage not to speak of studied accuracy in the statement of Christian truth.

Moreover, we find that the Muslim is compelled to criticize what is in his hands, which is often of the crudest description, and that, on the other hand, the Christian concludes that Muslim dogmatics are so crude as to be almost negligible. "We know not what each other says." How then can we meet ? What common language can we use ? How shall we ensure that there is a reasonable probability of our being intelligible when we address a theological message to Islam ? An aged Muslim friend said to the writer, "Until the theologians of both religions come together and speak with a common tongue, we must always be estranged ". These are practical points which have spurred the writer to write. He seeks to be a link though probably as a link he will have to take the strain on both sides.

Throughout, there has been no attempt to cultivate that neutrality which some call "objectivity", but the writer has tried to avoid cheap retorts and mere debating points. He feels that if people were to read this book without knowing that he believed in Christ it would be a tragedy. Muslims themselves are forthright in their confession of faith, and will honour one who makes his own confession, even when they do not agree with it. Thus it is hoped that there will be no suggestion in this book of the impartiality of one who has not made up his mind. On the other hand, the writer hopes he has been fair when he has had to state tenets in which he has no belief. Less would be ingratitude to many Muslims, from whom he has learned much. In most cases he has allowed the statements to stand in the words of those who subscribe to the beliefs.

A confession of the inadequacies of both writer and material presented is made with no false modesty. No one is more conscious than the author that a much better book could have been written. A better book would have had to be much longer and written by one better equipped in Oriental languages, in philosophy and in Christian theology. When theologians read what is written and feel that all the points have been gone into before *ad nauseam*, the plea of the author is that some things have been presented in a new context and some perhaps rescued from the dusty tomes of the study to turn to purpose in a living world which, maybe, the West has outgrown. Others may consider that liberal Islam has not been adequately represented. But liberal Islam has not yet evolved a system of doctrine other than a broad theism not differing much from any ethical monotheism of a Helleno-Semitic complexion with a head-dress of modern rationalism. Others will perhaps object to the presentation of the scholasticism of Islam and Christianity in the second part. But for this the author flatly refuses to apologize. The scholastic statement of Muslim doctrine has so many features in common with the similar statement in Christianity, in form, method and vocabulary, that it would have been absurd to attempt a work of this description without a full treatment of the mediæval development of systematic dogmatic by the exponents of dialectic. An examination such as will be presented to the reader may result in the rejection of the scholasticism which Islam offers, and it may lead to a corresponding rejection of those similar scholastic developments in Christianity. On the other hand, the reader will remember that, however scholasticism has been scoffed at, it was a system which came to fruition on one side in Spinoza, the profound influence of whose philosophy has had repercussions in modern times, and on the other hand, in St. Thomas Aquinas, who is rightly regarded as a theological genius. It may be that from our enlightened modern standpoint we may be able to discern in scholasticism deviations from what is central in Christianity, due to the attractions of a powerful philosophy which then held the field, but the minds which could use the great pre-Christian thinkers, Plato and Aristotle, in the criticism and systematization of their thought must not be dismissed with an airy gesture as beneath our notice. Finally we may see in the parallel systematization of doctrine in the two religions, evidence of which will be provided in abundance, a vocabulary, a method and a body of ideas which will make the intelligibility of one system clearer to the other, and throw into relief those matters which are vital to the creed of the Christian Church.

Other criticism will be offered by Orientalists, and they will no doubt be justified. For instance, the transliteration of words is a necessary evil, and no system is without its faults. Certainly the system adopted in the *Encyclopædia of Islam* is uncouth for English readers. The author will be content if his transliterations have made the original plain. By way of excuse for some deficiencies and the impossibility of making references to standard works in some instances, the writer would inform the reader that most of the work embodied in the following pages has been done in India, which is not yet famous for its theological libraries. Only by making elaborate notes when on furlough in England has it been possible to proceed at all, and sometimes at a critical point it has been impossible to refer to a book which was needed. The author has had, therefore, to trust to the accuracy of his notes without sometimes being able to check these at the final writing. He has also had to prepare all the typescript and indexes, and as his typing is of the one-finger variety, something of the exasperation involved may be imagined. The international situation has added to the difficulties, the first manuscript lying at the bottom of the sea. The author therefore craves the reader's kind indulgence.

It should here be said that the three " parts " of this work will each form separate units of a trilogy, though the main title is retained in each case. The materials for the remaining parts are all ready for the final writing, and it is hoped that they will follow soon after the publication of this present volume. The thanks of the writer are due in the first place to the Methodist Missionary Society, which has supported him for many years in the Henry Martyn School of Islamics, and has always helped him in his special work, and to the Rev. Godfrey Phillips of the Department of Missions in the Selly Oak Colleges, and indeed to many members of the staffs of those Colleges and their patron, Dr. Ed. Cadbury for much encouragement and aid. I would also express warm thanks to Dr. Richard Bell, Reader in Arabic at Edinburgh University, for help much appreciated. My colleagues on the staff of the Henry Martyn School have shown me great practical sympathy by allowing me to concentrate latterly to a great extent on this one task. I am very grateful to them. The names of the writers to whom I am indebted is legion. Evidence of this will be gathered from the following pages. If I have inadvertently used any words of theirs without due acknowledgment I humbly apologize and would point out that it is a proof of the efficacy of their teaching that now I cannot separate it from my own thinking.

Lastly, it is hoped that this book, in spite of faults, may stimulate the assistance of theologians in the task of presenting the evangel to Islam. The one who looks within for an infallible logic wherewith to reply to Islam will look in vain. He will not find it here. " We believe and therefore speak." He whom God guides to the truth will hear and believe likewise. Moreover, if there is anything here which is not of Faith, may God amend it, that He Who is the Truth may be all in all. And to Him be the Glory now and for ever. Amen.

J. W. SWEETMAN.

HENRY MARTYN SCHOOL OF ISLAMIC STUDIES,
ALIGARH, *October*, 1942

TABLE OF CONTENTS

PAGE

FOREWORD vii

SECTION ONE

INTERRELATIONS OF ISLAM AND CHRISTIANITY

A. RELEVANT HISTORICAL CONSIDERATIONS 1

B. THE EVIDENCE OF THE QUR'AN 6

(I) RELIGIOUS NARRATIVE 8

(II) WORSHIP AND RITUAL 14

(III) DOCTRINE 17

(*a*) *The Divine Being and Attributes* 17

(*b*) *Angelology* 22

(*c*) *Revelation* 24

(*d*) *Christological* 27

(*e*) *Eschatological* 33

(*f*) *Miscellaneous* 34

(IV) RELIGIOUS LAW 35

C. CHRISTIANITY AND MUSLIM TRADITION 36

D. THE CHRISTIAN THEOLOGICAL BACKGROUND TO EARLY ISLAM 42

(I) PRE-ISLAMIC CHRISTIAN CONTROVERSY 44

(II) THE GREAT SCHOOLS 46

(*a*) *Alexandria* 46

(*b*) *Cappadocia* 48

(*c*) *Antioch* 49

(III) THE EXISTING PHILOSOPHICAL THEOLOGY 50

(IV) CHRISTIAN HERESY AND ISLAM 57

(*a*) *Gnostic and Other Heresies* 58

(*b*) *Other Heretical Opinions on Christology* 59

(*c*) *Pelagianism* 61

(*d*) *Iconoclasm* 63

(V) JOHN OF DAMASCUS 63

(VI) THE APOLOGISTS 66

(VII) THE CHIEF POINTS AT ISSUE IN THE APOLOGISTS 71

(*a*) *The Person and Incarnation of Jesus Christ* 72

(*b*) *The Holy Trinity* 75

(*c*) *God, His Being and Attributes* 78

(*d*) *The Death and Crucifixion of Jesus Christ* 79

(*e*) *Scripture* 80

(*f*) *Muhammad* 82

(*g*) *Signs and Miracles to procure Faith* 82

SECTION TWO

THE INTRODUCTION OF PHILOSOPHY INTO ISLAM

PAGE

A. THE TRANSLATORS AND THEIR WORK 84

B. THE SHORTER THEOLOGY OF IBN MISKAWAIH 93

PART I. GOD

CAP. I. PROOF OF THE EXISTENCE OF AN ARTIFICER 93

II. UNANIMOUS CONSENT OF PHILOSOPHERS WITH REGARD TO THE EXISTENCE OF GOD 98

III. THAT THE EXISTENCE OF THE ARTIFICER CAN BE PROVED FROM MOTION 101

IV. EVERYTHING THAT IS MOVED IS MOVED BY SOMETHING ELSE AND THE MOVER OF ALL IS ITSELF NOT MOVED 103

V. THAT THE ESSENCE OF THE CREATOR IS ONE 106

VI. THAT THE CREATOR DOES NOT POSSESS A BODY 109

VII. THAT GOD IS ETERNAL 110

VIII. THAT THE CREATOR CAN BE KNOWN BY THE METHOD OF NEGATION AND NOT BY WAY OF AFFIRMATION 111

IX. THAT ALL THINGS EXIST BY MEANS OF THE CREATOR 113

X. THAT GOD MADE ALL THINGS BUT DID NOT MAKE THEM FROM ANY OTHER THING 116

PART II. THE SOUL

CAP. I. ON THE EXISTENCE OF THE SOUL AND THAT THE SOUL IS NEITHER BODY NOR ACCIDENT 118

II. THE SOUL PERCEIVES ALL EXISTING THINGS WHETHER HIDDEN OR PRESENT, INTELLECTUALLY CONCEIVED OR SENSED 120

III. HOW THE SOUL PERCEIVES THE VARIOUS PERCEPTIONS 122

IV. WHAT THE DIFFERENCE IS BETWEEN THE ASPECT OF REASON AND THE ASPECT OF SENSE, AND WHAT IS COMMON TO THESE TWO AND IN WHAT THEY DIFFER 125

V. THE SOUL A LIVING AND ENDURING SUBSTANCE, NOT SUBJECT TO DEATH AND MORTALITY. THE SOUL IS NOT IDENTICAL WITH LIFE BUT BESTOWS LIFE ON ALL LIVING THINGS 130

VI. THE THEORY OF THE ANCIENT PHILOSOPHERS AND THE ARGUMENTS BY WHICH THEY PROVED THAT THE SOUL DOES NOT DIE. . . . 133

VII. THE NATURE OF THE SOUL AND ITS LIFE, THAT LIFE WHICH IS THE PRESERVER OF THE SOUL AND BY REASON OF WHICH IT PERPETUALLY SURVIVES AND IS IMMORTAL 135

VIII. THE TWO CONDITIONS OF SOUL, ITS PERFECTION CALLED HAPPINESS AND ITS IMPERFECTION MISERY 139

IX. INCITEMENT OF DESIRE TO OBTAIN HAPPINESS AND AN EXPLANATION OF THE WAY IT IS OBTAINED 143

X. THE QUALITY AND CONDITION OF THE SOUL WHEN SEPARATED FROM THE BODY AFTER DEATH 148

PART III. PROPHETHOOD

		PAGE
CAP. I.	OF THE ORDER OF CREATED THINGS IN THE UNIVERSE AND THAT SOME OF THEM ARE CONNECTED WITH OTHERS	158
II.	MAN THE MICROCOSM	163
III.	THE FIVE SENSES RISE TO A COMMON POWER (COMMON SENSE OR SENSORIUM) AND BY GOD'S GRACE RISE EVEN HIGHER	167
IV.	WAHI	170
V.	REASON A KING WHO NATURALLY RULES AND DOMINATES ALL CREATED THINGS	173
VI.	TRUE VISION A PART OF PROPHETHOOD	176
VII.	THE DIFFERENCE BETWEEN PROPHETHOOD AND SOOTHSAYING	177
VIII.	THE PROPHET COMMISSIONED AND THE PROPHET NOT COMMISSIONED	180
IX.	OF THE KINDS OF REVELATION	180
X.	THE DIFFERENCE BETWEEN THE PROPHET AND THE FALSE PROPHET	182

INDEXES—

INDEX OF SUBJECTS	186
INDEX OF PROPER NAMES	192
INDEX OF AUTHORS AND BOOKS	195
INDEX OF SCRIPTURAL PASSAGES	207
PASSAGES FROM THE QUR'AN	209
ARABIC AND PERSIAN WORDS AND PHRASES	212
LATIN WORDS AND PHRASES	214
HEBREW WORDS AND PHRASES	214
GREEK WORDS AND PHRASES	214
ARABIC NAMES OF GOD	215

CONTENTS OF VOL. TWO

THE THEOLOGICAL POSITION AT THE CLOSE OF THE PERIOD OF CHRISTIAN ASCENDANCY IN THE NEAR EAST

INTRODUCTION

A. THE BEING AND ATTRIBUTES OF GOD
- (I) GOD, THE KNOWLEDGE OF HIS EXISTENCE
- (II) THE UNITY OF GOD
- (III) THE DIVINE ATTRIBUTES
- (IV) ANTHROPOMORPHISM
- (V) DIVINE TRANSCENDENCE AND IMMANENCE
- (VI) NEGATION AND AFFIRMATION

B. THE GRACE OF GOD
- (I) THE QURANIC TEACHING ON DIVINE FORGIVENESS
- (II) THE DIVINE MERCY IN THE QUR'AN
- (III) THE DIVINE FAVOUR OR APPROVAL
- (IV) THE LOVE OF GOD
- (V) THE MU'TAZILITE AND OTHER SECTARIAN VIEWS
- (VI) CONCLUSIONS

C. MEDITATION
(I) THE POWERS
(II) ANGELS
(III) EMANATION
(IV) TRINITARIAN DOCTRINE
(V) INCARNATION

D. LOGOS DOCTRINE, PROPHECY AND SCRIPTURE
(I) LOGOS DOCTRINE
(II) PROPHETHOOD AND PROPHECY
(III) SCRIPTURE
(IV) TRADITION

E. THE ORDERING OF THE UNIVERSE
(I) THE QURANIC DOCTRINE OF PREDESTINATION
(II) EARLY DEVELOPMENT
(III) NON-MUSLIM DOCTRINE

F. THE WORLD AND MAN
(I) COSMOLOGY AND THE MATERIAL UNIVERSE
(II) MAN
(III) THE SOUL

G. SIN, SALVATION AND JUDGMENT
(I) SIN
(II) FAITH AND WORKS
(III) SALVATION
(IV) LAST THINGS
(V) THE VISION OF GOD

CONCLUSION

SECTION ONE

INTERRELATIONS OF ISLAM AND CHRISTIANITY

A. RELEVANT HISTORICAL CONSIDERATIONS

For the purpose of understanding the complicated relations of Muslim and Christian theological ideas, it is necessary to sketch by way of introduction the primary historical relations of the two religions, and this is still further complicated by the intrusion of Judaism and Hellenistic influences, particularly Greek philosophy. In the following introductory chapters, therefore, only such matters are touched upon as seem to throw light on the subsequent development of a theological system in Islam in some intelligible relation with the theology of Christianity. It should be understood, therefore, that it is not the purpose here to present all the results of recent research into the origins of Islam and its historical relations with Judaism and Christianity. Those who wish to pursue this line of inquiry will find ample material available in the works of Bell,[1] Margoliouth,[2] Tor Andrae,[3] Jeffery,[4] Browne,[5] Barthold, Von Kremer, the studies in the life of Muhammad by Sprenger and others, and the Schwally-Nöldeke history of the Qur'ān.

It should first of all be observed that pre-Islamic Arabia was not isolated from the main currents of world-culture and religion. If we were to be content only with the evidence of the Qur'ān, with which we will deal more fully later, it would be at once clear that Muhammad had some sort of acquaintance with Judaism and Christianity. In the Qur'ān we find reference to his dealings with the Jews. There seem to have been several Jewish tribes in Arabia, and in Medina they constituted an influential trading caste. The *Kitāb ul Aghānī* contains some fanciful legends to account for the existence of the Jewish tribes of Yathrib and mentions the two tribes Nadir and Quraiza by name. Philostorgius says that when Theophilus, the Indo-Syrian missionary to South Arabia (A.D. 557–561) preached in the Himyarite kingdom, there were many Jews there. Dhū Nuwās (c. 521) a Himyarite king, probably embraced the Jewish religion from a political motive, because he was antagonistic to the aggressive Christian Abyssinians who were dominant for some time in South Arabia. It is thought by some that Sura lxxxv 5ff refers to a persecution of

[1] *Origin of Islam in its Christian Environment.*
[2] Schweich Lectures: *Relations between Arabs and Israelites,* especially Lect. III.
[3] *Ursprung des Islams.*
[4] *Foreign Vocabulary of the Qur'ān.*
[5] *Eclipse of Christianity in Asia.*

Christians in Najran for which Dhū Nuwās was responsible. Bishop Jacob describes such a persecution as occurring in A.D. 524. Some old Muslim writers say that a king called Abū Qārib (*c.* A.D. 450) was converted to Judaism. Inscriptions, however, would seem to indicate that he was a pagan. We find many Jews spoken of by early Muslim historians and all of them have Arab names. It is suggested that these may have been adopted or that their bearers were Jews by religion and Arabs by race, for proselytization was not uncommon. Muhammad himself may have been a proselyte or a would-be proselyte. Bearing in mind the fact that Christianity was identified with Rome on the one hand and with the Abyssinian enemy on the other, it should not be deemed surprising if resistance of a political and patriotic character to the missionaries who preached in pre-Islamic Arabia, may have encouraged the employment of Jews to refute the main tenets of Christianity and particularly the doctrines of the Holy Trinity and the Incarnation. When such ideas are opposed in the Qur'ān, it is not wildly improbable to think one hears the popular objections echoing the Jews.

Whether Muhammad knew Christianity at first hand or not must always be largely a matter of conjecture. Tor Andrae [1] considers that he may possibly have heard a missionary sermon, Sura xxiv. 35 f., may contain the vague recollection of the ornaments of a Christian church or of the altar, and the olive tree may be a mistake for the symbolic vine. Suras lvii. 27–29 and ix. 30–31 show some acquaintance with monastic life and even with the malpractices in monasteries. There are various legends describing how Muhammad met bishops and ascetics of the Christian faith. There is nothing improbable in this, but the Qur'ān, which must always be our first source of information on such matters, does not reveal any close and accurate knowledge of Christianity. But with this point we shall deal hereafter.

The relation of the Arabs with Christianity and Christian culture is not in doubt. It can be shown quite conclusively that Arabia had relations with all three of the main sections of the Christian Church, the Royal (Malkite) Byzantine Church; the Nestorian Church, which was an exiled branch having centres at Edessa in North Mesopotamia and later in Persia, and known for the wide ramifications of its missionary labours throughout the Middle East, Transoxania, Central Asia and China; and the nonconforming Jacobite Monophysite Church, of which Jacob Baradaeus (A.D. mid fifth century) was a great evangelist and missionary to the people of Arabia.

There were six provinces of the Nestorian Church, having centres in Seleucia, Jundishabur, Nisibis, Basra, Arbil and Karkuk. It is practically certain that there were Christians in Gilan and Bactria as early as A.D. 196. We read of Bishops of Rayy, Nishapur, Merv and

[1] *Muhammad: the Man and his Faith*, p. 49 ff.

Herat in the fifth century (A.D. 424), and of a Bishop of Samarqand before the time of the Prophet Muhammad. Indeed, when we consider the survey of missionary expansion which is given by Cosmas Indicopleustes of Alexandria, we may even say that Arabia stood fairly central in the geographical dispersion of Christianity, for up to the middle of the sixth century A.D. churches had been founded in Ceylon, Malabar, Socotra, Bactria, Mesopotamia, Persia, Scythia, Egypt and Abyssinia. It is highly improbable that so surrounded, Arabia should remain unaffected by Christianity, even if there were no evidence of Christianity within Arabia itself.

It is well established that there were many Christian churches along the trade routes in Arabia before Muhammad. Jacob Baradaeus and Theophilus have already been mentioned as missionaries to Arabia. A still earlier notice is that in which we are told that as early as A.D. 213, the great Origen was invited to preach in Arabia. Christian churches are mentioned at Najrān, San'a, Ma'rib, Hadramout, Aden, Ẓafār and other places. The Christians of Najran seem to have been specially influential.

During the centuries which preceded Muhammad, Christian culture had made a distinct impression on the East. Beside the famous Alexandria with its Neoplatonist school, and Antioch, a centre of Aristotelian learning, the metropolitan cities of the Nestorian Church were noted for their schools. In Jundishabur, where the Syrians of Antioch were brought into exile in the middle of the third century A.D., we find the Aristotelianism of Antioch transplanted ; and in the reign of Khusrū I (A.D. 531–579) a flourishing school of Græco-Syrian medicine and philosophy. Nisibis was also famous for its schools and its theological seminary. Basra had become a great centre of learning and was to be similarly famous in the Islamic era. Alexandria, Seleucia and Antioch were only inferior to Rome in point of size, and Edessa (now Urfa) was a most important centre of culture. It was situated east of the Euphrates on the main road from North Syria. It is said that its king, Abgar IX, was the first ruler to embrace Christianity (A.D. 179–216). One of its early famous sons is Bardesan (A.D. 155–222), the Gnostic, who was born a pagan and became a Christian and is credited with exerting a profound influence on Manichæism, with the rise of which he was almost contemporary. Edessa rapidly became one of the most influential of Christian cities. There in the fifth century was the Persian theological school, which was destroyed by Zeno, the Byzantine Emperor, in A.D. 489 ; whereupon its scholars fled to the protection of the Sassanids of Persia. The extant work of Job of Edessa (ninth century) introduces us to the physics, medicine and cosmology of the time, and shows the influence of the Greeks and particularly Galen. It also shows how long Edessa continued to be a cultural power. Thus Edessa was a meeting place of East and West, gathering the Greek learning from the latter and stretching out its hands with gradually increasing urgency to grasp the protecting robe of a Persia which before long would cease to be any one's protector.

The Sassanids were open to foreign influences, and when they brought their captives from Antioch and other cities, they set them to enrich the Persian nation with the arts and philosophy in which they were expert. The arm of Persia reached even to Egypt, and shortly before the advent of Muhammad there was a Persian viceroy in Alexandria. In the flux and ferment of war and invasion between Persia and Byzantium we see the Nestorians more and more identified with Persia, and the cultural elements diffused as a sort of Hellenistic leaven there before the coming of Islam, and all the seeds scattered for the crop of eclectic systems which later grew within the bounds of Islam; for in addition to what we have observed, Buddhism lingered long in Persia and the Oxus valley, and the Syrians had their colonies in India. The sixth century saw the Indian fables of Bidpai translated into Persian and the Aristotelian works of Paul the Persian in which he sought to prove the superiority of knowledge over faith.

Alongside the Hellenistic tendencies, we have evidence of strong Semitic reactions in the Middle East at the time when Islam arose. The potent elements of Semitic monotheism, resisting what it deemed paganizing tendencies, seem to have been at work even before the iconoclastic controversy, and it seems worth remarking that Leo the Iconoclast was a Syrian. Obscure hints that Jews were used to refute Christian doctrine point in the same direction. It is quite possible that the preoccupation of the Church in the East with metaphysical questions, hair-splitting discussions of the mode of the Incarnation, the two-natures controversy and other similar subtleties, gave a chance to the broad simplification of the Muslim declaration of the Unity, the Majesty and the Judgment of God. The knots of controversy were cut by a positivism which had a Semitic urge and zeal behind it.

The necessity for an apologetic against Gnosticism and paganism, seen so early at Alexandria, was responsible for various schools of philosophical theology throughout the areas served by the Church in the East. The creation of literature was stimulated. Alongside the sacred lore treasured in the Greek tongue there were soon to be found books in the Nubian and Ethiopic, in Armenian and Georgian, in Coptic and Syriac. Some of these were translations from the Greek. Barthold tells us that inscriptions which may be ascribed to the sixth century A.D., make it clear that Arabic was a language in common use in the Church. We have, however, no evidence of a Christian literature in Arabic, and in particular, there is no trace of an early translation of the Scriptures into Arabic. Sura xcvi. 3–5 would perhaps indicate that writing was as yet a recent innovation, and it is quite possible and even probable that the Qur'ān was, properly speaking, the first book actually written in Arabic. But with this exception, it is indeed remarkable in how many languages of the lands which were afterwards to become Muslim there was a preparatory Christian literature—even in Sogdian, Turkish and Northern Chinese—during the seventh century.

Even in the earliest days of the Muslim expansion we find that mighty upsurge of monotheistic fervour expressed in the strange blend of rhapsody and story, the struggling articulation of a new nation's reasons for its birth, found within the pages of the Qur'ān—itself not yet fully developed into a theology—meeting with a highly complicated theological system which had drawn Plato, Aristotle, Plotinus and Proclus into its service. Thus, while Islamic thought is in its infancy, we find the great eastern theologian of orthodoxy, John of Damascus, in the very city where the first dynasty of Muslim monarchs held its court. The Prophet Muhammad died in A.D. 632, and the Damascene was born in A.D. 665 and lived, in all probability, till he was ninety years of age. The Umayyads held sway till the middle of the eighth century. The Damascene's dialogues in refutation of Islam and support of Christianity are extant, and thus, within the shortest possible time, Islam and Christianity join issue in theological debate. As yet the debate was rather one-sided and could not well be otherwise. The free-thinking Umayyads do not seem to have been unduly disturbed. In these early days the highly educated Syrians, well-versed in Roman law, skilled in medicine, practised in literary arts, and on this account useful in the administration of the strange new territories into which the predominantly illiterate Arabs had thrust as conquerors, were welcomed for the contributions they could make to the State. They held for a long time a privileged position and the attitude towards them was generally one of toleration.[1] Having no national culture themselves, the Arabs needed help. The valley of the Euphrates became a centre for the gathering of world culture. Here there were to be found Christian, Jewish and Manichæan universities, and here the Muslims began to learn the Greek sciences taught in the main by their Christian subjects.

Up to the first half of the ninth century it is broadly true that non-Muslims and non-Arabs were more cultured. The sense of superiority led to nationalist movements (*shu'ūbīya*). Barthold remarks that such nationalist and communal tendencies were to be found at this time among Christians of various nationalities and sects as well as among Persians, Jews and the Hellenistic pagan survivals represented by the town of Ḥarrān. To this recrudescence of narrow nationalism the

[1] Al Akhṭal, a Christian, was poet-laureate to the Umayyads at Damascus, *Kitāb ul Aghān* ixiv. 122.

broadening influence of the Muslim State, embracing as it did a great variety of racial elements in its process of gradual absorption, opposed its power. As Muslims advanced in culture we see the gradual usurpation of the Christian intelligentsia and "internationale". When the conquest had been consummated, the racial varieties within the Muslim fold ensured a greater virility and a broader culture, and the lesser nationalisms and communalisms were submerged until it became the turn of the Christians to become exclusive and conservative and less than catholic; but this was not before Christianity had had a decisive influence on the future of Muslim thought and particularly Muslim theology.

B. THE EVIDENCE OF THE QUR'AN

Christian and other Biblical and Apocryphal influences are clearly evident in the Qur'ān and in the traditions of Islam. It is not meant to maintain the claim that the Qur'ān has been immediately and consciously devised by reference to those various particulars which it will be our duty to set forth shortly in some detail. Many of the matters mentioned must have become part of the common religious stock of the times. Some of the terms used and the ideas expressed must have been equally the possession of Jews and Christians and other religious people in the times immediately preceding and contemporary with the compilation of the Qur'ān and the Ḥadīth. It is, of course, possible that there was some literary dependence, but more than this cannot be said. Exact literary dependence is not in the main what should concern us here. Moreover, when likeness to Judaism and to Christianity is pointed out, it must not be assumed that Islam is nothing but a slavish imitation. Our chief purpose is to gather together similarities which, however they are to be accounted for historically, present us with a body of ideas which cannot be attributed exclusively to Islam, and which show points of contact of some significance for the further comparative study of the theologies of Islam and Christianity. In a survey of these there will become evident, despite the similarities, a variation in the data from which Islam and Christianity start. In these similarities and this variation we find much that determines the later course of development. Narrow divergence at the source will to some extent determine wider estrangement as the stream of development flows on. Occasionally the similarities will bring the two streams almost to a confluence. Whether these introductory remarks are justified it is left to the reader to judge, as the argument moves through the wider ranges of theological thought in the two religions, and in the final and critical and reconstructive section of this book the importance of data will be discussed.

Jeffery [1] has gathered some 300 pages dealing with foreign words in

[1] *Foreign Vocabulary of the Qur'ān.*

the Qur'ān, many of which must have been in use in pre-Quranic Arabic, but quite a number also must have been used little or not at all before they were used in the Qur'ān. The bewilderment evinced by commentators when they try to explain these words is sufficient evidence for this.[1] For us questions of etymology and derivation are of secondary importance. The fact that the ideas expressed necessitated the use of foreign words is, on the other hand, of primary importance.

If we take for example technical words of a general religious signification we shall find that some of these belong to a common original Semitic stock. The best example of this is perhaps in the case of the great act of worship in Islam, the *Ḥajj*, the pilgrimage to Mecca and the rites associated with it. This name *Ḥajj* is from the Semitic root denoting the making of a circuit. The very word is used in the story of the Israelites at Sinai (Ex. xxiii. 14). The feast of booths is called *Ḥajj* in the Old Testament (Judges xxi. 19, etc.). The details mentioned in Exod. xix, abstinence from sexual intercourse, washing of garments, and the pause (verse 15 *cf. wuqūf*) before God, are all similar to the visit to Arafat enjoined among the rites of the Muslim pilgrimage. Other details such as the *tarwiya*, the libations at Zamzam, the stoning, etc., are capable of explanations which relate them to very early Semitic solar or fertility cults. Here then we have an example of something really primitive and not original either to one or other of the religions which maintained the practices.

But with many technical terms this is not the case. Let us notice some of these technical terms of a general religious signification. *Islām* and *Muslim* can be traced to Syrian Christian usage[2] in the sense of resignation or submission as found in Sura ii. 106 and 125. *Āya*, "sign" in Sura. ii. 37; iii. 9; xxxvi. 33, etc., is the Syriac equivalent for the Scriptural σημεῖον. *Shuhudā'* with the meaning of "martyrs" echoes the Syriac, as e.g., Suras iv. 71; iii. 134; xxxix. 69; and lvii.18. *Tajalla* signifying divine self-revelation, and later an important technical term among the mystics, has similarly a Syrian origin:[3] see Suras vii. 139 and xcii. 2. Geiger[4] has pointed out that the term used for religious instruction, *darasa*, is akin to the term *midrash* familiar in Rabbinical usage; see Sura iii. 73, etc., and Jer. xxix. 13 and Gen. xxv. 22. *Dīn* in both its meanings, namely, religion and judgment, particularly in the common phrase "*yawm ud dīn*"—day of Judgment, has its origin in the Syrian religious vocabulary. Christianity was often spoken of as the "Way," and the word *sabīl* in Sura ii. 102, etc., recalls this to mind. *Sajada*, used for prostration

[1] *Vide* As Suyūṭī: *Mutawakkilī passim.*
[2] Horovitz: *Koranische Untersuchungen*, 55.
[3] Mingana: *Syriac Influence on the Style of the Qur'ān*, 86.
[4] *Was hat Mohammed aus dem Judenthume aufgenommen?* 51, cf. *madrasa.*

in adoration, is most probably derived from the Aramaic, though Gaster[1] considers that the technical use was primarily Samaritan. Similarly *sifr* (cf. *sepher*), Sura lxii. 5, for " book " is Aramaic. The term *mathal* used in Sura iii. 113, etc., for " parable," derives from Christian[2] sources. When used for " religion " or " sect " that now most familiar term *milla*, which is to be found in many places in the Qur'ān, e.g., Suras ii. 114, 124 ; iii. 89 ; xxxviii. 6, etc., is the Syrian technical term for religion. *Qissisūn* (Sura v. 85) is the common Syriac for " presbyter ". The word *qalam*, " pen ", which is used allegorically in the Qur'ān and became an important symbol in the Muslim cosmology, is the Greek *kalamos* transmitted through Syriac, and the usual term for the cosmos, viz., *'Ālam* could be of Hebrew, Rabbinical or Syriac origin.[3] The term *furqān* used in the Qur'ān at Sura viii. 29 and 42 in its primary significance of " deliverance ", but used elsewhere obscurely, e.g., Suras ii. 50, 181 ; iii. 2 ; xxi. 49 ; xxv. 1, was a puzzle to commentators, although it has now become a common name for the Qur'ān. It is to be found in the Targum of 1 Sam. xi. 13 for the deliverance which Saul was instrumental in procuring through the divine aid, just as it is used in the Qur'ān for the victory of the Battle of Badr, but in regard to the other obscure signification it is most interesting to find that it is the regular Nestorian Syriac for " salvation ". Other general terms which are worth noting are *ṣawāmiʿ* " cloisters " (Sura xxii. 41), *ṣalaba* " to crucify " (Suras iv. 156 ; v. 37, etc.) and *ṣibgha* " baptism " (Sura ii. 132).

But while these are suggestive they are the least important. In addition there is a wide range of reference embracing religious narrative, ritual and worship, doctrine and religious law, examples of which it will be convenient to take in that order.

(i) Religious Narrative. In the narratives of the Qur'ān we have many stories which have their origin in the Old Testament and a few which are faintly reminiscent of the New Testament. The field of reference is, however, broader than the Biblical text and includes Talmudic additions and so-called New Testament apocrypha. While there seems to be a preponderance of tales about Old Testament characters, there is little indication that these have come directly from Jewish sources. An examination of the names reveals the surprising fact that they are almost without exception transmitted through a Christian medium. There are three names, Qārūn, the Quranic name for Korah, Uzayr, usually translated " Ezra ", and 'Isā, the regular Quranic name for Jesus, the forms of which are very difficult to explain. But if we take the rest, Lot, Elijah, Elisha, Job, Solomon, Noah, Aaron, Jonah, Michael, Pharaoh and Gabriel are

[1] Art. *Samaritans* in Encycl. of Islam, cf. *masjid*.
[2] Mingana : *op. cit.*, 85.
[3] Jeffery : *op. cit.*, 209.

represented in the Qur'ān by names which plainly show Christian influence. Horovitz has a special study of the names used in the Qur'ān.[1] From an examination of the evidence he presents it will be seen that it is not always possible to state categorically that a name has come from a Christian source simply because it has lost some of the marks of the original Hebrew name. We have to allow for the fact that names may have been Aramaicized by Jews themselves. But even when this is taken into consideration it is remarkable that the Old Testament stories, particularly the story of Lot, show Christian influence. Another point to be borne in mind is that in the Old Testament the interest is more purely historical than when such stories are retold either by Christians or Muslims. Now the purpose is to point a moral or to illustrate a point. In the Qur'ān they are brought forward to support the prophetic claim or to symbolize the divine Judgment. Occasionally they are amended to present some doctrinal point. E.g., The angels who visit Abraham do not eat with him as in the original story (see Sura xi. 72) because it is now held that angels do not eat.

The following examples will show to what extent the Qur'ān draws on the treasury of Jewish and Christian story. The story of the creation of Adam is to be found in Suras xvii. 62 ff., xxxviii. 71–79, and here we find elements introduced which are not in the original story, namely, the jealousy of the angels and the refusal of Satan to worship Adam. Reference may be made to the *Talmud*[2] and the *Midrash*[3] for the former of these, and for the latter it is interesting to note Heb. i. 6: "And again when He bringeth the firstborn into the world, He saith: Let all the angels of God worship him." There are many early and pre-Islamic stories which offer us similar material to that found in the Qur'ān. Thus, e.g., *Vita Adæ et Evæ* xiv. 1–xvi, a very early apocryphal document,[4] contains the following: "God the Lord spake: Here is Adam. I have made thee in our image and likeness. And Michael went out and called all the angels saying: 'Worship the image of God as the Lord God hath commanded.' And Michael himself worshipped first; then he called me (Satan) and said: 'Worship the image of God the Lord.' And I answered, 'I have no (need) to worship Adam.' And since Michael kept urging me to worship, I said to him, 'Why dost thou urge me? I will not worship an inferior and younger being. I am his senior in the creation; before he was made was I already made. It is his duty to worship me.' When the angels, who were under me, heard this, they refused to worship him. And Michael saith, 'Worship the image of God, but if

[1] *Koranische Untersuchungen*, p. 78 ff.
[2] *Sanhedrin*, 59b.
[3] *Midrash Rabba* on Num. para. 19.
[4] Charles: *Apocrypha and Pseudepigrapha*, Vol. ii, 137.

thou wilt not worship him, the Lord God will be wrath with thee.' And I said, 'If He be wrath with me, I will set my seat above the stars of heaven and will be like the Highest. And God the Lord was wrath with me and banished me and my angels from our glory.'"

The story of Cain and Abel (Gen. iv. 3 ff.) with the names transformed into Qābil and Hābil may be found in Sura v. 30–36. It is commonly assumed that the Idrīs of Sura xix. 57–58 is the Enoch of the Old Testament. The story of Noah and the Flood is told at great length in Suras xxix. 13; vii. 57 ff.; iii. 30, etc. The name used for the Deluge (*ṭūfān*) is a foreign word and is found in the *Targum* of Onkelos Gen. vii. and in the *Talmud*.[1] Likewise the statement that the waters of the flood were hot (Sura xi. 42) agrees with *Sanhedrin* 108 and the *Targum* of Jonathan b. Uzziel on Gen. vii. When considering the question of the source of such matters as we find recorded in both the Qur'ān and the *Talmud* it should be remembered that both the Palestinian and Babylonian *Talmud* were completed before the advent of Islam and so the presumption is that the Quranic narrative is not original. There always remains, however, the remote possibility that additions have crept into the text of the *Talmud* from Islamic sources. It should further be noted that very often there is evidence pointing both to *Talmud* and to Christian sources. Thus both the name Nūḥ for Noah and the word *ṭūfān* can be traced in the Syriac usage.

Since it was one of the claims of the Prophet Muhammad that he had revived the religion of Abraham, it is not surprising to find that a good deal of space is given in the Qur'ān to stories of the Patriarch. The chief references are: Suras xvi. 124; ii. 128; iii. 60; vi. 79; lxxxvii. 19; xxxvii. 99; xi. 72. Points additional to the Biblical narrative are that books are ascribed to Abraham (lxxxvii. 19). The Rabbis used to claim that Abraham wrote *Sepher Jazira*. We are told also that Abraham's father was an idolater and that Abraham wished to be the means of his conversion to monotheism. This addition may be traceable to the *Midrash Rabba* on Genesis (para. 38). An unexplained divergence in the traditional interpretation is that it was his son Ishmael who was offered as a sacrifice and not Isaac. It may be that some of the details in the stories are from a body of primitive Semitic tradition or folklore. There is some confusion about Jacob as to whether Ishmael was one of his ancestors (Sura ii. 126) in the order Abraham, Ishmael, Isaac and Jacob. The whole of Sura xii. is devoted to the story of Joseph with sundry elaborations, which Geiger is disposed to think come from Rabbinical sources. These accretions are: the attraction Zulaikhā had for Joseph, the amazement of the Egyptian women at the beauty of Joseph, the child who gave testimony of the innocence of Joseph, the advice which

[1] *Sanhedrin*, 96a.

Jacob gave to his sons not to go in at one gate [1] (Sura xii. 67), and that Jacob by revelation knew that Joseph was alive. Thus we find that the *Midrash Tanchuma* quoted in *Midrash Yalkut*, cap. 143, says : " He knew that he continued to live by the Holy Spirit."

There is perhaps more space given to Moses in the Qur'ān than to any other of the Old Testament characters.[2] Thus we have his drawing of water from the rock in Suras ii. 57 and vii. 160 ; of his receiving the Law we read in Sura vii, and in this same Sura how he prayed to see the glory of God. Other references for the same story and for the episode of the Golden Calf are Suras ii. 48 ff., xx. 82 ff. and iv. 152. In Sura vii. 154 we find the appointment of the seventy ruling elders and in Sura v. 23 ff., the forty years' wandering. Sura xxviii. 76–85 gives an account of the dispute with Korah (Qārūn). Divergences from the Biblical story are fairly numerous. Thus Pharaoh's wife is substituted for his daughter as the one who showed kindness to Moses. In the Biblical narrative it was the vision in the Bush which directed Moses to leave Midian, whereas in the Qur'ān he had the vision when already on his way back to Egypt. Like the Quranic account, the Rabbis record how the hand of Moses became leprous white before Pharaoh. This is not Biblical. Pharaoh claimed divinity, according to the Qur'ān, and this is in line with the Jewish legend contained in the *Midrash Rabba on Exod.*, para. 5. The Qur'ān also states that Pharaoh repented (Sura x. 90 ff.) and with this should be compared the similar tale in *Pirke Rabbi Eliezer*, sect. 45. Showing how the material in the Qur'ān was somewhat confused, probably because it was received by hearsay, one might point to the uncertainty as to the number of the plagues of Egypt, since Sura xvii. 103 refers to nine and Sura vii. 130 to five. God's threat to let Mount Sinai fall on the rebellious Israelites is recorded in Jewish tradition.[3] The Qur'ān records the story of Moses' threat to kill Aaron, and the *Talmud* [4] tells us how Aaron saw Hur killed and thought the same fate would befall him (cf. Sura xx. 95 ff.). Some Muslim commentators go so far as to say that Moses was accused of killing Aaron, who died alone on Mt. Hor. The Rabbis, according to Geiger, also tell this story.[5]

Before leaving the Moses cycle it should be observed that when the Qur'ān speaks of Maryam, it confuses the Virgin Mary with the sister of Moses (see Sura lxvi. 12 ; xix. 29 and iii. 30 ff.).

We have the story of Saul (*sic*) and Goliath (Tālūt and Jālūt) in Sura ii. 248 ff. Note how there is a confusion with the story of Gideon

[1] *Midrash* on Genesis, para. 91.

[2] The other references are : Suras vii. 101, 125, 127–139 ; ii. 46–49 ; x. 76–93 ; xi. 99–101 ; xx. 8–82 ; xxiii. 47–51 ; xxvi. 9–69 ; xxvii. 13–15 ; xxviii. 2–45 ; xl. 24–49 ; xliii. 45–55 ; lxxix. 15–29.

[3] *Abodah Zarah* ii. 2.

[4] *Sanhedrin*, 5.

[5] *Midrash Tanchuma.*

in ii. 250. David, as writer of the Psalms, a prophet and king, gifted in the art of making armour, is spoken of in the same context and in Suras iv. 161; v. 82; vi. 84; xvii. 57; xxi. 78, 79; xxvii. 15 and 16; xxxiv. 10–12; and xxxviii. 16–29. In the last-mentioned passage we have the story of the ewe lamb, but no mention of the affair of Bathsheba. Solomon in the Qur'ān is a romantic figure, as he was in Jewish and Christian legend. He was a great magician who had control of demons and spirits and winds (Sura xxxviii. 35). This should be compared with the account in the *Second Targum of the Book of Esther* and is probably derived from a mistaken interpretation of Eccles. ii. 8. We are told that he understood the language of birds (Sura xxvii. 13–16, cf. 1 Kings v. 13). The story of the visit of the Queen of Sheba to Solomon (Sura xxvii. 20 ff.) is similar to the record in the *Second Targum of Esther*. Other Quranic references to Solomon are Suras ii. 96; iv. 161; vi. 84; xxi. 78–81; xxxiv. 11.

The above is not by any means an exhaustive statement of the stories and characters common to the Old Testament and the Qur'ān, but the examples given should be sufficient to suggest the large amount of material which was held in common and is still held by Muslims, Jews and Christians.

Narratives with a New Testament background are much fewer in the Qur'ān. Nöldeke is reminded of Luke xvi. 24–25 by Sura vii. 48: "But the fellows of the Fire shall call out to the fellows of Paradise, 'Pour out upon us water, or something of what God has provided you with'," and Sura xlvi. 19: "And the day when those who disbelieve shall be exposed to the fire: 'Ye made away with your good things in your worldly life, and ye enjoyed them; wherefore to-day shall ye be rewarded with the torment of disgrace, for that ye were big with pride in the earth without the right, and for that ye did abomination.'" It may be that we have a garbled version of the parable of the wicked husbandmen in Sura xxxvi. 13 ff. and similarly of the foolish virgins in lvii. 12 ff. In the Surat al Mā'ida (Sura v) we have undoubtedly, towards the end, a confused memory of the Table of the Lord mingled with the miracles of the feeding of the multitudes and the provision in the Wilderness. The basis of this may very well have been an instruction or homily heard on the Holy Communion, in which it is not unusual to find gathered together by way of illustration such elements as we find in the Quranic narrative. This view is strengthened by the fact that the word *ma'ida* is the technical term used by the Abyssinian Christians for the Table of the Lord. Even the very expressions used in the conversation which is reported between the Lord Jesus and his disciples recall the phrases of the last discourse of our Lord as recorded by St. John. A comparison should be made of Sura v. 112 ff. with St. John xiv., etc. Thus we find the subject opened with a reference to the manifest signs which corresponds with

St. John xiv. 11: "Believe me for the very works' sake." In the Quranic account the disciples ask Jesus whether God is able to send them a "table", and the reply of Jesus is: "Fear God if ye be believers". This should be compared with St. John xiv. 1: "Ye believe in God believe also in Me." In the Qur'ān the disciples are represented as saying: "We desire to eat therefrom that our hearts may be at rest" (cf. John vi. 34 f.). The coming down out of heaven is prominent in both the Quranic and the Johannine passages (e.g. John vi. 41, "I am the bread which came down out of heaven"). We are reminded of John xiv. 2, "If it were not so I would have told you", by the Quranic passage—words put in the mouth of the disciples —"That we may know that what thou hast told us is the truth", and the "festival" of verse 114 of the Sura recalls to mind the Eucharist. The miracles of Christ are frequently spoken of, but in summary fashion. They are said to include giving sight to the blind from birth, cleansing lepers and raising the dead (see Sura iii. 43). The story of the Annunciation and the Nativity finds its place in Suras iii. 30–44, xix. 1–39. In the latter there is nearer approximation to the story in the Gospel according to St. Luke, but, generally speaking, there is a great deal of extra-biblical material. The account in Sura iii opens with the story of the immaculate conception of the Virgin Mary as found in the *Protevangelium of James*, which is an apocryphal book of the second century A.D. After her birth "her Lord received her with a good reception and made her grow with a good growth and Zakariya took charge of her". That Zakariya was the custodian of Mary is also related in the *Protevangelium*. The form of the Annunciation, and in particular the reference to "the Word", is similar in the same apocryphal book. "O Mary! verily God gives thee the glad tidings of a Word from Him" (Sura iii. 40). "Fear not, Mary, for thou hast found grace before the Lord of all things and thou shalt conceive of His Word" (*Prot.* xi. 2). There follow the Miracles of the Infancy, namely, that Jesus spoke in the cradle, made clay birds and breathed life into them. These are parallel to the stories in the *Arabic Gospel of the Infancy* (xxxii) and in the apocryphal *Gospel of St. Thomas*. The general claim of Jesus is to heal the blind from birth and lepers, and even to raise the dead and tell hidden things. This also accords with the *Arabic Gospel of the Infancy*. Other details are added in Sura xix. Some of these remind us of the story of Hagar and Ishmael, and it may be that in popular story there was a conflation of the story of the wanderings of Mary after the birth of Jesus with the story of the exiled Hagar and her son. Here we read of the spring [1] which provides the water and the lamentation of the Virgin, and how dates drop from a tree to give her food. Here again reference should be made to the *Arabic Gospel of the Infancy* (xxiv)

[1] See also Sura xxiii. 52.

and also to the *Gospel of Pseudo-Matthew* (xx). Other points in the Quranic story which should be noted are that Mary was in retirement at the time of the Annunciation and that when she conceived she went away to a desert place. After the child was born and she brought Jesus to her relatives, they were shocked, but He spoke in her vindication.

There are other stories of Jesus in the Qur'ān, but as they are of a distinctly polemical character we leave their consideration to a later section.

(ii) Worship and Ritual. The ritual recitation of Scripture is expressed in somewhat similar terms in the Samaritan, Jewish, Syrian, Christian and Muslim cults. Thus we have the Synagogal *Qeri'a,* the Muslim *Qirā'a,* the Samaritan "*beshem Adonai eqrā*" I recite in the name of the Lord,[1] while we have, of course, similarly the word *Qur'ān,* which is not only used for the inspired recitation of the Prophet, but also for the Syrian lectionary.[2]

Ṣalla with *ṣalāt* from which it is derived and which together represent the common terms for ritual worship in the sense of "bowing down", we may with unanimous authority refer back to Aramaic as its origin and to Syrian Christianity for its usage.[3] To laud and praise God is expressed in Syriac by cognates to the familiar Islamic *ṣubhān* and *taṣbīh.* But even where there is no etymological connection in the terms used, the common ideas are sufficiently remarkable. Both Guillaume and Geiger point out that the rules for the performing of ritual worship are very similar in Islam and Judaism. Among such rules are the following: A man should dismount from a beast to pray; he should shorten his prayers in time of war or alarm; he should not pray when ceremonially unclean or drunk (cf. Sura iv. 46 and the rules in the first five sections of *Berachoth* and *Erubin* in the *Talmud*). He should also be properly orientated—though perhaps the insistence on the proper direction for prayer was more emphasized by the Samaritans than the Jews. Before performing the ritual prayer, a Muslim must make his intention (*nīya*) to proceed with such and such a prayer. There are parallels to this in the *Kawwana* of the Jews and the *intentio* of the Christians.

Ablutions before prayer are commanded in the *Talmud*[4] and in Sura v. 8 of the Qur'ān. Prayer is in both the religions a matter of obligation to all who can understand the meaning of the words they use, including women, children and slaves.

Sura lxxiii. 1–4 and 20 ff. refer to night vigils which recall monastic practice. The prayers which were regarded as canonical in the Christian Church were at the third, the sixth and the ninth hours of the day.

[1] See Gaster: Art. *Samaritan* in *Encyc. of Islam.*
[2] See Jeffery: *Foreign Vocabulary of the Qur'ān,* p. 233.
[3] For authorities see Jeffery: *op. cit.,* p. 198 text and note.
[4] *Berachoth,* 46.

In Islam the Ahl ul Qur'ān, who base their practice on the Qur'ān, hold that only three canonical prayers are obligatory in Islam. To the primary three hours of prayer in Christianity were later added two periods of night prayers. "Solemn prayer at midnight is enjoined, 'inasmuch as the Fathers have handed down that at that hour all creation pauses for a moment to praise God, and all the angelic host does Him service—along with the souls of the righteous, hymning God Almighty at that hour'. Prayer also at this hour fulfils the Lord's words, 'At midnight a cry arose. . . . Therefore watch, for ye know not at what hour He cometh'. 'Cockcrowing' is the last of the series of hours, the second of the night hours."[1] It is therefore most interesting to note that these five hours correspond in most respects to the number and times of the canonical prayers in Islam, which has also added two to the Quranic three.

In regard to the manner of prayer, it may be remarked that *prostration* was common in the Christian Church and among the Jews. Thus in the Old Testament at Lev. ix. 24 we find the record of the prostration at the dedication of the tabernacle when the people "fell upon their faces". The Jews recited the declaration of the Unity of God *standing*, following thereby the custom of the disciples of the Rabbi Shammai. This *'Amidah*, as it is called, corresponds to the Muslim *qiyām*. Sitting, with the body resting on the heels or on the inside of the feet, was another posture of prayer among the Jews (see 2 Sam. vii. 18), and Ps. xcv. 6 speaks of *kneeling*, which was ordinarily with the body bent forward so that the head might touch the ground. These two postures correspond to some extent to the *jalsa* and the *sijda* of Muslim ritual worship. The marks of prostration on the forehead of the worshipper were a sign of his great piety, and are referred to in Sura xlviii. 29. "Their marks are in their faces from the effects of adoration. That is their similitude in the Law and their similitude in the Gospel."[2] Evidently the practice was observed by both Jews and Christians.

Though fear and awe as motives to religious worship have been somewhat disregarded in favour of love, self-dedication and mystical familiarity among some modern Christians, they are not absent from the New Testament nor from later Christian experience; thus no unfavourable comparisons should be drawn between Islam and Christianity in this particular in such an absolute fashion as to suggest that one motive prevails to the exclusion of the other in either of the two religions. Thus, while it may be said that Muhammad calls men to fear and awe before the Judge of all mankind, he only echoes, as

[1] *Vide* art. *Worship* (*Christian*) in ERE. xii. 770.

[2] Tor Andrae: *Mohammed: The Man and His Faith* (Eng. trans.), 122. He gives references for the Christian practice to John of Ephesus in *Patrologia Orientales*, xvii. 40 and to Cheikho: *Al-nasraniyya*, p. 178.

Tor Andrae [1] abundantly shows, the "Christian ascetic piety" of the Syrian Church. The two aspects of the devotional spirit are brought out in the story of Abba Joseph told by Thomas of Marga.

"When I lived in the service of the monastery, I used to pasture a few cattle . . . in the valley near the cemetery, and I heard from within the thicket the sound of bitter weeping, like that of one fastened in the stocks. At the noise of the mournful outcries, I went softly into the thicket and found Abba Joseph sitting on the ground among the grass and plants and flowers . . . and I saw him gathering dry grasses from among the green grass, which he brought with his hands before his face, and weeping bitterly he said, 'The days of man are like the grass, and he groweth up like the herb of the field, which when the wind hath blown over it is not, neither is its place known', and again, 'Man is like unto a vapour, and his days pass like a shadow'; and he laid them down on the ground. And again he gathered other grasses and after he had weeded out all the old, he passed his hands softly over the new, and embracing them said, 'Verily the generations of flesh and blood are like unto the leaves of trees, some of which fade and fall and some of which grow up'; and he repeated these words with mournful sighs and groans, while tears flowed down from his eyes abundantly. And again he took some of the beautiful flowers and, looking at them sweetly, he groaned, and said to God, 'Glory to Thee, O Creator of all, how beautiful are Thy works!' Now I, standing silently above him, marvelled at the wonderful things that I saw, and how that holy man was able to weep over such contemptible and despicable matters with so great a weeping which others could not have wept even had they been beaten. And after his great weeping and his bitter outcries, he started up with gratitude to God, and there sprang up gladness within him, and like David, his mouth was filled with laughter and his tongue with praise, and . . . he lifted up his voice and sang in metre the whole of the hymn of the Hosannas, 'The rose, and the lilies and the blossoms, and the spring flowers are very lovely in their appearance'." [2]

Barlaam and Ioasaph,[3] attributed to John of Damascus, gives evidence of the same in many places. The frequency with which tears and contrition, awe and judgment, occur in the *agrapha* attributed to our Lord and abundantly quoted by Muslim writers, leaves us in little doubt that this element in worship is to be ascribed in a marked degree to the Eastern Christianity in the midst of which Islam came to birth.[4]

In brief it may be said that in both the ritual itself and in the expe-

[1] *Op. cit.*, 114 ff.

[2] Thomas of Marga: *Book of Governors* (ed. and trans. Budge), Vol. ii, 566 f.

[3] x. 84–85 (Loeb Library ed. p. 142 ff).

[4] Cf. the collection made by Asin y Palacios taken mainly from the *Iḥyā 'Ulūm id Dīn* of Al Ghazzālī and entitled *Logia et Agrapha Domini Iesu*.

rience of adoration there are strong resemblances to each other in the three religions.

Before leaving this subject of worship it should be remarked that the word *ṣawm* employed for fasting in Arabic is derived from the Aramaic and was in use in the Syrian Church. The word *qurbān* also, used in the sense of "oblation", is Aramaic and Christian.[1]

(iii) MATTERS OF DOCTRINAL SIGNIFICANCE. While it is broadly true that the Qur'ān is not a theological book in the strictest sense of the word, but rather rhetorical and exhortative, this should not be taken to mean that there is nothing of a theological character to be found therein. On the contrary, polemic and apologetic and even theological argument can be found within its pages. It has already been pointed out that the narratives of the Qur'ān are didactic and used to clinch the arguments advanced by the Prophet, and in their hortatory and oracular form they bear comparison with the form of Old Testament prophecy. The fact that such narratives in such a setting and with such a purpose should have been used in the proclamation of the message Muhammad felt called to deliver, places him alongside the Prophets of Israel with their conception of divinely-ordered history. Indeed it is not the least of the achievements of Muhammad that he succeeded in inculcating into the Arab people the sense of Divine election and theocracy which is the basis of the prophecy of the Old Testament.

(*a*) *The Divine Being and Attributes.* Much of what is found in the Qur'ān concerning God expresses the main conceptions held just as tenaciously in Judaism and Christianity. Ideas at which the Christian looks askance are in the main such as retain the idiom of the old dispensation and many of them can be paralleled in the Old Testament. Comparisons made within the narrower range of the three religions yield much discrepancy and even disharmony and contradiction but, taking the three religions in the wider background of world religion, important doctrines stand out clearly and are the basis of a fundamental harmony. Considerations of space forbid that the whole subject of the Quranic doctrine of God should be dealt with here. It may be found possible to devote more space to the subject later on, though how to bring the vast mass of material into reasonable compass is somewhat of a problem. Here we will simply make some suggestions prompted by a close examination of the Qur'ān in comparison with the Old Testament. The period lying between the two and represented in the Syrian development must be left to the further research of competent scholars who, nevertheless, may find in the suggestions which follow clues of which they may make some use. The main concepts which, as expressed and emphasized in Islam, are open to criticism from a Christian point of view, but which nevertheless are

[1] Wensinck: *Encyc. of Islam,* ii. 1129.

not to be denied as fundamental principles, may be summarized as follows. God is One and Supreme, the Sovereign Creator and Preserver. He is Transcendent and Mighty, Wise, All-knowing and All-seeing, working His will in all things and executing judgment and retribution, the Author of life and death. He is also Guardian and Guide, Forgiving and Merciful. It would be a work of supererogation to make references to the Bible supporting these main conceptions.

Coming, however, to particulars, certain matters must be borne in mind. Firstly, owing to the rhapsodical and ecstatic style of the Qur'ān much of the material available in that book for the formulation of a doctrine of God, is of an ejaculatory character and no clue is afforded in the context as to the particular sense in which certain words and names are to be taken. Thus, secondly, in interpreting these words and names Muslim commentators who turned to the linguistic material available in the common idiom of Arabic, would be liable to content themselves with that material supplemented, of course, by what the traditions could provide in elucidation of difficulties. In this way, if in the mind of the prophet there were certain foreign ideas associated with the names he used for God, these could not be well known, and if he introduced a new sense, in the absence of his own explicit assertion to this effect or of adequate explanation in the Quranic context, such ideas and significances would be lost. A case in point is the use of the term *Quddūs* (holy) for God. The only material provided for the explanation of this is to be found in Suras lix. 23 and lxii. 1, in both of which passages the ejaculatory phrase occurs "the King, the Holy" or "the Holy King". With regard to this term there is a wealth of material to be drawn upon in the Bible, and we can trace a most instructive line of development in the Old Testament. Thus from the idea of untouchability and inaccessibility (cf. 2 Kings xix. 22; 2 Sam. vi. 6ff.) we move to the sublimely ethical (cf. Amos v. 6–11; Isa. l. 10–17; Jer. xxxi. 31f. and Hab. i. 12–13). Now there is little doubt that under the influence of Arabic usage a term which had become religiously and theologically so significant in North Semitic development reverts to the more primitive meaning of transcendence in the hands of Muslim commentators. So far as we have learned none of them has given the term an ethical interpretation.

It is possible that a reference to the Hebrew may yield a meaning to a name which is a puzzle to the commentators, e.g., the name *al Mu'min* as used for God. But *mu'min* ordinarily means "believer". That is a most inappropriate name for God. Therefore Muslim commentators consider that some other meaning such as "the One who keeps in peace" must be understood. But when it is realized that the root is used in Deut. vii. 9 and Isa. xlix. 7 (cf. also Psa. xxxvi. 5 and lxxxix. 1) for the "faithfulness" of God, light is cast on an obscurity.

Such names as *Jabbār* (Heb. *gibbor*) "mighty" (Sura lix. 23 and frequently in the Old Testament, e.g., Jer. xxxii. 18; Zeph. iii. 17; Psa. xxiv. 8; Deut. x. 17; Isa. ix. 6, etc.), *al Fattāḥ*, the opener (Sura xxxiv. 25 and frequently in the Old Testament, e.g., Gen. xxx. 22; Num. xxii. 28; Deut. xxviii. 12; Psa. li. 15; Psa. civ. 28; Ezek. xxxiii. 22, where God is represented as opening the mouth to prophesy and praise, or opening His hand to lavish His gifts, etc.), *al-Bārī*, the Creator (Sura lix. 24 and ii. 51, cf. Eccles. xii. 1; Isa. xl. 28; and Gen. i. 1, where the same root is used), *al Muṣawwir*, the Former (Sura lix. 24 and a common Aramaic name for God used by the Rabbis, cf. the cognate Hebrew root used in Gen. ii. 7, etc.; Psa. xciv. 8; Isa. xliii. 1, etc.), *al Qābiḍ*, the Gatherer (Sura xxv. 48 and xxxix. 67, where the root is verbally used; cf. Ezek. xxii. 19–20; Deut. xxx. 3–4; Psa. cvii. 3; Isa. liv. 7; lxvi. 18; Jer. xxxii. 37; Joel iii. 2; Micah ii. 12; in which passages God gathers the exiled people and gathers men to judgment, etc.), *al Basīṭ* (verb from the same root used in Sura xlii. 26 and the Hebrew cognate in Job xix. 9, though here the meanings would seem to differ), *al Wahhāb*, the Bounteous Giver (Sura iii. 6; xxxviii. 8; cf. the Aramaic cognate used in Dan. ii. 21, etc.), *as Samī'*, the Hearer (often in the Qur'ān and the conception represented with equal emphasis in the Old Testament, e.g., Exod. xxii. 23 and 27; 1 Kings viii. 30 ff.; Job xxxiv. 28; Psa. xciv. 9, lxv. 20 and Isa. lxv. 24), *al 'Ālī*, the Exalted (Sura ii. 256; xxii. 61; xxxiv. 21f.; xl. 12; xlii. 2 and 50–1; cf. Hosea vii. 16, xi. 7; Psa. xlvii. 9, xcvii. 9, etc.), *al Kabīr*, the Great (frequently in the Qur'ān; cf. Job xxxvi. 5), *al Ḥasīb*, the Reckoner (Sura iv. 88; xxxiii. 39; iv. 7; cf. Num. xviii. 27; Lev. vii. 18 and xvii. 4, where it represents God's taking into account the sacrifices of His people, and Psa. xl. 17, where there is more of gracious consideration), *al Barr*, interpreted by the commentators as Benign, but probably "the Pure" (Sura lii. 25–28; cf. Psa. xviii. 26, "With the pure Thou wilt show Thyself pure"), *at Tawwāb*,[1] the One who is apt to turn or relent (Sura ii. 35, 51, etc.; iv. 20, 67; ix. 105, 119; xxiv. 10; xlix. 12; cx. 3, cf. the technical use of terms meaning "to turn" and "to repent" in the Old Testament Aram. TWB, Heb. SHWB), *al Muntaqim*, the Avenger (Sura xxxii. 22; iii. 3; v. 96; xiv. 48, etc.; cf. Lev. xxvi. 25; Isa. xlvii. 3; lxi. 2; Jer. v. 9; ix. 9, where the same root is used in reference to the divine action,) *al Wāsi'*, the Ample or Bounteous (Sura liii. 33, where God is said to be Bounteous of forgiveness, and Sura iv. 129; cf. the words from the root YSH' used in the Old Testament in the sense of salvation and lying at the base of such names as Joshua; Judges iii. 9, "The Lord raised up a *Saviour* to the children of Israel", and see also Psa. lxii. 2, iii. 8, lxxii. 4), *al Ḥayy*, the Living (Sura xl. 67; ii. 256, xxv. 60; cf. Deut. v. 26; Jer. x. 10; Daniel vi. 20, 26 and

[1] Jeffery: *Foreign Vocab. of Qur'ān*, p. 87.

frequently); all the foregoing would appear to be names which have no sort of originality in Quranic usage, but to rest on the foundation of a common stock of ideas. And in addition, even the anthropomorphisms of the Qur'ān and the Old Testament are similar, both speaking of God's hand, His face and His being seated upon the Throne. So strong, indeed, is the Biblical influence (not, of course, by direct literary dependence) on the formulation of the canonical list of the Divine Names usually called *al Asmā ul Ḥusnā* (the Ninety-nine Beautiful Names) that we find therein names which have little or no foundation in the Qur'ān, but have in the Old Testament, e.g., *al Māni'*, the Hinderer (cf. Num. xxiv. 11; Ezek. xxxi. 15; 1 Sam. xxv. 26; whereas in the Qur'ān even the verb is not used with God as the subject, *al Muqaddim*, the Preceder or Preventer—in the old sense of going before—(cf. Psa. lix. 10, xxi. 3) "For Thou preventest him with the blessings of goodness".[1] Before leaving words used for God, which are linguistically similar in the Old Testament and in the Qur'ān, reference should be made to the very important name *al Rāḍī*, which is used to express the Divine acceptance, willingness or good-pleasure. Derivatives from this root are common in the Qur'ān, e.g., Sura v. 119, "God is well-pleased with them and they with God"; xx. 108, "Only one towards whom God is propitiated shall be heard as he speaks in the day of judgment," etc. The "goodwill" *riḍwān* of God is the subject of many passages. We find a similar frequency in the Old Testament, but in the Hebrew the root is RTSH. Out of fifteen instances of the use of this, thirteen are applied to God, and the idea is the propitiation of God, e.g., Jer. xiv. 10; Ezek. xx. 40–41, "As a sweet savour will I *accept* thee"; Ezek xliii. 27, "The priest shall make your offerings upon the altar and your peace offerings; and I will *accept* you saith the Lord God"; 2 Sam. xxiv. 23; Psa. cxix. 108; Eccles. ix. 7.

In some cases the linguistic relation is not found or is less distinct. Thus God is *Al Ghaffār*, the Forgiver, which the Hebrew represents by the root KPR. *Aḍ Ḍārr* represents God as the Afflictor, while Lam. i. 5, Psa. xliv. 2 and Ruth i. 21 present this idea with a different word. *Al Bāqī*, the Abiding, is the Quranic expression applied to the "face" of Allah (Sura lv. 27), while Psa. cii. 26—"They shall perish, but Thou shalt endure"—expresses the idea in other terms. Both Qur'ān and Old Testament declare that God is the First and the Last, e.g., Sura lvii. 3 and Isa. xliv. 6. Both speak of God's guidance with constant reiteration, e.g., Sura vi. 38 and Isa. lxiii. 11. The anger of God, though differently expressed, is to be found in both. Both insist that it is the prerogative of God to bring low, e.g., Sura iii. 25, which has its parallel in 1 Sam. ii. 7. In the Qur'ān the watchfulness of God is represented by the name *al Khabīr*, whereas the same idea is expressed in other terms in Daniel ix. 14; Jer. xxxi. 28, and Gen. xxxi. 49.

[1] *Aṣ Ṣabūr*, the Patient, not found in the Qur'ān, is another example.

The name *al Muqsiṭ* is not in that precise form found in the Qur'ān, but is derived from the foreign word *qisṭ*—justice, and used for the divine equity on the authority of the justice mentioned in Sura x. 48 and the just balance of Sura xxi. 48. The word is of Aramaic origin (cf. Daniel iv. 37). *Al Muhaimin*, the Preserver (Sura lix. 23) is obscure in its origin, but is certainly not Arabic.

In addition to the names mentioned, *Malik* and *Malakūt* representing kingship and kingdom (Suras lxii. 1 and xx. 113, etc., and xxiii. 90, etc.), *al Fāṭir*, Creator (Sura vi. 14, xii. 102, xxxix. 47, xlii. 9, etc.) an Ethiopic meaning of the root, *al Qayyūm*, Self-subsisting, *ar Razzāq*, Provider of daily bread, may all be classed with words which, if not foreign in every particular, have not the original significance in Arabic which they acquire by their use in the Qur'ān, in which they most commonly represent a technical sense in one of the cognate Semitic languages, usually Aramaic.[1] We have also the authority of Margoliouth for the Christian origin of *Rabb* in the sense of Lord.[2] The form of the name *ar Raḥmān*, Merciful, points to the fact that it is not pure Arabic. A Christian origin is probably to be traced for this name, but the borrowing was pre-Islamic.[3] Words not used as names of God, but associated with the divinity such as *Sakīna* (*Shechinah*) in Suras ii. 249; ix. 26, 40; xlviii. 4, 18, 26, which is manifestly from Biblical usage, *Ḥanān* (in Sura xix. 14), which is the sole survivor of the "grace" of the Old Testament (*ḥēn*), and *Kibriyā'* (Sura x. 79, xlv. 36), which departs from the ordinary meaning of the Arabic root and signifies "Glory", add emphasis to the foregoing examples which show to what a remarkable degree parallels may be drawn between the Quranic doctrinal statements and the language of Judaism and Christianity; for the latter has made no repudiation of the Old Testament, but rather acknowledged, and for the most part welcomed, the light which the Old Dispensation throws upon the New. Any embarrassment which may have been felt at certain elements in the Old Testament has been compensated for by an instructed realism and a theory of historical development which has enriched religious thought. But such considerations really belong to a later stage in the development of the argument of this book.

It cannot be maintained that the Quranic insistence upon monotheism is unique. Deut. vi. 4, "Hear, O Israel: the Lord our God is one Lord," is echoed in Mark xii. 29. Polytheism is denounced with all the vehemence at the command of the Hebrew Prophets, e.g., Ezek. viii. 5–18 and Isa. xliv. 9, 20. The Christian Scripture is no less certain, e.g., 1 Cor. viii. 4–6. All three religions maintain the doctrine

[1] For further information with regard to these, see Jeffery: *Foreign Vocabulary of the Qur'ān* at the appropriate places.
[2] *ERE* vi. 248.
[3] See Jeffery: *op cit.*, p. 140 f.

of Creation, e.g., Sura vi. 95 ff.; xvi. 3 ff.; xci. 1 ff.; lxxxviii. 16 ff.; lxxx. 24 ff.; lxxix. 27 ff., among which we find some of the sublimest passages in the whole of the Qur'ān and where not only is God extolled as Creator, but where His providential care is expressed in vivid fashion. Comparable passages in the Bible are Isa. xl. 12–26; Psa. xix. 1 ff.; Matt. vi. 26 ff.; Hebrews xi. 3, etc.—in addition to the Creation story of Genesis which is the inspiration of much that we find on the subject in the Qur'ān (cf. Sura x. 3 and xli. 8–11).

Equally emphasized in Qur'ān and Bible is the doctrine of the Judgment of God. While this forms a continuous theme in the Quranic proclamation, e.g., Sura xxxix. 47; ii. 107; xxii. 55, nothing there equals the magnificent oracles of judgment of the Hebrew Prophets, particularly Amos and Isaiah, and neither should the stirring passages in the New Testament be ignored or forgotten in vindication of the righteousness of God, while recognizing that the Grace of God is the abiding theme of the New Testament Scriptures. It would, moreover, be most remiss if one were to declare that the Grace of God finds no place in the teaching of the Qur'ān, though it must be admitted that the retributive justice of God is uppermost in that book. The Prophet is constantly recalling the mercy of God even if the sound Christian foundation for the declaration of His mercy is apparently unknown. The Prophet believed that God had dealt graciously with him (cf. Sura xciii.), and it was this which sustained him when all seemed to be lost (cf. Sura ix. 40 ff.). When the Qur'ān uses the name *Ar Ra'ūf* for God, the gentler and more pitiful aspect of God's dealing with men is prominent. Thus God will not suffer man's faith in Him to be in vain (Sura ii. 138); out of His compassion He sent signs to men (Sura lvii. 9); His providential protection is by His kindness and compassion (Sura xxii. 64), and the pity of God is maintained in the most unlikely contexts as, for example, in Sura xvi. 48–49 and iii. 28 where the subject is the retributive justice of God. What we find to be lacking in the main is the primary emphasis on grace, righteousness and truth, the *ḥeṣed*, *tsedeq* and *ᵉmeth* of the Old Testament round which all that is distinctive (together with the conception of God's mercy) in the Old Testament conception of God is gathered, and into which the Christian enters as into a rich and everlasting heritage. One or two meagre passages are all which can be offered for the wealth of the older Scripture, e.g., Sura iii. 89, "God speaks truth," and vi. 115, "The words of thy Lord are fulfilled in truth and justice".

(*b*) *Angelology*. There was a considerable cult of angels in Judaism, and after the Nestorian controversy in the Christian Church the office of angels was magnified, and there grew up a certain measure of worship of both saints and angels. It is interesting to note that when Ibn Qayyim comments on Sura xxi. 98, where it is declared that both the worshippers of others beside God *and what they worship* will go down into the fire, he makes a distinction between the idol which is the object of worship and those objects of worship which possess personality or sense and reason. Of these latter he specially mentions Ezra and Jesus, who were really good and should not therefore be cast into Hell. He also mentions angels, and asserts that they exist but should not be worshipped. This, however, does not exclude the intercession of angels. Muslim tradition has amplified what is found in the Qur'ān on this subject and in Rabbinical fashion describes the occupation of God in heaven. In three of the twelve hours into which the heavenly day is divided, God contemplates the sins of the world, and when His throne shakes and gets heavy with His wrath the angels sing praises to Him for the next three hours. While this is not Quranic, it gives the atmosphere of the age, and is in harmony with much that we find in the Qur'ān. There we are told that the angels bear the Throne of God and continually worship Him (Sura lxix. 17), that they are the messengers of Allah to guard and help His servants (Sura vi. 61).

The word used for angel in the Qur'ān is *malak* (ii. 33), which is not pure Arabic, but which may be referred back to Christian Ethiopic usage. Gabriel and Michael (*Jibrīl* and *Mīkāl*) are mentioned by name, e.g., in Sura ii. 91 and 92. Men have guardian angels (Sura xiii. 12), and this was a common belief in pre-Islamic times. In the *Life of Adam and Eve* (xxxiii. 1) we read " God the Lord gave us two angels to guard us. The hour came when the angels had ascended to worship in the sight of God ".[1] Similar ideas in amplification of the Qur'ān are found in Muslim *Ḥadīth*. The intercession and mediation of angels is also taught in the Qur'ān (Sura xlii. 3). This idea is common in Jewish pseudepigrapha. Reference should be made to the *Apocalypse of Moses*, xxxv. 2 and to the *Third Book of Baruch* (*passim*). It is an idea not altogether absent from the Bible as Zech. i. 12 and the *Book of Revelation* bear witness. In Sura lxxxii we read of the two recorders of men's deeds and so also in the *Testament of Abraham*, 12. The Holy Spirit is considered to be an angel, and he is later identified with Gabriel as the agent in revelation, about which more later. Here it should suffice to draw attention to 1 Kings xxii. 21 and to the Talmudic " speaking spirit "[2] whom the Rabbis identified with Gabriel. Quranic references of interest are Sura v. 109 and xvi. 104.

No very clear and absolute distinction is made between angels and *jinn* if we can take the two passages, Sura ii. 32, where Satan is one of the angels, and Sura xviii. 48, where he appears as one of the *jinn*, as any evidence. A similar confusion appears in the pseudepigrapha, where (in the *Book of Jubilees* ii. 2) we read of the angels of natural phenomena and (in the *Book of the Secrets of Enoch*, A xxix. 3) that they were made of fire. This was regularly held in regard to the *jinn*.

[1] A further reference is the *Book of Jubilees*, xxxv. 17.
[2] *Sanhedrin*, 44.

Geiger points out the similarity between the Talmudic and Muslim ideas about the *jinn*. They possess three angelic qualities and three human. They have wings, can know the future, and have power to fly from one part of the earth to another. These are their angelic qualities. They also eat and drink, have children and die. The *Talmud* also says that they listen behind the curtain when instruction is being given, while Muslims explain shooting stars as the stoning of the *jinn* by angels when they are eavesdropping (cf. Sura lxxii). In verse 19 of the Sura mentioned, the curiosity of the *jinn* in listening to teaching is narrated. Whether the guardians of Hell are to be classified as angels or *jinn* is not perfectly clear (Sura lxxiv. 30–31). Such guardians are described as of gruesome aspect in the *Book of the Secrets of Enoch* (xlii): "I saw the guardians of the keys of Hell standing by the gates like huge serpents, their faces like lamps that are gone out, their eyes like smouldering flames, and their teeth naked down to their breasts."

Satan is spoken of in the Qur'ān under the name Shaiṭān, which is the equivalent, and the name Iblīs, which is a corruption of the Greek *diabolos*. He is represented as head of a host, and it is interesting to find that the plurality of satans, *Shayāṭīn*, in the Qur'ān has a parallel in the *Book of Enoch*. In that book the references are numerous; typical ones are lxv. 6 and lxix. 14.

Sufficient has been said on this subject to show that a great deal of the angelology of the Qur'ān has its parallels in popular belief among the People of the Book. The stories of dissension among the angels at the Creation have already been referred to.

(*c*) *Revelation*. The explicit reference to the Law of Moses (*Tawrāt*), the Psalms (*Zabūr*) and the Gospel (*Injīl*) in the text of the Qur'ān immediately puts us on familiar ground. Implicit in the stories of the prophets of old as Muhammad related them is the first part of the conception of revelation found in Heb. i. 1–2: "God, having of old times spoken unto the fathers in the prophets by divers portions and in divers manner, hath at the end of these days spoken unto us in His Son." When one reads the list of the Hebrew Prophets one cannot be at a loss to know whence the Prophet Muhammad had his conception of Prophethood. If we note the language which is used, namely, *nabī*, prophet, and *nabuwwa*, prophecy, there can be no doubt that these are borrowed from the older religions, and we are probably correct if we accept the opinion of Wright [1] that they are of Jewish Aramaic origin, though Jeffery, for good reasons, points to the Hebrew,[2] to which, of course, both must ultimately be referred. If *nabuwwa* is to be regarded as a prophetic document rather than the office of a prophet, then 2 Chron. ix. 29 is significant, but we incline to the latter view.

[1] *Comparative Grammar*, p. 46.
[2] *Foreign Vocabulary of the Qur'ān*, p. 276 f.

We have already made allusion to the idea that the Holy Spirit was the agent in revelation. Jeffery considers that the Quranic usage of the name may be best explained by reference to the Christian usage, but it must be remembered that in extracanonical writings the same idea is to be found. It is true that the use of the word *Qudus*, holy, suggests the Christian origin, but if we refer, e.g., to the *Fourth Book of Ezra* we find that Ezra is represented as praying: "Send unto me the Holy Spirit that I may write all that has happened in the world" (4 *Ezra* xiv. 22). With this should be associated the many references to an angelic agent in revelation, e.g., *Book of Jubilees* xxxii. 21, where the angel is said to bring down seven tablets of revelation to Jacob. We would therefore incline to refer the Quranic idea of the angelic holy spirit as the agent in revelation to such sources rather than to the Christian pure and simple. No doubt when the Holy Spirit is spoken of as aiding Christ there is closer proximity to the Christian point of view. It would, however, be too much to expect a clear conception to be afforded to us in the pages of the Qur'ān.

The mention of "tablets" recalls the fact that the common notion of tables of revelation finds its place also in the Qur'ān. In the Old Testament we read of the tables of stone on which the ten words of the Law were inscribed by Moses. The word *Lawḥ* used in the Qur'ān represents these tablets of Moses in Sura vii, and heavenly records or the Book in Heaven from which piecemeal the Qur'ān (and probably all the revelations to the prophets) was given to the Prophet Muhammad, in Sura lxxxv. 22. The word in its religious significance is used in Hebrew, Aramaic and Syriac and, as already said, represents a familiar idea. The written tablets which the scribes prepare are spoken of in 4 *Ezra* xiv. 21 ff., and the tablets in heaven which were brought down to Jacob are mentioned in the *Book of Jubilees* xxxii. 21, and in a fragment of the *Prayer of Joseph* preserved in *Philocalia* (cap. xxiii. 15) we may read: "For I have read in the tablets of heaven all that shall befall you and your sons." This agrees with the reference in Sura vii. 142, where the heavenly tablets are said to contain "details of everything". We find references to the heavenly tablets four times in the *Book of Enoch*, twenty times in the *Book of Jubilees* and three times in the *Testament of the Twelve Patriarchs*.

Similar remarks may be made with regard to "the Mother of the Book", *Umm ul Kitāb*, the Heavenly Prototype of all revelation. Though exact linguistic resemblance is not in evidence, we have the concept in Philo and the *Wisdom of Ben Sirach* of Wisdom as the Mother of the Divine Logos,[1] and "He that taketh hold of the Law findeth Sophia and she will meet him as a mother"[2] and "All these things (of Sophia) are the Book of the Covenant of God Most High,

[1] *de Fuga et Inventione*, 108 f.
[2] *Sirach* xv. 1.

the Law which Moses commanded as a heritage for the assemblies of Jacob."[1] Thus it is not too highly improbable that we have the literalizing of an allegory in popular imagination based on such language. The Rabbinical idea was that God's statute book was something which existed before creation, and it is in accord with this that He creates and governs and finally judges the world. Thus the transcendent Book is a Book of Fate as well as a Book of Law. There are many passages in the Qur'ān which speak in such an absolute fashion about " the Book " that it is difficult to escape the conclusion that some such transcendent book is referred to, of which the Scriptures are only partial representatives. Thus Jews and Christians are People of the Book. In the Annunciation, Sura iii. 43, we find the words, " He (i.e. God) will teach him the Book, and wisdom, and the law and the gospel, and he shall be a prophet to the people of Israel." In this passage the Book is mentioned separately from the Law of Moses and the Gospel. In Sura iii. 183 we read : " Those who have had the Book brought them before you " and we have in Sura xxii. 69 : " Didst thou not know that God knows what is in the heavens and the earth ? Verily, that is in a book, verily, that for God is easy," which plainly refers to a book in which all is written. That it is a book of legal precepts seems evident also from Sura xxxiii. 6 : " Blood relations are nearer in kin to each other by the Book of God than the believers and those who fled," and Sura ix. 36, " The number of months with God is twelve months in God's Book." That it is a book of Fate seems clear from Sura xxxv. 12 : " No female bears or is delivered, except by His knowledge ; nor does he who is aged reach old age, or is aught diminished from his life without it is in the Book," and Sura xxxv. 28 shows that what was given to the Prophet was *from* the Book : " What we have suggested to thee from the Book is the truth." This does not mean that there is complete consistency in the references, and it is quite obvious that sometimes the reference intended is to some book, like the Law of Moses or the Gospel, which is in the hands of the Prophet's hearers. But it will be noted that a like duality is to be found in the Jewish references to the Tablets, which are at one time spoken of as being in Heaven and at another time as being the writing of the prophets or the Scribes. And the Targum of Canticles v. 10 speaks of God studying in the day time the twenty-four books of Scripture and by night the six *sedarim* of the *Mishna,* while the Qur'ān often states that God's knowledge is in a book, Sura xxii. 69 ; xxvii. 76 ; l. 4 ; xi. 5–8.

Commenting on the " tablets " as they are spoken of in the *Book of Enoch*, Charles [2] points to Exod. xxv. 9, 40 and Daniel x. 21, and speaks of the " heavenly tablets of God's plans ". The references to the *Book*

[1] *Sirach,* xxiv. 23.
[2] Charles : *Apoc. and Pseudep. of O.T.*, Vol. ii, pp. 262–3.

of Enoch are xciii. 2, lxxxi. 1–2, ciii. 2–3, cvi. 19. One other reference may be given to the *Book of Jubilees* v. 13: "And the judgment of all is ordained and written on the heavenly tablets in righteousness . . . and all their judgments are ordained and written and engraved."

The Qur'ānic conception of successive verification and confirmation of revelation and the line of prophets is based on material which the Bible supplies. It is true that occasionally odd persons appear as prophets in the Islamic lists, such as Alexander the Great and Luqmān, and that there is a marked absence of reference to the writing prophets of Israel. It is also noteworthy that some Old Testament characters figure as prophets in the Qur'ān who have little claim to be regarded as such. Nevertheless, with all these provisos it is still possible to see the dependence on the older religions for the conception of prophecy, and Muhammad is explicit in his appeal to the older in his own defence and to establish his own right to the office of a prophet. In one place (Sura ii. 130) we read: "Say ye: 'We have believed in Allah and what has been sent down to us, and what has been sent down to Abraham and Ishmael and Isaac and Jacob and the Patriarchs, and what has been given to Moses and Jesus, and what has been given to the prophets from their Lord, making no distinction between any of them.'" Jesus, it will be observed, is one of the line of prophets. "In their footsteps we caused Jesus, the Son of Mary, to follow, confirming the Torah which was before Him, and We gave Him the Gospel, containing guidance and light, confirming the Torah which was before it, and as guidance and warning to those who show piety" (Sura v. 50). Not only is there this doctrine, but the manner of the Old Testament prophets is readily discernible in Muhammad's teaching, in the way natural calamity is cited as a disclosure of the divine will and judgment. A comparison of Zech. xiv. 12–19; Hag. i. 10–11 and ii. 17; Hab. viii.; Jer. xxv. 17–38 and many other passages with Suras xvii. 5 ff., 70 f.; xli. 12 ff.; xxix. 39 and the like, will make this abundantly plain. Moreover the hard way Muhammad has to take before he can convince the people to whom he is sent is compared to similar rejection of the prophets of Israel, e.g., Sura v. 73 ff., where he speaks of the slaying of the prophets by the Jews. So completely conscious is Muhammad of the background of the older religions that he declares that the former scriptures contain prophecies of his advent (Sura lxi. 6 ff.).

(*d*) *Christological*. The source from which Muhammad derived his ideas about Jesus Christ—if he depended on a source and is not simply expressing his own ideas—is likely to remain a mystery. Nevertheless Sura xix. 38 proves at least this much that Muhammad was aware of a controversy: "The sects have disagreed among themselves." Whether he was aware of the terms of the controversies which were raging we cannot declare with any assurance, and simply advance what information is available, for what it is worth as casting light on the Quranic statements.

Is there an echo of the manifold controversies on the Person of Christ? We know that Arianism persisted for a long time in various forms, and that the Nestorian controversy was still proceeding. Questions about the dual nature in Christ were being asked. Nestorius argued that there was a union of humanity and divinity in Christ, but not a union in essence. Cyril of Jerusalem asserted a metaphysical and physical union insomuch that God *became* man.[1] In the incarnate Christ there was one subject having one nature and that divine-human. Nestorius disagreed because he held that this would destroy the divine immutability. It was Nestorius also who protested against the use of the title *theotokos* for the Virgin Mary, and it was the Nestorians who had had such great influence in the Middle East at the time when Islam arose. Furthermore, the Monophysites were popular in Palestine, in Egypt and in Antioch. In the sixth century they formed sects in Syria and Egypt. The Jacobites also—as explained above—were influential in Arabia, and they were monophysite. Have we in the Qur'ān an incompletely informed mind expressing an opinion about current controversies?

Whatever answers may be given it is interesting to examine the conception of Christ set before us in the pages of the Qur'ān with such a background in mind.

At first blush it may seem to be expressing the obvious when it is affirmed that the Qur'ān teaches that Jesus Christ was only a man. In Sura xliii. 59 it is roundly asserted: "He is only a creature to whom we have been gracious." In Sura xix. 36: "God could not take to Himself a Son. When He decrees a matter, He has only to say Be!", and in Sura v. 79: "The Messiah is only a messenger." Such passages seem conclusive enough, but a closer examination presents many checks. Thus, for instance, if we look closely at the context of the first reference we find that there is a mysterious allusion to the raising up of *angels*: "He is only a servant on whom We have bestowed favour, and have appointed him to be a parable for the Children of Israel. *If We willed, We should appoint angels from among you* in the land to succeed." If the words of verse 60 were uttered immediately after those of verse 59 (which Bell doubts) then we should have a significant movement of the Prophet's mind revealed to us, and it might be suggested that Muhammad thought immediately of an angelic nature when he thought about Christ. On the other hand, in the context of the third reference above we have the plain declaration that "both of them ate food" which refers to Mary and her Son. This, taken in conjunction with the story of Abraham's angel visitants, who

[1] *ἐγένετο ἄνθρωπος, οὐ συνήφθη ἀνθρώπῳ.*

do not eat food because they are angels, would constitute a plain denial of the angelic nature of Christ.[1]

Similarly it seems quite conclusive when we read Sura iii. 52: "Verily the likeness of Jesus with God is as the likeness of Adam. He created him from earth, then He said to him 'Be' and he was," that the humanity of Christ is taught. But here also it must be remembered that the Qur'ān gives a pre-eminent place to Adam, as we have already seen. He was created in a Heavenly Eden amid the court of Heaven. He was represented as superior to the angels, who were called upon to worship him, and he was the occasion of the fall of Satan. Apocalyptic literature busied itself excessively with the doctrine of the person of Adam, and we know that there was great emphasis laid upon the doctrine of the Christ as the Second Adam within the Christian Church. This was particularly true of the theologian Theodore of Mopsuestia, who represents the Eastern Church in regard to this point. Thus if the likeness of Adam is to be pressed, it has a twofold aspect. For Adam was a direct creation of God and did not come to exist by ordinary generation, and the same is held to be true of Christ. Thus it might be held that we have here something approaching an Arian conception.

Nor is this by any means the only complication. Christ is declared to be "a Spirit from Him", Sura iv. 169, and sometimes in the Qur'ān "spirit" means an angel, and the Holy Spirit is identified with Gabriel. There may be here, however, a reference to one of the "seven substances" from which, according to the *Book of the Secrets of Enoch*,[2] Adam was composed, the previously mentioned "earth" being one of them, and the Spirit which was from the Spirit of God another. Moreover, in Sura xxiii. 54–5 the Spirit is said to be "*amr rabbī*", which might be translated "the word of my Lord", for *amr*[3] is one of those words in the Qur'ān which is used in a variety of meanings and certainly in some places suggests the term "*Memra*" used as equivalent for "*Logos*". And then, to come full circle, Christ is spoken of as "the Word". This, as already pointed out, is in the terms of the Annunciation in Sura iii. 40: "O Mary, Allah giveth thee tidings of a word from Himself whose name is the Messiah" and is also in Sura iv. 169: "The Messiah, Jesus, Son of Mary, is only the Messenger of Allah and His Word which He cast into Mary." In these two passages, however, the less ambiguous *kalima* is used and not *amr*.

[1] Cf. also D. B. Macdonald: art. 'Īsā in *Encyc. of Islam*, Vol. ii, 524. Note particularly Sura iii. 40. *Muqarrabun* is a title for angels.

[2] xxx. 8 ff.

[3] A complete list of references for the word is: xxiii. 54 f.; xiii. 2; x. 3; vii. 52; xviii. 48; lix. 15–16; iii. 42; xxxii. 23–24; xlv. 16; xxii. 66; xx. 65; xvi. 35; xx. 92; vi. 57–58; ii. 63; xi. 43, 45; xix. 56; xi. 69, 78, 84, 123; lxv. 1; xviii. 15; vii. 28; xxxiv. 11; xvii. 87.

It is commonly held that the use of the word *'abd* (servant) in xliii. 59 settles the matter, and that this word alone implies humanity. In comments on such texts both Nöldeke and Bell [1] and many others suggest " man " as an equivalent. But there is clear evidence in the Qur'ān that angels were called *'abd*, e.g., Sura iv. 170 : " The Messiah will not disdain to be a servant of Allah, *nor will the angels* who stand in His presence " (cf. also Sura xix. 94). Neither is the statement in Sura v. 79 decisive when it says that the Messiah is only a messenger (*rasūl*), for that very term is used for angels in Sura xxii. 74 : " Allah chooses messengers from among the angels and from among the people." [2]

It has often been pointed out that there seems to be a docetic element in the Quranic denial of the crucifixion of Christ. Thus we find in Sura iv. 156 : " 'Verily, we have killed the Messiah, Jesus the Son of Mary, the Apostle of God.' But they did not kill Him and they did not crucify Him, *but a similitude was made for them.* And verily those who differ about Him are in doubt concerning Him ; they have no knowledge concerning Him, but only follow a conjecture. They did not certainly kill Him. Nay, God raised Him up unto Himself ; for God is Mighty and Wise." With such a statement should be compared Christian statements such as that Christ would not see corruption and that He could not be holden of death. It is perfectly feasible that a Christian might say of the Jews that they did not succeed in their object because God raised Christ up. From the time of Muhammad back to the early docetism is a far cry, but we do not know whether statements which appeared in pseudo-gospels and acts were embodied in popular tales of Christ and persisted up to the time of the Prophet Muhammad. We might point, e.g., to the apocryphal *Acts of Peter* [3] and *Acts of John*, particularly the latter, in support of the idea that the cross was only a phantasm. In the *Acts of John* we find explicit statements. Our Lord is represented as talking to John in a place apart while the people are supposed to be crucifying Him. He says : " Unto the multitude in Jerusalem I am being crucified and pierced with lances and gall and vinegar is given Me to drink. But unto thee I speak " (97). " Neither am I He that is on the cross, whom now thou seest not but only hearest a voice. I was reckoned to be that which I am not, not being what I was to many others " (99). " Nothing, therefore, of the things which they will say of Me have I suffered " (101). But apart from these remote statements we have evidence of heretical doctrines held by people close to the days of

[1] Note to Sura L. 8 in his translation.

[2] As a matter of interest one might refer to the words of Jalāl ud Dīn Rūmī in the *Mathnawī* (vi. 2972 Nicholson's ed.), " Jesus in the form of man was homogeneous with the angels."

[3] James : *New Testament Apocrypha*, p. 334. *Acts of Peter* was written about A.D. 200.

Muhammad and these, the aphthartodocetists as they were called, held that the body of Christ was incorruptible and insensible to the weakness of the flesh. This question was a live one about the time when Islam arose. Justinian (A.D. 483–565) belonged to this school of thought, and even tried to enforce his opinion. We read that Eutychius lost his bishopric through opposing him. Even a father of the Church so justly famed as Gregory of Nyssa [1] had the naïve idea that Christ, by assuming human form, deceived Satan into thinking that he had only an ordinary human being to deal with. Julian of Halicarnassus (d. *c.* A.D. 518), the founder of the sect of the Julianists, held that after the incarnation the body of Christ was not susceptible to corruption. There seems to have been some sort of idea that the suffering of death would be derogatory to the dignity of Christ, and it may be that Muhammad thought that it would be derogatory to the prophethood of Christ. Indeed we have early evidence that such arguments were used by the Caliph Mahdī (*c.* A.D. 781) [2]: "It was not honourable to Jesus Christ that God should have allowed Him to be delivered to Jews in order that they might kill Him" (cf. Sura v. 74, where it is stated that the Jews killed the prophets). However this may be, it is clear that certain docetic elements persisted to within a short time of the advent of Islam. Not that Justinian denied the crucifixion, for he was one of those responsible for the formula "God was crucified for us" (A.D. 564), which would be an added stumbling block to the acceptance of the crucifixion, if it were expressed in that way, but can hardly be the occasion for the Quranic protest. Nevertheless we might legitimately conjecture that if Jesus Christ was regarded as more than man, such a docetic element as we find in the Quranic denial of the crucifixion might be expected.[3]

It is not intended, however, to assert that the Qur'ān does not deny the divinity of Christ. The denial is most categorical. Sura ix. 30–31: "The Jews say that Ezra is the Son of God and the Christians say that the Messiah is the Son of God. That is what they say with their mouths, imitating the statements of those who misbelieved before. . . . They take doctors and monks for Lords rather than God." (The latter part of this is probably a misunderstanding of the Syrian use of the word *Rabb* as in *rabbi* and *rabban*, the word *Rabb* being most commonly used of God in Arabic, but used in a secondary sense for "lord" by Jews and Christians.) Sura v. 76: "Assuredly they have disbelieved who say: 'Allah is the Messiah, the Son of Mary.' . . . Assuredly, they have disbelieved who say 'Allah is the third of three'." Sura iv. 169: "Do not say 'Three!' Refrain, it will be better for you; Allah is only One God; glory be to Him (far from) His having a son!"

[1] *Or. Cat.*, cap. XXVI.
[2] *Timothy's Apology for Christianity*, ed. and trans. Mingana, p. 42.
[3] The Qur'ān says nowhere explicitly that Christ was only a man.

Sura v. 116 : " When Allah said : ' O Jesus, Son of Mary, was it thou who didst say to the people : " Take me and my mother as two gods apart from Allah " ? ' He replied : ' Glory be to Thee ! It is not for me to say what to me is not true (*or* what I am not entitled to say) ; if I did say it, Thou knowest it ; Thou knowest what is in my soul, but I know not what is in Thy soul ; verily it is Thou Who art the Knower of secret things. I did not say anything to them but what Thou didst command me : " Serve Allah, my Lord and your Lord." ' " The last phrase reads almost like a translation of John xx. 17. In these passages along with the denial of the Trinity there is a denial of the divinity of Christ and His Sonship (see also Sura xix. 36).

The Qur'ān, misconceiving the Trinity as Father, mother and Son, feels called upon also to deny the divinity of the Virgin Mary. Wherein lay the misconception and wherefore the necessity for such a denial is difficult to state with any certainty. It has been hazarded that because *Rūḥ* (Spirit) in Syriac is used in the feminine there was a misidentification of the Holy Spirit with the Virgin. It has been pointed out that in the *Gospel to the Hebrews* Christ is made to refer to " my mother, the Holy Spirit ". Others point to Aphraates' doctrine of the Spirit [1] and his *Treatise of Virginity against the Jews*, where he says : " When a man hath not yet taken a wife, he loveth and honoureth God his Father and the Holy Spirit his Mother and he hath no other love." [2] Others would hear in the words of the Qur'ān an echo of the Nestorian protest against the title *theotokos* for the Virgin. It is well known that the worship of Mary was greatly emphasized after the Nestorian controversy.[3] On the other hand, it may be that a sort of divine family similar to that found in pagan myths was in the mind of the prophet in his protest against the Trinity. We must remember that such notions might have been familiar to Arab paganism and that the Prophet would be right in protesting either against tritheism or against such a pagan idea, and that Christians themselves could also protest against such a misreading of the doctrine of the Trinity as that found in the pages of the Qur'ān, or against an incarnation through the conjunction of a god with a woman.[4]

Finally, for completeness, reference may be made to the fact that Jesus is known throughout the Qur'ān as the Messiah and that the form of the name shows it to have been derived from Christian Syriac. There is no evidence in the Qur'ān that Muhammad knew the signifi-

[1] Burkitt : *Early Eastern Christianity*, 88.

[2] Note that the Old Syriac has the reference in John xiv. 26 in the feminine and that the Peshitta has the feminine in Luke iv. 1 ; John vii. 39.

[3] Cf. Fisher : *History of Christian Doctrine*, p. 172.

[4] Further reference for the topics mentioned may be made to Epiphanius *Haer.* xix. 4, etc. There we find the Ebionite ideas about the Heavenly Man or Adam applied to Christ, the idea of Christ as a gigantic angel and the conception of a woman Holy Spirit.

cance of this term.[1] As already said, Christ is a worker of miracles (Sura ii. 81, etc.). Since it involves a possible confusion in regard to the identification of the Holy Spirit, we should also note the claim of Muhammad in Sura lxi. 6 ff., to be the fulfilment of a prophecy that one should come after Christ: "And when Jesus, Son of Mary, said, 'O children of Israel, I am Allah's messenger to you, confirming the Torah which was before Me, and announcing the good tidings of a messenger who will come after Me, bearing the name Ahmad.'" The name would be a translation of *periklutós*, a misreading for the correct *parákl̄etos* in John xiv. 16 and commentators have explained it in this way. That the Muslim interpretation is quite impossible hardly needs repetition. The points to note, apart from the actual text, which is well established from ancient manuscripts, are John xvi. 26, where the Comforter or Paraclete is identified with the Holy Spirit; xv. 26 and xvi. 13, where the identification is with the Spirit of Truth; xx. 22: "Receive the Holy Spirit" and the giving of the Holy Spirit on the Day of Pentecost. It should also be remembered that though the word "paraclete" has become a proper name for the Holy Spirit in Christian usage, it is actually an attributive and not a proper name, and is used as such not only for the Holy Spirit, but also for Jesus Christ Himself, in 1 John ii. 1. For other uses of the word in the form *peraqlīt* the *Talmud* may be consulted at *Shabb.* 32a, *Zebaḥim* 7b and also *Pirke Aboth* iv. 15 and Philo: *Vita Mosis* iii. 14.

(*e*) *Eschatalogical.* The doctrine of the final Judgment looms large in the proclamation of Muhammad. Macdonald compares him in this respect to a revivalist preacher who pictures the torments of the damned and seeks to strike terror in the hearts of his hearers. That such teaching was common in the Christianity of that age is quite clear. The pages of *Barlaam and Ioasaph* are full of such allusions. Tor Andrae quotes the translation of a Coptic text,[2] "I am afraid of the road whereby I shall depart to God and of the Powers that stand on it, because I am flesh and blood and like every other man, and no man is sinless in the sight of God. There is specially the great river of difficulty and of the great abomination of this river of fire, whereon roll waves on waves and the burning flames which no man can escape. . . . O this throne of fire which is full of trembling and horror! O this throne of terror!"[3] Equally vivid are the descriptions of the Prophet Muhammad. The judgment comes like a blow (Sura xiii. 31), is overwhelming (xii. 107), and deafening (lxxx. 33). It is the day of the diagnosis (4 Ezra vii. 104, the *Yawm ul Faṣl* of Sura xxxvii. 21), the day of reckoning (*yawm ul Ḥisāb*, Sura xl. 28), etc. In this all men will appear before God after the resurrection of the body (Sura

[1] Refs. for the name: iii. 40; iv. 156, 169, 170; v. 19, 76, 79; ix. 30–31.
[2] *Ursprung*, 267 ff.
[3] Budge: *Coptic Texts* v. 726 f.

iv. 10; xxi. 104; lxxxv. 10–13, etc.). That day is also described as "the Hour" *sā'a*, the familiar term in Christian usage (see John v. 28, Mark xiii. 32 and Sura liv. 46; xlii. 17; vi. 31, etc.). Bell[1] draws attention to the word used in Sura lxxiv. 1–7, *rujz*, which is the Syriac word used in Matt. iii. 7. It is also significant that Christ is spoken of as a sign of the "Hour" (Sura xliii. 61) which would appear to be a reference to His second advent (in which Muslims believe) if the pronoun refers back to Christ.[2]

When we come to the descriptions of the celestial cosmology in the Qur'ān we find there also elements from the older religions. Geiger sees in the reference to seven Heavens, circles, strongholds or courses (Suras ii. 27; xvii. 46; xxiii. 17, 88; xli. 11; lxv. 12; lxvii. 3; lxxi. 14; lxxviii. 12, etc.) affinity with the *Talmud*.[3] Reference, however, should also be made to *Slavonic Enoch* 3–21.[4] Geiger also refers the seven hells of the Qur'ān to the same sources[5] (see Sura xv. 44). The name *Firdaus*, Paradise, may in all probability be attributed to a Christian source.[6] A Paradise described in sensual imagery was not foreign to some Eastern Christians, as Tor Andrae points out,[7] quoting the *Hymns of Paradise* of Ephraim the Syrian. And when the pleasing virgins of Paradise are described in the Qur'ān at Sura lvi. 36 an unusual term is used (*'arūb*) which shows affinity with the Hebrew of Ezek. xvi. 37 and Cant. ii. 14. It should not be forgotten that when Jerome commented on Matt. xix. 29 he promised the recompense of a hundred wives! "*Ut qui unam (mulierem) pro Domino dimiserit centum recipiat in futuro.*"

The term used for resurrection, *qiyāma*, is a technical term in Christian Aramaic,[8] and the insistence on the resurrection of the body is distinctly Christian and needs no reference to establish it.

With regard to other details in the description of the Last Things, *Yājūj* and *Mājūj* (Sura xviii. 93–97) are the Gog and Magog of Ezek. xxxviii and xxxix. It is highly probable that Mālik the guardian of Hell (Sura xliii. 77) is the Moloch of the Old Testament.

(*f*) *Miscellaneous.* We would conclude these illustrations—which are not to be taken as at all exhaustive—with some miscellaneous references of interest for comparative doctrine. The vanity, uncertainty and inconstancy of this present world is compatible with the

[1] *Origin of Islam*, 88.
[2] See, however, Bell: *The Qur'ān* ii. 495.
[3] He refers to *Chagiga* ix. 2.
[4] Charles: *Apoc. and Pseudep. of O.T.*, Vol. ii. 432 ff.
[5] *Erubin* xix. 1. The names are *Sheol, Abaddon, Beēr-Shakhath, Bor-Shā'on, Ṭīṭ-ha yāwen, Tsalmaweth* and *Erets teḥtīth*, cf. 2 Sam. xii. 6; Job xxviii. 22; Psa. lv. 24; Psa. xl. 2 (two); Psa. xxiii. 4; Deut. xxxii. 22; and Psa. lxxxviii. 6 for the origin of these names. *Hāwiyā* (Sura ci. 6) as a name for Hell may have been created on the same principle from the "mischief" of *Ezek*. vii. 26; and Isa. xlvii. 11.
[6] Jeffery: *For. Voc. of Qur'ān*, 224.
[7] *Muhammad*, p. 120 f.
[8] Schwally: *Idioticon*, 82, referred to by Jeffery, *op. cit.*

ascetic spirit in the Syrian Church which, though in some sort repudiated by the "no monkery" of the Prophet Muhammad, shows again and again in the pages of the Qur'ān (Sura xl. 82; lxviii. 17 ff.; ii. 268, etc.).[1] *Fājir*, wicked (Suras lxxi. 28; lxxxii. 14, etc.) is the technical Syriac for "fleshly". *Suḥt* is variously attributed to the Syriac meaning "depravity" and to the *Talmud* where it has the significance of "unlawful" (see Sura v. 46, 67, 68). *Ṭāghūt* (ii. 257, etc.), idolatry, has also, in all probability a Talmūdic origin (cf. *Sanhedrin* x. 28d). *Khaṭi'a*, "to miss" represents fairly closely the ἁμαρτία of the New Testament (see Suras iv. 94; ii. 286; xxviii. 7; xvii. 33; iv. 112 and lxix. 9, etc.).[2] And similarly the terms for purification and purity, *dhakkā* and *zakā*, both Tor Andrae and Bell consider to be due to Christian Syriac usage.[3]

The special use of *kaffara* in Sura xlvii. 2 importing "absolution" is associated with Jewish or Christian ideas of atonement, and the word *qurbān* in the sense of oblation has also a backing from the particular Aramaic and Christian usage of the term[4] (cf. Mark vii. 11 and many places in Leviticus and Numbers, e.g., Lev. ii. 4, also Neh. x. 34 and Ezek. xx. 28 and xl. 43, where both the Hebrew and the Aramaic occur).

If these examples are studied it will be seen what a considerable body of evidence of a doctrinal dependence on the older religions is presented by the text of the Qur'ān or, if that is too great an assumption, at least what remarkable parallels can be presented to prove the common idiom of the thought and even, in some cases, of the religious speech. It will also be seen that the connections with Christianity are closer than one would at first expect, although we have already given the warning that there may have been a growing approximation in religious speech between Christians and Jews.

(iv) Religious Law. For completeness we may give a few examples of similarity in religious law between the precepts of the Qur'ān and the older religions. It should first be noted that the very conception of the Qur'ān as the *Sharī'a*—a Code—is a return to the conception of revelation as Law such as we find in Judaism and the extreme reverence for the Torah. But the Qur'ān in itself could not supply all that was required in a complete religious Code, and so we have the gradual enlargement of the preceptive element in the *Ḥadīth* and the later systematized *Fiqh* of Islam. As this enlargement and development took place the older and well-established religions wielded a stronger and more far-reaching influence than in the Qur'ān.

[1] Cf. *Barlaam and Ioasaph* xv. 127.
[2] See under the appropriate headings in Jeffery, *op. cit.*
[3] Bell: *op. cit.* 51, and Tor Andrae: *Der Ursprung des Islams und das Christentum* (in *Kyrkohistorisk Arsskrift*, 1925, p. 106).
[4] Cf. Wensinck in *Encyc. of Islam*, Vol. ii, 1129, and Mingana: *Syriac Influence on the Style of the Qur'ān*, p. 85.

Ablutions and bathing are prescribed in Judaism and Islam (Sura v. 8 and 9, cf. many passages in the Mosaic law). The prohibited degrees of marriage are the same in Islam and Judaism (Sura iv. 26–27). The prohibitions with regard to certain food show similarities with the Jewish Law (Sura ii. 167) particularly in the prohibition of what dies of itself and swine's flesh (see also Sura v. 89 f.). For marriage with a female slave compare Sura iv. 28 with Deut. xxi. 10 ff., and for divorce Sura ii. 226; 228 f. and iv. 24 with Deut. xxiv. 1. The period of waiting before a woman can be remarried is three months according to the Qur'ān (Sura ii. 228), and we find the same law in the *Talmud.*[1] The period for the suckling of a child is two years (Sura ii. 233). This is also to be found in the *Talmud.*[2] The laws of inheritance in the Qur'ān and the Old Testament differ radically, but are in agreement as to the order in which relatives of the deceased person shall receive their portions (Sura iv. 12 ff., etc. and Deut. xxi. 15–17 and Num. xxvii. 8–11). The duty of almsgiving is laid down in all the three religions (Sura ix. 5, 18, 60, 104; ii. 269 f.; vi. 138 ff.; iii. 86; lvii. 7; cf. Lev. xix. 9 f. and Deut. xiv. 28 f.).

For the Law of Retaliation, Sura ii. 175; iv. 94 and v. 49 should be compared with Deut. xix. 4–13 and 15–21, etc.

C. CHRISTIANITY AND MUSLIM TRADITION

The traditions of Islam give much evidence of the influence of Christianity during the period of the formulation of Muslim tradition. This is not simply in the acceptance of Christian ideas, but also in antagonism, for the early traditions reflect the controversies of the times. An instance of this may be given in regard to the question of miracles. The Qur'ān contains the disclaimer of Muhammad to be a worker of miracles, but the common argument for the unique personality of Christ which was adduced from His power to work miracles, finds an answer in the stories of the miracles of Muhammad. Thus we have evidence from the *Apology* of Al Kindī (late tenth century according to Massignon) of stories of the following miracles: The wolf and the ox speaking in confirmation of the prophethood of Muhammad, the tree which moved towards him, the shoulder of goat's flesh which warned Muhammad that it had been poisoned, and the miraculous production of water whereby the Prophet satisfied the thirst of his followers. We have also the story of the healing of the leg of Salmā after the battle of Khaibar by the Prophet blowing upon it, and of healing imparted by the Prophet's clothes which remind us of Mark vii. 23 and Acts xix. 12. On the other hand, in his *Apology* before the Caliph Mahdī (A.D. 781) made by Timothy the Nestorian Patriarch,

[1] *Gebhamoth* iv. 10.

[2] *Kethuboth* lx. 1. See Geiger: *Was hat Mohammed aus dem Judethume aufgenommen?* 90.

he is able to say that the Qur'ān has not been confirmed by miracle without, apparently, any contradiction from the Caliph.[1]

Guillaume says that the early narrators of *Ḥadīth* "borrowed events from the life of Jesus, attributing them to their own Prophet"[2] and Goldziher has gathered a number of illustrations from "a great wealth of examples",[3] and says in a footnote that Ibn Ḥajar[4] agrees with more ancient authorities in acknowledging the share which the Christian proselyte Tamīm ud Dārī had in the formulation of Muhammadan eschatology. The same writer shows how even the phraseology which speaks of men doing anything "in God" (*fi'llāh*) reflects the Christian phrase "in Christ". Thus we have, "God has servants who eat in God, drink in Him and walk in Him".[5] "Fellowship in God" becomes a Muslim phrase.[6] In the *Ṣaḥīḥ* of Muslim and the *Mishkāt*[7] we have the tradition attributed to Abū Huraira: "The Apostle of God said, 'God Most High said, "I have prepared for my righteous servants what eye hath not seen, nor ear heard, nor hath it entered into the heart of man."'" This is almost a literal translation of 1 Cor. ii. 9. It is possible, of course, that by "God said" we have an indication that this is quoted from former scripture. Other matters in *Ḥadīth* and *Fiqh* which are worthy of note are to be found in Guillaume and Goldziher. They are far too numerous to be adequately represented here. They embrace versions of the parables of Jesus Christ and His sayings. Some of these latter are such as we find in the Gospels and some are "unwritten" sayings of Jesus.[8]

As time passes there is strong evidence for more accurate knowledge of the Christian records. Thus Al Ya'qūbī in his *Tārīkh*, which was written in the latter part of the ninth century, describes how Christians do not hold that Christ spoke in the cradle, gives outlines of the earlier parts of the four Gospels, and then summarizes, giving the miracle of the raising of Lazarus, and the betrayal of Christ by Judas; he shows acquaintance with the discourses at the Last Supper, the scene in Gethsemane, the trial of Jesus and His crucifixion, without any attempt to reconcile the narrative with the Qur'ān.[9] There is a very full account to be found in the forty-fourth treatise of the Ikhwān uṣ Ṣafā (*c.* A.D. 1000).[10] In this we find an appreciation of the fact that Christ found the Jews devoted to the externals of the Law of Moses

[1] Mingana: *Woodbrooke Studies*, Vol ii, p. 37.
[2] Guillaume: *The Traditions of Islam*, p. 133.
[3] Goldziher: *Muhammadanische Studien*, Vol. ii, 382 ff.
[4] i. 372.
[5] Al Fashanī: *Commentary on the Forty Traditions*, 52.
[6] Muslim v. 236.
[7] *Book of Seditions*, on the *Creation of Paradise and the Fire*.
[8] The collection made by Asin y Palacios, *Logia et Agrapha Domini Iesu* should be consulted.
[9] See *Macdonald Presentation Volume*, contribution by Dwight M. Donaldson, p. 89.
[10] *Risā'il Ikhwān uṣ Ṣafā* (Cairo, 1928), Vol. iv, 94 ff.

and with little interest in the inwardness of religion. They were following slavishly the traditions which had come down to them and had but little knowledge of the bearing of these things on the Hereafter. When the Messiah observed them He saw no difference between them and the people who had no knowledge of religion and prophecy, and who did not accept the Book and the Sunna, the Way or the Law. They had no knowledge of renunciation of this present world or zeal for the next. So he was grieved at their state and had compassion on them. He knew it was useless to rebuke them, as they already had the rebuke of the Law before them. It was no use to lay prohibitions upon them and threats, for these, too, were in the Law and the Prophets. He saw that he should manifest himself to them as a healing physician. So he began to go to the homes of the people and meet them individually. He would find a man and preach to him, exhort him and teach him in parables, rousing him from his ignorance. He would lead him to be converted from this present world and would inspire within him a desire for the hereafter and its peace.

There follows a description of how Christ taught the necessity of inward purity : " Because you have washed your bodies and whitened your garments, and have put them on when your souls are defiled with the corpses and filthy things which pertain unto ignorance, blindness and dumbness, and are made vile by those things which are associated with evil dispositions, such as envy, hatred, treachery, fraud, greed, avarice, meanness, suspicion and lewdness." . . . " Can you feel a desire for the Kingdom of Heaven wherein for those who dwell therein there is neither death nor weakness from old age, neither pain nor sickness, neither hunger nor thirst, neither fear nor grief, neither poverty nor need, neither trouble nor affliction, neither remorse nor envy ; and where there is likewise no hatred, no boasting and no arrogance, but where men live as friends, in harmony, happy and joyful in their spirit, their fragrance, their graciousness, their gladness and their pleasure ? . . . And you can be with them living for ever, never growing old, never dying, never suffering pain, never thirsty, never sick, never fearful and never sad."

" He gave them much counsel, and His word had effect on their souls. It was customary for the Messiah to go every day from one town to another. He healed them and preached to them ; He warned them and summoned them to the Kingdom of Heaven. But the King of the Children of Israel, supported by a mixed rabble, wanted to arrest Him. Once when He was at a public meeting, this crowd set upon Him, but He escaped. . . . They would lose sight of Him then till He would be heard of in another place whence they would go to seek Him. This passing from one place to another went on for about thirty months.

" At last, when God purposed to bring about His end and raise Him up unto Himself, He gathered His disciples to Him in Jerusalem.

There, in an upper room with His chosen companions He said, 'I go to my Father and your Father and before the separation of my divinity (*lāhūt*) I give a charge to you, and I make a covenant and an agreement with you. Whosoever accepts my charge and fulfils my covenant shall remain with me to-morrow, and whosoever accepts not my charge, I shall not be with him in anything.' They said then to Him, 'What is the charge ?' He said, 'Go to the kings in the uttermost parts of the earth and inform them from Me of what I have told you and summon them to that to which I have summoned you. Fear them not neither be in awe of them, for when my human nature (*nāsūt*) [1] is separated, then I shall be in Heaven on the right hand of the Throne of my Father and your Father. And I shall be with you wherever you go, your help in giving victory and strength, by permission of my Father. Go to them and summon them by means of your friendship and cure them and command them to good and forbid them from evil, though you yourselves may be killed or crucified or banished from the earth.' But they said, 'What is the proof or confirmation of what you command us ?' He answered simply, 'That I will be the first to do this.' . . .

"It was in this fashion that His human nature was crucified. His hands were nailed to the wood of the cross and He remained hanging on the cross from early in the day until the evening. He asked for water but He was given vinegar to drink and He was pierced with a spear. Then He was buried in a rough unfinished place and forty men were on guard at the tomb.

"All this occurred in the presence of His companions and His disciples. . . . They were assured that He had not ordered them to do something other than He would do Himself. Afterwards they assembled for three days in the place where He had promised to appear to them and they saw this sign which was between Him and them ; so the news spread among the Children of Israel that the Messiah had not been killed. So the grave was dug up and even His human nature was not found. There was therefore some difference of opinion among them and much controversy arose, the account of which would be lengthy.

"It was then that those from among His disciples who accepted His charge went abroad among the towns. Each one of them went where he was sent. One went to the towns of the West, another to the towns of Abyssinia, two went to the habitations of the city of Rome, two went to the kingdom of Antioch, one to the towns of Persia and one to the towns of India. There were two others who stayed in the regions of the children of Israel."

It will be seen that this account is fairly accurate, and very

[1] *Lāhūt* and *nāsūt* are the regular Syriac terms for the divinity and humanity of Christ.

slight concession is made to the different account of the crucifixion to be found in the Qur'ān. A statement of facts which do not agree with the Quranic account is made quite objectively. From this it would appear that the Qur'ān was not accepted—at least by these men—in the way it is accepted to-day.

In passing it may be mentioned that the legend or legends, for they are various and extraordinarily copious, of the supernatural journeys of Muhammad, the Isrā' and Mi'rāj [1] have their roots in earlier stories—notably *Slavonic Enoch*—and will in later days be found to have been given back to Christian story, e.g., in the *Divine Comedy*.[2]

One matter of particular importance is the evidence of the ascetic tendencies in early days due to the Christian ascetic ideal and practice. There are passages in the traditions which show that the asceticism of Christian monks had caught the imagination of the first generation of Muslims and though the Islamic trend is usually away from asceticism and the injunction from the Prophet "No monkery in Islam" is most influential, the Prophet is credited with sayings which could be pressed into the service of the "rule of poverty". He is recorded as having said, "I stood at the gate of Paradise and observed that the majority of those who gained admittance by it were the poor, whereas the wealthy were turned away." [3] In addition we have the record from 'Abdullāh b. Mas'ūd: "As though I beheld the Prophet of God imitating one of the most ancient prophets, who was tortured and beaten by his people, but only wiped the blood from His face, and said, 'God forgive My people, for they know not'," which teaches Christian meekness [4] and obliquely applies the saying to the Prophet. A large proportion of the sayings attributed to Christ by Al Ghazzālī in his *Iḥyā* are of an ascetic character. "It is related that Jesus, may the blessing of God and peace be upon Him, went out and prayed for rain. When they grumbled, Jesus, upon whom be peace, said to them: 'Whoever among you has committed sin let him go back.' They all went back, and no one remained with him in the desert except one. Then Jesus said, 'Is there no sin in thee?' And he said: 'I swear before God that I do not know of anything, except that on a certain day I was praying, when a woman passed by me and I looked on her with this eye, and when she again passed by me I stuck my finger into mine eye and, plucking it out, threw it after the woman.' Then Jesus said to him: 'Then pray to God while I say "Amen" to your prayer.' And so he prayed and the heaven became covered with clouds and then poured forth rain and they quenched their thirst." [5]

[1] *Ibn Hishām* i. 168 and versions in Bukhārī, the *Mishkāt* and many other collections.
[2] Miguel Asin: *Islam and the Divine Comedy* contains a mass of information which may be usefully consulted.
[3] Bukhari: *Riqāq*, 57.
[4] Bukhārī: *Anbiya*, 54.
[5] *Iḥya 'Ulūm id Dīn*, Vol. i, 277–281, cf. Jno. ix. 31; Matt. v. 28 f.; xviii. 9.

In the same writer we find[1]: "Take Christ as your pattern. For it is said that He had no purse and for twenty years He wore the same woollen shirt; on His journeys He took with Him nothing but a cup and a comb. One day when He saw a man drinking out of the hollow of his hand He straightway threw His cup away and used it no more. Then He passed a man who was combing his beard with his fingers and immediately He cast away His comb and used it no more." In the *Mishkāt* there is an attribution of a similar asceticism to Muhammad in the section which deals with the excellence of poverty and the Prophet's manner of life. "It is related from Umar that he said: 'I went in to the Prophet of Allah and lo! he was lying on his side on a mat made of reeds. There was no bedding between him and it; and the mat had marked his side. He was propped up on a pillow made of skin stuffed with the rinds of dates. And I said, "O Messenger of Allah, pray Allah to give abundance to thy followers, for verily the Persians and the Greeks have been given abundance although they worship not Allah." He answered "O Ibn Khaṭṭāb, art thou yet in this condition? Those are people whose good things have been given to them quickly during this world's life."[2]

In seeking to understand these traditions it is well to remember that we have evidence of a native simplicity as distinct from ascetism in the early days of Islam. 'Umar himself from whom the above tradition is reported was not a man likely to attach too much importance to worldly show. We are told that this persisted even in the Umayyad Caliphate. 'Umar b. 'Abd ul 'Azīz stripped the Mosque of Damascus of much of its ornament and melted down the golden chains of the lamps because "he considered such show to be opposed to the spirit of Islam".[3] We also read how Ibn Ḥanbal left a banquet which was being given in his honour because silver plate was being used. So, though Islam protested against monasticism and celibacy, it exhibited a spartan or even puritan spirit in many respects.

As examples of how matters which were of interest among Christians were taken over into Islam, we may take the question of the age of the resurrection body and the question of whether a wicked man may be a minister of religion. In regard to the former we have the words of Theodore of Mopsuestia: "In the resurrection the Creator will by His power remove all the defects which the bodies of men had in this world, and will quicken the bodies blameless and perfect in form at the age of thirty years." If someone asks "How do you know this?" we will answer, "Immediately after the creation of Adam (God's) order was imposed on him. Further, after the law was given to the Israelites God ordered them that a man of thirty years should do the

[1] *La Perle Précieuse*, p. 53 (trans.).
[2] *Kitāb ur Riqāq fi Faḍl ul Fuqarā'* (Arab. text 447).
[3] Margoliouth: *Early Development of Muhammadanism*, p. 168.

work of the tabernacle and the priesthood. Our Lord also came to baptism at the age of thirty years. . . . Adam was created at the age of thirty years . . . there is there (Paradise) neither old nor young, but all mankind will rise up at the same age."[1] In the *Mishkāt* (and in Tirmidhī) we find the following: " It is related from Abū Sa'īd that the Messenger of Allah said, ' The meanest of the dwellers in Paradise is the man who will have eighty thousand servants and seventy-two wives . . . and they who die whether old or young, of those who go to Paradise will all return in Paradise to thirty years of age. They will never exceed that age.' "[2] In a Ḥanafī book of instruction we find: " In the traditions we find that the ritual prayer is obligatory (*wājib*) behind every Muslim whether righteous or wicked, although he may be guilty of the greatest sins, but it is not correct to recite the ritual worship behind a heretic, a denier of *Ḥadīth* or a Shi'a."[3] In Theodore we read: " If a priest is false because of his odious conduct, the baptism which he administers is true because of the (imposition of the) right hand, and if his works are sinful, the sacrifice which he offers is genuine. . . . If the priest is a sinner, his iniquity, like his justice, is upon himself alone. . . . Those who assert that the sacrifice of a sinful priest is not holy, assert wrongly. . . . If a hand is imposed upon Satan there is in him the hand of priesthood, and if he breaks the sanctified bread and give me of it, I shall receive it from him and regard it as lacking nothing."[4] Many similar instances could be given, but considerations of space forbid.

D. THE CHRISTIAN THEOLOGICAL BACKGROUND TO EARLY ISLAM

No doubt a great deal in Islam is to be attributed to the genius of Muhammad and to the Qur'ān as a sacred book, but these were not the only elements potent in the production of the Islam which we now know. Already some evidence has been produced for this statement. After the compilation of the Qur'ān in the first generations of Islam that religion grew and developed in a partially Christian environment. During this time it exacted a service from Christianity which it employed in its own systematization. So, though it might be possible to maintain that Muhammad was only influenced in a small degree by Christianity and Judaism, and that it is certain that his knowledge of Christianity was of a superficial character, it is in no wise possible to say the same about the early period of Islamic development. There the influence of Christianity was profound and far-reaching.

Thus it now falls to our lot to discuss in somewhat fuller detail

[1] Mingana: *Synopsis of Christian Doctrine in the Fourth Century*, according to Theodore of Mopsuestia.

[2] *Kitāb ul Fitan fi ṣifāt il Janna* (Arab. text, p. 497).

[3] *Huquq wa Farā'iḍ ul Islam*, p. 127.

[4] *op. cit.*

than in the opening remarks on relevant historical matters, that Christian theological setting which will give us the clue to much we shall afterwards encounter in our study of Islamic theological beginnings and lines of development. If we institute a comparison of Christianity and Islam by taking what Christianity now is after centuries of development and comparing it with an Islam which has been similarly developed, we set ourselves to examine the streams at their mouths which are far apart, rather than at the sources which are close together. If we wish to know why one stream flows to the West and the other to the East, we must make a survey of the watershed, so far as that is possible, because this particular watershed lies in country which is almost inaccessible, and convulsions have diverted the streams from their old beds. In fine, there is much that remains unexplored, and we have to manage with the sparse information which we have been able to gather. New discoveries might be greatly revealing.

When, also, we find a somewhat naïve description of Christianity in Muslim writers and smile with superiority because we have first-hand knowledge of Christianity as it *is*, we should remember that it is possible that our knowledge of what Christianity *was* may be deficient. Not that we consider that the eternal and immutable truth of Christianity is not a fact but that the form of doctrine has exhibited much that is transient and subject to change. We may doubt very much indeed whether that Muslim theology which was formulated *contra Christianos* was adequately formulated in opposition to what is fundamental in Christianity and yet we must know that it was formulated in antagonism to the form of Christianity with which it was familiar. Whether Christianity was properly and truly presented to that age or not must not be taken for granted either one way or the other—indeed it may be utterly impossible to make a positive statement or form an assured judgment on that question in general. In some respects and by some people Christianity may have been correctly presented, but in other respects and by other people quite incorrectly. By some it may have been exhibited as it is in truth and by others a mere travesty of Christianity may have been set before the critical eyes of the first Muslims. There is much valuable information to be gathered from Dr. L. E. Browne's book on this subject,[1] and with the main findings of that book we are in agreement. In an historical examination of this matter ethical, political and racial matters must find a place, but here our sole purpose is theological, and it is to data of that description that we will devote our attention in the main, only touching on other matters when they seem to have some bearing on our inquiry. It may be further remarked that it is not intended to give complete descriptions of heresies, schools of theology and great theologians in the pages which follow, but simply to indicate the broad

[1] *Eclipse of Christianity in Asia.*

outlines and to deal with matters in more detail when they show parallels with thought in Islam.

(i) PRE-ISLAMIC CHRISTIAN CONTROVERSY. For more than three centuries before the advent of Muhammad the Christian Church was agitated by controversy after controversy. We find at the beginning of that period a Church which had passed through years of suffering and persecution at long last emerging from its lowly estate in the world and coming to recognition as the religion of a mighty enpire. It was indeed significant that in the early fourth century one of the first acts of Constantine when by his presence he gave countenance to the new status of the Church at the Council of Nicæa, should be the receiving of numerous petitions of complaint from bishops against their fellow bishops. It is recorded that he burned them.

We must not, of course, attribute all the controversies to the period which began with the fourth century. The Marcionites with their peculiar Gnostic tenets had disturbed the Church of the second century and they lingered on into the seventh century. The Gnostics had already been stimulating enough to provoke the books on heresies which were the foundation of theology—even as early as the latter part of the second century in the work of Irenaeus. Justin Martyr, Clement, and Origen to mention only a few had all taken part in resisting false doctrine, or in defending Christianity against Judaism and paganism, or in adapting the message of Christianity to current philosophical thought. And someone has described the third century as one of the most unhappy of the Christian era. It was this century which saw the beginnings of the controversy about the relation of the Son to the Father. The question of the divinity of Christ took first place in theological discussion. There was unanimous agreement that Christ came from God, that He had brought a divine revelation, and that He was both Saviour and Lord, but the problem was raised as to how this recognition of Christ as Saviour and this worship of Him as Lord could be explained in relation to a religion which had asserted at the cost of its own blood a pure monotheism against the polytheism of the Roman world? Eusebius says that during the years of peace which preceded the Diocletian persecution, the Church fell on evil days and showed signs of degeneracy. It is during this period that we see the rise of the heretical schools of Adoptianism, which asserted that God chose Christ to be His Son because of His virtue, and Sabellianism, which maintained that Christ was simply a manifestation of the One God. We witness also the controversy of Dionysius of Alexandria with Paul of Samosata (*c.* 250). Here we have the beginnings and they came to a head in the fourth century. Nicaea which should have brought about a settlement was the prelude to some sixty years of unremitting dispute and contention. Nor did this end it, for there immediately followed the Christological controversies with regard to the relation of the humanity to the divinity in Christ, and these lasted till after the rise of Islam.

The Church was now clothed with temporal power. It had powers to enforce doctrine in the interests of unity—always a primary consideration to those who rule. It had a major doctrinal battle to face and the instruments it used were not the gentle apostolic persuasion of a fellowship in the Grace of God, where all must be subordinate to the glory of God and the praise of the Gospel. It now seized on the instruments of disputation and set in motion the processes of councils. It had escaped the dangers from without and was now to be subjected to an inward purging and feel the agony of dangers from within. Its unity, promoted by the necessity for closing its ranks in protective fellowship against an antagonistic world, was now to be broken by the incursion of nominal Christians in ever-increasing numbers. With the friendship of Constantine Christianity had become fashionable, and we should never forget that he who lent his support to the settling of the disputes in the Church at Nicaea was not yet a baptized Christian. The age of shrines and images, relics and charms and the cult of saints was upon the Church, and all these things would find supporters in the new adherents of what was shortly to become the State religion. For, before the end of the fourth century, we find that paganism is proscribed even as Christianity had been and that the Emperor (Theodosius) is commanding that all his subjects should be orthodox Christians. Heresy is henceforth punishable by the State and so the definition of heresy becomes all-important.

One of the sad features of this period is the rivalry of the great schools. They seemed to delight in setting themselves in opposition to one another. Alexandria seems jealous of Antioch; the Oriental bishops respond with opposition to Athanasius the Alexandrian bishop, the Greeks and Syrians almost hound him. At one time Irenaeus could look to the bishops as the guardians of sound faith and, apparently, expect some unanimity from them, but now it is the bishops who seem to be the irreconcilables and unanimity is far to seek. Antioch, which was soon to play so potent a part in influencing the Church of the East, the Nestorians and the Syrians, who were to be the closest in their contacts with Islam, and at whose feet the early Muslims were to sit when they set themselves to systematize Islam, was most unhappy in its relations with Alexandria, to which also Islam became the heir in many things, particularly in its mysticism and Neoplatonism.

We find another outbreak of contention and dispute in Constantinople when Nestorius of Antioch became the bishop of that great city and startled the Church with his protest against the use of the title Theotokos—God-bearing—for the Virgin. The dispute led to the scandalous council of Ephesus in 431. The Alexandrians arrived at the Council before the Syrian supporters of Nestorius and condemned and excommunicated him. When the Syrians arrived they reversed this decision, and then Cyril of Alexandria compounded with the Syrians, and Nestorius was left in the lurch! The decision finally reached in condemnation of Nestorius amounted to the affirmation of the principle that the humanity and divinity in Christ were inseparably united. Then the question arose as to how they were united?

There follows the attempt of Eutyches to explain this mystery. He held that Christ was God and man, but that when the union of the two natures took place in the incarnation the stronger submerged and absorbed the weaker, so that Christ was all divine. Dioscorus of Alexandria supported this, and Constantinople, led by Flavian, opposed it and excommunicated Eutyches. The Council at Ephesus in 449 reversed this decision, and Leo the Great of Rome called it a Council of Bandits.

In addition to these the Pelagian controversy must be mentioned, for though it perhaps agitated the East less than the West, nevertheless it had a profound influence on it and is associated with the Nestorian Church, the Church which more than any other was brought into touch with Islam in its early years.

Such was the continual gnawing strife and controversy which rent and wore down the Church, which imperilled its unity and which sapped the energies of the Church of the East at a time when a clear, patient, vigorous and united witness was required of it in face of the imminent rise of Islam.

(ii) THE GREAT SCHOOLS. The three great schools of Christian theological thought which should be considered in relation to the study we have in hand are the School of Alexandria, the School of Cappadocia and the School of Antioch.

(*a*) *The School of Alexandria.* Alexandria was the centre of Greek, Graeco-Semitic and Christian culture and learning for centuries. Indeed it was the meeting place of East and West and the great colony of Jews was largely instrumental in achieving a wonderful blending of Semitic religion with Greek philosophy. It was in this place that the Greek translation of the Old Testament scriptures was made, in which—and in the Wisdom literature—we see the beginnings of the attempts to reconcile Moses and Plato. Islam was later to exhibit in its development a similar synthesis of Semitic and Hellenistic elements, and for this the ground had been prepared by at least six centuries of theological and philosophical thought. Its great names are Philo (*c.* 20 B.C–*c.* A.D. 50), Valentinus the Gnostic (*c.* A.D. 120–160), Basilides (117–138 at Alexandria), Clement (*c.* 150–213), Origen (185–254), Plotinus (*c.* 205–270).

The School was strongly marked by eclecticism. Here truth was regarded as a river fed by many streams and every flower yielded honey to the bee. Its philosophical background was a Platonism systematized by Aristotelianism and supplemented by the ethical emphasis of Stoicism. It was in the *Timaeus* that its Platonism found its centre, and this Platonism never ceased to be the predominant feature of the teaching associated with the School. It had its trinitarian exponents such as Numenius, Moderatus, Nicomachus, and probably the greatest of all, Plotinus. But it also had unitarian Platonists of some note as witness Celsus with whom Origen disputed. It is from Alexandria that the Neoplatonism arose which was afterwards to exercise such a profound influence on the philosophy of religion in later years, both in Christianity and Islam, and which must always be taken into consideration when Islamic mysticism is examined. Even Islam with its rigid unitarianism could not resist the inroads of the trinitarianism of Neoplatonism into its orthodoxy, its Sufism and its philosophical schools, as we shall have occasion to show in some detail later on. Ideas of emanation and procession prominent in philosophy and theology in both the religions or their unorthodox offshoots have their source in the main in this School. In Islam we may trace them in al Fārābī, in Ibn Sīnā (Avicenna), in Ibn Rushd (Averroes), in Ibn 'Arabī the great mystic and many others. They even find their way into traditions put into the mouth of the Prophet Muhammad, as, e.g., "The first thing which Allah created was the Reason." Even when regarded as errors they form the subject of discussions by the theologians. And when Neoplatonist elements have been noted in Islamic thought it should not be thought that the fount of origin has been reached in Pseudo-Dionysius, or Proclus or Plotinus, whose influence certain scholars have rightly observed, for behind Dionysius and the others there are Clement and Origen and behind Clement and Origen, Philo.

Philo was the author of many a tenet which we find later in Islam. His angelology, his thoughts on prophethood and the principles of exegesis are all traceable in the religion of the Prophet, and the discussion is in the idiom which Philo rendered familiar and which the Rabbis and the Christian Alexandrians transmitted with their own comments and additions. Thus many things which strike our ear strangely, or perhaps scandalize our orthodoxy, or—as is sometimes the case—are represented by certain writers as marking the complete difference of Islam from Christianity, such, for instance, as the utter transcendence of God, these very things can be found in the Christian writers of the Alexandrian School. Shortly we shall take doctrine after doctrine and show that this is so.

It should further be noted that the School of Alexandria is strongly characterized by pure intellectualism and abstraction. Sense is regarded as of little account. This world is a shadow of realities which lie beyond and the world of sense and corporeality is valuable solely as a gate whereby entrance may be made into the purely incorporeal (see Philo, *de Somniis*, 32). This idea was to become almost proverbial in Sufi thought with its oft repeated *al majāzu qantarat ul Ḥaqīqa*, " the phenomenal is the bridge to the real ".

But Christian Alexandrians accepted the Incarnation, which Islam has shown no disposition to accept. For the Christians of that school the Incarnation was fundamental. It was the touchstone whereby they shaped all the rest of their theology after what they had laid down about the transcendent Monad. Though they did not ignore the humanity of Christ, yet the Divine Logos provided them with the key to all the theological mysteries and to the interpretation of Scripture. In this they differed from the School of Antioch, where the first consideration was the revealed Scripture which was examined for the truth about the historical Jesus. It is as if the starting point of the Alexandrine system of philosophical theology was the *a priori* principle of the Divine Logos as mediator, whereas the Antiochene School preferred to work *a posteriori*. Howbeit, in this too the Alexandrians had a share, for we are probably right in holding the work of Origen to be of the greatest importance, greater even than that of Clement, since his scriptural theology, his methods of exegesis, his care in textual criticism, his emphasis on grammar and linguistics, his theories of types and allegory, were all such as would be of the greatest interest to a religion like Islam in which such stress was laid on Scripture. Much of the work of Origen must have formed the precedent (taken in conjunction with Philo on the Jewish side) for what we shall discover in the systematization of the like thoughts in Islam. Moreover, many of these things were carried over into the Schools of Antioch and Cappadocia by thinkers who honoured the great saint and found inspiration in the work he had done.[1]

(*b*) *The School of Cappadocia*. The name of this school is not happy, but if it were called the School of Caesarea, so many towns were called by that name, we should not be much better off. The name applies to a School of Christian theology represented by three great names, Basil of Caesarea, Gregory of Nazianzus and Gregory of Nyssa, who was the greatest theologian of the three. Their date is from A.D. 362 to 394. We mention them here because we shall have occasion to refer to them later and because the school represents some points of difference from Antioch. It carried on in many matters the work of Origen, reviving it for the fourth century. It is more philosophical and metaphysical than Antioch, while at the same time showing marked Aristotelian influence. Thus we find in Basil a distinction made between *ousia* and *hypostasis* showing that the former is related to the latter as the universal is to the particular. Another instance is in the

[1] Origen's theology is to be found in his commentaries on John and Matthew. His *de Principiis* is partially available in Rufinus' translation.

employment of the Aristotelian terms "form" and "elements" in the discussion of the sacrament of Holy Communion. But in their attempt to restate the doctrine of the Trinity, they used Platonism as well as Aristotelianism. In their mysticism they form a link between Alexandria and Pseudo-Dionysius. A special point of interest is their insistence on tradition as a source of Doctrine. This might be written or oral. In this we see the influence of Philo and those Jews who held that beside the written law there was an oral instruction which had been handed down. Gregory of Nazianzus speaks of a secret or esoteric discipline.[1] We find the same idea recurring in Islam, and the *sunna* may be said to be based on such an assumption. The Sufis also appeal to an unwritten tradition to support their peculiar tenets. In contrast to Alexandria we see a strong emphasis on the humanity of Christ. We have also a better systematized doctrine of human nature. The idea that the whole of humanity was created ideally by God, recalls the conception of the Heavenly Adam which has had some influence in Islam. Similarly we have man described as the microcosm,[2] which theory we find in Philo and in the earliest theological thought of Islam. Their eschatology also will present points of interest when we come to examine that subject shortly. Finally, although this school is unswerving against Arianism, it should be remarked that Gregory of Nazianzus points out particularly the human limitations of Christ, His lack of knowledge and His growth therein, His subjection to temptation, His grief and all the human elements of the Gospel story.

(*c*) *The School of Antioch.* Antioch was as old as Alexandria, and it had an ancient rivalry with the latter city. But as a centre of learning its history was shorter and it could hardly dare to vie with the great names associated with Alexandria. Its importance as a school of thought was due to its Christian associations rather than to classical learning. It claimed to be the first city of Christianity, and it certainly was the first centre of Gentile Christianity. The controversies within the Church from the fourth to the sixth centuries coincided with a growing interest in Aristotelianism as distinct from Platonism. While Alexandria remained the great Platonist School, Antioch developed its philosophy along the lines of Aristotle. The results of this are seen in the methods which the Christian Antiochenes used in the examination of material data as the foundation of their systematic theology.

Antioch had associations with the early Gnosticism. Its schools of rhetoric and dialectic must have been founded at an early date. It is known from Eusebius[3] that there was a school of this description in A.D. 269 when Paul of Samosata was condemned. This Paul seems

[1] *Orations* xl. 45.
[2] In *al Insān ul Kamil* by Jīlī and Ibn Miskawayh; see *infra*, p. 163 f., etc.
[3] *Eccles. Hist.*, vii. 29.

to have paved the way for the distinguishing emphasis of the Antiochenes upon the historical Jesus and their dislike of metaphysics. Not that it must be supposed that this dislike was carried too far, for pseudo-metaphysical subtleties are in evidence from the teaching of those who looked to Antioch as their theological mother. We find them in Nestorian apologists *ad nauseam* ; and quite apart from such crudities the nurture of Antioch must be seen in the Syrians who were the agents in opening the treasuries of Greek philosophy to the Persians and Arabs. It would seem also that at a later date, when adversity brought low the pride of Alexandria and of Antioch, Alexandria was instrumental in A.D. 720 in bringing back Greek learning to Antioch. It is probable that here we should look for the new (and somewhat degenerate) synthesis of Neoplatonism and Aristotelianism of an uncritical character which we find in the early Muslim period and with more complications as the Muslim system unfolds itself. It may be, of course, that this synthesis has a much earlier beginning and that we may refer it more closely to the influence of Origen on Antioch. It is certain that the School carried on the tradition of Origen in respect to solid historical and linguistic research. Thus, Lucian the Martyr (311–312) was probably concerned in the revision of the Syrian text of the New Testament. There is also traceable in Lucian the *logos* Christology of Origen.

Lucian was the teacher of Arius and these early Arians show acquaintance with Aristotelian dialectic. It is also at this period that we notice that, however much allegorism had been sanctified by Origen, the school prefers to take the other elements of his exegetical teaching, and there soon arises a preference for grammatical and literal exposition of the Scriptures. The typology of Origen, however, survives.

For us the association with Arianism must be significant. How much vigour had it in the period immediately preceding Muhammad? Another significant association is with Nestorianism. Diodorus (378–394) has often been regarded as a precursor of Nestorianism, and it is certain that Theodore of Mopsuestia (*c.* 429) was the immediate forerunner of Nestorius in his Christology. Not only was the school influential through its teaching in Greek, but both Diodorus and Theodore had their works translated into Syriac by Ibas of Edessa in 457 or thereabouts, and so the theology became more widely known and spread eastward with the exile of Nestorianism into Persia. The migration from Antioch to Jundishabur, where an Aristotelian school was founded, has been already mentioned, and we may also note that Nisibis became the heir of Edessa, and so the teachings of the school were planted in the heart of the new Muslim Empire.

We shall have to refer to the teachings of the School at some length presently, and therefore these preliminary remarks must suffice.

(iii) THE EXISTING PHILOSOPHICAL THEOLOGY. From the foregoing it will be clear that before the advent of Islam there was a considerable body of philosophical theology in existence. A modern Indian Muslim has written on Muslim theology and has said: "It is the opinion of the majority of people that the tenets of theology (*'ilm ul kalām*—more strictly 'dialectical theology') are derived from the Greeks. The basis of this is that in Al G͟hazzālī's *Madnūn aṣ Ṣag͟hīr wa'l Kabīr* and his *Jawāhir ul Qur'ān* he has derived his exposition of *Nabuwwa* (prophethood), *Waḥī* (revelation), *Ilhām* (inspiration), *Rūya* (vision), *'Ad͟hāb wa T͟hawāb* (retribution and reward) and *Mu'jiza* (miracle), from Ibn Sīnā and Al Fārābī and what they wrote in a Greek philosophical vein. But this opinion is greatly in error. No doubt Al G͟hazzālī did get these from Ibn Sīnā and Al Fārābī, but these matters are original discoveries of these philosophers and have no connection with Greek philosophy. Ibn Rushd writes in *Tahāfut ut Tahāfut* 'As for the rest the ancient Greek philosophers have said nothing about miracles. I know not a single one of the ancients who accepts what Al G͟hazzālī has taken from the philosophers of Islam about Vision. G͟hazzālī thinks that philosophers deny the resurrection of the body but there is no statement of the ancients on this subject.' The truth is that though Muslims have looked on Aristotle and Plato with respect and have taken all their tenets, their discipleship has been limited to mathematics and physics and the like. When divinity was so imperfect among the Greeks, how could Muslims reap advantage from it? The doctors of *Kalām* always looked down on Greek theology. Although Ibn Taimīya does not agree with the exponents of *Kalām* (*mutakallimūn*)—for he says in his *Ar Raddu 'ala'l Manṭiq*, 'Many things in the *mutakallimūn* are nonsensical'—nevertheless, just after this passage he writes, 'The *Kalām* of Aristotle and the *mutakallimūn* are both before me. In comparison with Aristotle's the latter's is based to a far greater degree on assured premisses.' In *Tahāfut ul Falāsifa* the doctrines of prophethood, miracles and the hereafter which Al G͟hazzālī ascribes to the philosophers of Greece are not their discovery at all, but are Ibn Sīnā's, and originally not even of his invention, for Ibn Sīnā changed the findings of the older *mutakallimūn* and expressed them in a new way. Ibn Taimīya writes in *ar Raddu 'ala'l Manṭiq*, 'Ibn Sīnā dealt with matters of theology, prophethood, the hereafter, and the Law (*sharī'a*), of which those before him (perhaps Greek philosophers) had not spoken, neither did their intellect reach to it, but Bū 'Alī Sīnā derived these things from Muslims.' Ibn Taimīya is not generally regarded as an expert in the rational sciences, so perhaps his testimony may not be trusted, but Ibn Rushd (Averroes), the greatest of Muslim philosophers in his *Tahāfut ut Tahāfut* has made it clear in regard to many tenets that Ibn Sīnā derived them from the *mutakallimūn*, e.g., in *It͟hbāt ul Fā'il*[1] he says,

[1] Beirut edit., p. 54.

'In this, both (i.e., Fārābī and Ibn Sīnā) followed our *mutakallimūn*.' In another place he writes, 'And this is the method which Ibn Sīnā derived from the *mutakallimūn*.' [1]

"This gift of *Kalām* will ever remain for a memorial. By means of it liberty was won from enslavement to Greek philosophy. The Greek philosophy had gained such acceptance in the world, and such publicity that its doctrines were considered to be inspired. Muslims looked at them in the same way and thought of Aristotle and Plato as the gods of learning. Someone asked Fārābī, 'What is your relation to Aristotle?' He replied, 'If I had lived in Aristotle's time I would have been a worthy disciple of his.' Ibn Sīnā in his *Shifā* on a similar occasion wrote, 'Though such a long time has elapsed, there cannot be a particle of addition to Aristotle's findings.'" [2]

The purpose of this long statement is clear. Because certain theological matters are not to be found in the Greek philosophers, it must be concluded, says the learned author, that the Muslim theology is underived and original to the early exponents of the dialectical theology in Islam. This would lead one to suppose that before these early theologians of Islam there had been no exposition of the matters mentioned. Our lengthy references to the theological schools and our present intention in setting forth the existing philosophical theology before Islam is to show that such a contention is unsupported and that already matters of theological importance to both Christianity and Islam—not to speak of Judaism—had been under discussion for centuries. Our later examination of the details will give overwhelming evidence on this point.

From the earliest time men of religion had sought to relate their religious conceptions to the philosophy of the day. To be intelligible one must not only use the language of the people to whom one addresses oneself, but have a knowledge of the ideas which the words one uses are likely to suggest. The Fathers of the Christian Church had this task when they sought to present the new message of Christianity and even earlier than their time, we find the necessity imposed upon the writers of the New Testament. A teacher like Irenaeus, who had little patience with the metaphysical and held strongly to the inability of reason and the absolute need for revelation, could not avoid taking into consideration ideas of emanation current in his day when considering the mode of the generation of the Son, even while holding that it was incomprehensible.[3]

The Jews of Alexandria started with the twin conceptions that Scripture was a divine revelation and that Greek philosophy was true. Since this was the case, their task resolved itself into the reconcilia-

[1] Beirut edition, p. 276.
[2] Shiblī: *'Ilm ul Kalām*, p. 153.
[3] *Adv. Haer.* iii. 18, 7.

tion of philosophy with the Law, Plato with Moses. Philo thus took the logos doctrine already existing—although he claims he had it by divine revelation [1]—and uses it in his exposition of Judaism. A second result of the acceptance of the two principles mentioned was that it was concluded that there must be a twofold means of acquiring truth. There was a way of ascent by the human reason and a way of bestowal from above by divine revelation. These two factors we find presented in a philosophical manner in Philo.

The case was similar with regard to the Christian Alexandrians. Harnack says : [2] " The Church appears as the insurance society for the ideas of Plato and Zeno." Some of the early Christian scholars came to Christianity by the path of philosophy. This was the case with Clement, and Justin Martyr describes his itinerary *via* Stoicism, Peripateticism, Pythagoreanism and Platonism. In this last they found most to attract them Origen was in the like case.

That there were dangers in this must be obvious, and sometimes one wonders whether the content as well as the form of philosophy did not intrude itself to the detriment of what was fundamental in Christianity, and press revelation into the background The reservations permitted to Synesius of Cyrene (d. 412) when he was appointed bishop, in regard to the resurrection of the body and the creation of the world, contrary to the Christian tradition, are illustrations of this. Harnack says that these early philosophizing theologians " made Christianity a deistic religion for the whole world without abandoning in word at least the old teaching of the Christians." [3]

Indeed it is quite clear that there were protests from some early Fathers. Tertullian is an opponent of such philosophizing tendencies, though he was the first to use the term " person " with regard to the Trinity. His synthesis was rather with Jewish elements, and for him Christianity was the New Law. That difference of opinion as to the legitimacy of philosophy can be heard from Muslim lips in later centuries, and the question is one which was not raised originally by Muslims, but one which they received as part of their inheritance from these centuries of Christian and Jewish inquiry. On the one side we have the work of Clement and Origen and on the other the protests of Hermias, Tertullian and the orthodoxasts of Alexandria.

Neither are the Muslims the authors of dialectical theology.[4] In Christianity there were dialectical schools at a very early date. Origen informs us that in the schools of instruction in Alexandria there were ordinary schools where the creed was taught with simple commentary, and that there was also provided a dialectical instruction for those who

[1] *De Cherubim* ix. (i. 144).
[2] *History of Dogma*, Vol. ii, 228.
[3] *History of Dogma*, Vol. ii, 224.
[4] *Vide infra*, p. 64, for the Aristotelian dialectic of John of Damascus.

were fitted to receive it and profit by it. These were initiated into scientific, mathematical, physiological, astronomical and philosophical study. Definitions were proposed and discussions ensued on ethical subjects. We have already mentioned the dialectical school at Antioch where gradually philosophical propositions were regarded as of less account than scriptural exegesis. The methods of exegesis have their reflection in the schools of Muslim theology as we shall show presently. Traditionalism was also not neglected in the Cappadocian School. Thus it is not too much to say that the subsequent legalistic, philosophical and mystical elements in later Islam show parallels with similar elements in pre-Islamic Jewish and Christian schools. In early Christianity we see the Tertullian point of view and the vigorous Hellenistic influences. We have literalism favoured by a school like Antioch and allegorism favoured by Alexandria. For one the Mosaic Law is the schoolmaster and for the other the Greek Philosopher is the tutor. For Clement revelation is by the medium of Scripture and abstract reasoning. There is a covenant of God covering the patient search for truth in the philosophers and the Mosaic Law.

So long as the unity of truth was proclaimed, one might argue that little harm could be done, but when we find that there was a tendency to divide truth according to the various grades of men so that what was "the truth, the whole truth and nothing but the truth" for one class was certainly not so for another, we can see what dangers lurked. The "two lives" of Philo and then in Clement, which the latter sought to justify by the distinction between "milk" and "solid food", "Faith" and "understanding all mysteries", "the spirit of bondage" and "the spirit of adoption" could do a great deal to unsettle the conception of the unity of truth. The practice of "reserve" and "accommodation", while it might have some justification as applied to teaching so that simple minds might not be burdened with matters which they could not well understand, might on the other hand become a subtle enemy of truth. The division into the common people, who could exercise faith as a sort of inferior discipline and obedience to authority, and the privileged wise with their mystical or intellectual *gnosis*, has its reflection in the *'āmm* and *kh̲āṣṣ* of later Muslim writers and in the practice of "*taqlīd*"—unreasoning obedience to authority, and the *taqīya* whereby a man concealed his real opinions. There is a danger here that faith should be regarded as just inferior understanding. Even Al G̲h̲azzālī who achieved some measure of emancipation from mere intellectualism, is not unable to escape the snare. He has his plain dogmatic and ethical teaching in one group of his writings, attacks the philosophers in others, in yet others condescends to philosophize, and even in *Mishkāt ul Anwār*, where he brings his readers to the threshold of an advanced mystery, hints that there is a further stage which could not then be revealed, and which we have not found explained in any of his extant works. Place side by side the types and antitypes of Origen and Al Ghazzālī's similar indulgence in symbolism. Consider Clement's doctrine of gnosis alongside the words Al Ghazzālī uses in addressing his reader in *Mishkāt ul Anwār*.[1] "You have assayed to climb an arduous ascent, so high that the height thereof cannot be so much as gauged by mortal eyes. You have knocked at a door which is only open to those who know and are 'established in knowledge'. Moreover, not every mystery is to be revealed or divulged", and add to this the *disciplina arcani* of Gregory of Nyssa and, with all the differences encountered, it can be seen that there is the common attraction of the esoteric which might lead to contempt for simple truth which could be grasped by the "vulgar horde". The pride of intellect which thinks certain "truth" is "good enough" for common people is not a sign of any great ethical superiority.

The esoteric doctrine, reserve, the "two lives", the grades of the vulgar and the elect, allegorism and typology, all these go together. And when it is asked "Of what profit has been your allegorizing? What has it revealed?" the only answer that can be given is that it has "revealed" such subjective imaginings as contribute to the conceit of superior wit or piety, and constitutes a convenient method of reading into the Scripture what you wish to find there.

The principle of "accommodation" has more to commend it. When Origen says, "The holy apostles in preaching the faith of Christ declared with the utmost clarity whatever they considered was necessary for salvation even to those who were slack in investigating divine knowledge and left the reason for their statements to be discovered by those who showed themselves worthy of the excellent gifts of the Spirit"[2] or to Celsus, "For our prophets and Jesus Himself and His disciples were careful to adopt such a style of address as would not merely convey the truth, but which would be suitable for the winning of the common people, until each one, drawn and led onward, should reach up as far as possible to the comprehension of the mysteries which lie behind the seemingly simple words", and Ibn Miskawayh[3] (in almost identical terms): "The honoured prophets, on whom be peace, had to adopt a style of explanation which was near to the understanding and could benefit all classes of men in common, in order to proclaim their message and teach men. So they used proverbs and riddles which, beside being commonly understood, satisfied the elect also. Each man was informed by the prophet's word according to the extent of his intelligence," so long as there was no idea of exclusiveness, and there was nothing to be withheld absolutely but only until the preliminary instruction had done its work, then there was no violence to

[1] Gairdner's translation, p. 44.
[2] *de Principiis* i. 3.
[3] *Vide infra*, p. 173.

the unity of truth. It is doubtful, however, whether this was always the uppermost thought in the minds of these philosophizing theologians. It may be with such ideas as these in mind that Shiblī suggests in the quotation we have made that an emancipation from philosophy was desirable, but the further contention that this emancipation was achieved either in the earlier Christian or the later Muslim theologians is not one which we can possibly admit. The philosophizing of theology had gone a long way before Islam and in Islam it continued on the same path in spite of the protests of Al G͟hazzālī.

It is true that protests have taken place in both the religions, and that sometimes the protest against the use of reason in religion is added to the dislike of philosophy in religion particularly in Islam. It has formed a classical question in Islam as to whether what is right and wrong is recognizable by reason, with few except the Mu'tazilites, who are not reckoned orthodox, maintaining the affirmative. This is to press matters to a crude extreme. The principle which Clement, for instance, accepts is that nothing is to be believed of God which is unworthy of Him and that reason must be the judge of what is worthy of Him. Thus reason is the judge of revelation.[1] This question will be taken up later. It must suffice here to indicate the problem. Is revelation to be regarded as merely a confirmation of what the reason discovers? Or is revelation to be accepted only when we can in some way read into it what has already been rationally conceived? Or is the mistake we make in thinking of revelation as static? Or does revelation mean the stimulation of right reason? All these indicate some of the problems which arise and which must be faced. But the easy way out, to regard as allegory all which does not exactly square with some preconceived logical or philosophical scheme is erroneous as a method and multiplies error.

For all the appeal to philosophy it should be recognized that in these early schools there was a decided lack of rigidity. The case of Synesius has been mentioned and is, by the way, a comment on Shiblī's statement that the question of the resurrection of the body was not one which had been discussed. There is evidence that though philosophy was pressed into service a great deal had to be regarded as only an interim statement. The data of Christianity to which the Apostle's Creed is witness were not lost, and they did a great deal towards the reshaping of philosophy, and though it is easy to say, for instance, that Neoplatonism influenced Christianity, it is possible and indeed probable that Christianity influenced Neoplatonism. In general it seems that *solvitur ambulando* was a tacit principle in the evolution of Christian theology. As a heresy arose or a wrong statement was made or a wrong term used, criticism was exercised, and out of the criticism emerged a more assured understanding of the genuine content of the

[1] *Stromateis* vi. 15, 124; vii. 16, 196.

faith. Thus was realized in one way the promise of the guidance into all truth which was Christ's bequest to His disciples. The lack of rigidity is illustrated by the defence of Dionysius of Alexandria by Athanasius,[1] although he used the term " created " of Christ, and thus it seems clear that though metaphysical terminology might imply unorthodoxy, the terminology was not regarded as the all-important thing. Indeed, it would seem that difficulties increased when the approval of orthodoxy was transferred to the acceptance of philosophical statements. Earlier, what seems to have been asked is whether something " novel " (cf. the Muslim *bid'a*) was being introduced into the faith. Certainly this was the case with Tertullian. The above remarks will imply that to some extent " heresy " contributed to the development of the theology. Similarly in Islam : the early books of theology in Christianity were books on heresies, and in Islam also we find the same compilations.[2]

One of the results of an excessive emphasis on *gnosis* in the Alexandrian School particularly, but this is true to some extent of all the Eastern schools, is a deficient soteriology. Too often we find the substitution of monastic discipline and virginity and an ascetic intellectualism usurping the place of the redemptive self-giving of God. The incarnation is in the main held out as a sort of promise of the deification of man. Cosmological considerations are of more importance than the atoning grace which brings back the individual sinner in reconciliation to God. The East had too little of Augustine and too much metaphysical speculation. It puzzled itself about the mode of the Incarnation to the neglect of the doctrines of grace. For the faith of trust there was substituted the faith of assent, and now when the Muslim comes face to face with the Christian he has little to ask of the God Who is Saviour and everything to ask about problems of the Trinity, the mode of the Incarnation, the difficulties of the union of divine and human.

(iv) Christian Heresy and Islam. When the question is asked as to whether Islam may not have been adversely affected to Christianity by heresy, if this refers to the rise of Muhammad and his direct relation to heretical sects in Arabia, one may reply that there was as much likelihood (or more) that he would have acquaintance with orthodox Christianity. If, however, the question refers to the later development of Islam there is more possibility that in the early clash between Islam and Christianity on theological grounds Muslims may have become acquainted with heresies which could be used to support the

[1] *de Sent. Dionys.*, 4. Cf. also *ERE* viii. 779.

[2] There is a temptation to follow here with a discussion of early Christian mysticism in relation to Sufism, but if mysticism were dealt with this book would be enlarged beyond all due proportions. The works of Nicholson, Massignon, Margaret Smith, Horten (of Bonn) are recommended to the student who wishes to include these in his study.

Muslim position. Something has been said under the heading of the Christology of the Qur'ān about the influence of Gnosticism especially in its docetism. Here it must be added that though the Gnostics seem to be too early to have had—in the absence of literature available to Muhammad—any direct influence on him, it would seem that some of these ancient heresies often had a very tenacious life. In certain cases it may have happened that the impulse which was powerful in the rise of Islam may have been at the same time within other movements which appear in ecclesiastical history as Christian heresies. In order to form some sort of judgment on the matter we shall glance at some of the heresies which may be thought to exhibit characteristics similar to those shown in Islam.

(*a*) *Gnosticism and Kindred Heresies.* Gnosticism arose very early, and beside the Christian variety we find pagan gnosticism and Jewish. The great names in the early period are Valentinus, Basilides and Theodotus. It is interesting to find in the first Epistle of St. John evidence of the existence of gnostics at that early date. Ignatius[1] in his epistles had occasion to utter warnings against docetic heresy. He shows that he attached great importance to the physical facts of Christ's death and resurrection. "Why am I ready to face the beasts if Christ did not die in the flesh?"

Theodotus (end of second century) exhibits many likenesses to the Ebionites. He held that Christ was a mere man and yet believed in the miraculous conception. He denied that Christ could be called God. These Ebionites and the Marcionites show a keen dislike for the Old Testament. The former held that it was a forgery by an evil spirit. The Pseudo-Clementines declared that it had been interpolated by false prophets who had added the stories of the sins committed by Adam.

The whole view of prophethood contributed by these sects is of special interest. The Ebionite prophets were Abraham, Isaac, Jacob, Moses, Aaron and Joshua. This should be compared with the Muslim ideas and the exclusion in Islam also of the writing prophets of the Old Testament (with one or two exceptions). The Sethians held that Mani, Adam, Seth, Noah, Abraham were prophets. (Al Biruni quotes Mani for Buddha and Zoroaster as prophets.) The inclusion of Seth is interesting because we find him in Islam also and to quite a marked degree in later mysticism.[2] We have evidence in Mas'ūdī[3] and Baghdādī[4] that early Islam was acquainted with the Marcionites.

When we realize the affinity that the later sect of the Paulicians had with Marcion, and their adoptianist tendencies, and the tradition which relates the sect to Paul of Samosata, it is not unfitting that he

[1] *Ad Smyrn.* v. and *ad Trall.* x. Cf. also Ep. of Barnabas, v. 10 ff.
[2] Epiphanius: *Haer.* xxxix. 1.
[3] *Les Prairies d'Or* vi. 385 f. Cf. also i. 200 and viii. 293.
[4] *Al Farq baina'l Firaq*, 349.

should now be considered. His tenets were also akin to the Monarchians—indeed many of these heretical sects show many points of similarity—in the fact that he denied personal distinctions in the Godhead. He held that Christ was born of the Virgin and that the Logos inspired him. The Logos is considered to be an impersonal attribute of the Father. Paul averred that hymns to Christ were an innovation. This list of beliefs is remarkable, for the Muslim could hold all this and even affirms it. Paul held strongly to the opinion that the light which was in Christ was not the Logos in its essence.[1] The differences between his ideas and the Muslim conceptions are that he would agree that Christ could be called God by virtue of the clothing of Christ with divine dignity by union with God. Although Adoptianism proper rose in Spain in the eighth century A.D. where in the middle of the century Migetius denied the divinity of the Word, the beginnings of adoptianism should be looked for much earlier and Paul of Samosata lies in the path of inquiry.

We come finally to the Paulicians.[2] In affinity with the Marcionites they held a critical view of Scripture. In Christology they are adoptianist. God sent an angel to be born of a woman and adopted Him as His Son. Scott[3] says that they were strongly anti-Catholic and anti-clerical. They rejected the worship of images and repudiated monasticism. Their affinity for the Muslims was such that they fought on the side of the Muslims against the Byzantine Empire. They represented a popular movement which had a great following in Armenia and in Syria. The date of the rise of the sect is obscure, but if Constantine Silvanus (possibly *c.* A.D. 640) was the founder, then we may see in Islam and the Paulician movement movements which sprung almost simultaneously from common causes. Among other tenets of the sect may be mentioned the rejection of the doctrine of the perpetual virginity of the Virgin, the rejection of purgatory and the intercession of saints.[4]

(*b*) *Other Heretical Opinions with regard to the Incarnation and the Person of Christ.* The Arian heresy is the first which falls to our notice. In previous pages we have had occasion to refer to this doctrine. The main tenets of Arianism which concern us here are the attribution of an inferior deity to Christ. The Father is the "unbegotten" and the Son is "begotten". The Arians were often nicknamed "Porphyrians", and the significance of this is probably that the doctrine suggested a scheme of emanation on the Neoplatonist pattern. We have seen how the controversy distracted Christendom. It was not settled at Nicaea but continued for many a long day. We read that

[1] Athanasius: *de Decret.* c. v. 24.
[2] Scott in *ERE* ix. 695 ff.
[3] *Loc. cit.*
[4] Cf. Qur'ān Sura ix. 30–31. "They take doctors and monks for Lords rather than God."

in A.D. 359 Constantius, the Byzantine Emperor, was instrumental in gaining the assent of the bishops to a creed which was virtually a repudiation of the divinity of Christ. During the reign of Valentinian, Rome adhered to the doctrine of Nicaea, whereas at Milan there was an Arian bishop. Towards the end of the fourth century Constantinople was almost wholly Arian.

In regard to this doctrine, in addition to the remarks we have already made under the heading "Christology of the Qur'ān", we would point out that in the philosophizing theologians of Islam it is not uncommon to find schemes on the emanational pattern which allow some possibility of a vicegerent of a supernatural character mediating between the transcendent One and creation. Even with regard to the Prophet Muhammad we find that there is advanced a doctrine of his pre-existence in *al Ḥaqīqat ul Muḥammadīya* or the Light of Muhammad. These ideas are to be found in some of the great mystics. Ibn Sīnā in *Kitāb ul Ishārāt* identifies the Aristotelian *'Aql* (Primal Reason) with the Light of Allah spoken of in Sura xxi v. 35. Traditions have been put into the mouth of the Prophet such as "I was a prophet while Adam was between water and clay." In Jīlī, the great mystic, the *Ḥaqīqa* is described in terms which are distinctly Arian, and Porphyrian. "One of his names is Word of God (*Amr Ullāh*) and He is the most sublime and exalted of all existences. He is supreme in regard to dignity and rank and there is no angel greater than He. He is the chief of all archangels and in all devices is superior to the angels. . . . He has different guises and is manifested in various habitations."[1]

The Monarchians were for the most part opposed to any sort of logos doctrine. They are said to have been students of Aristotle. God, in their creed, was a single person just as He was a single being. Some Monarchians held that Christ was a mere man whom God had inspired and who was specially elect of God—a good definition of the prophet in the Muslim system. Others held that Christ was a mode of the divine manifestation, not really distinct from God the Father except on the plane of manifestation. The former rejected the fourth Gospel and were nicknamed *alogi*.[2] The latter are better known as Sabellians after Sabellius, who was the chief exponent of the school. The Monarchians had a very long history. They are attacked by Tertullian,[3] and they were condemned by the Lateran Council as late as A.D. 649. It is interesting to note that an early Bishop of Bostra in Arabia, Beryl (a contemporary with Origen), held to the views of the modalist Monarchians. He said that the personality of Christ was purely human.

[1] *Al Insān ul Kāmil*, Vol. ii, Capp. 51, 60, etc.
[2] Epiphan: *Haer*, li.
[3] *Adv. Prax.*

The schools which over-emphasized the humanity of Christ have also been mentioned. This was peculiarly the tendency of the school of Antioch. This school did great service in recalling Christendom from a metaphysical view of Christ to consider Him as He was portrayed in the pages of the Gospel. Paul of Samosata was associated with Antioch, and so was Nestorius. It has been said that "Nestorianism was the characteristic heresy of the school which looked to Antioch for leadership". Both Diodorus and Theodore of Mopsuestia had laid special stress on the manhood of Christ, not, however, to the exclusion of His divinity, but with a great deal of ambiguity with regard to all that was fundamental in the idea of Incarnation. The idea set forward that there was a moral bond of union between two persons, which became the regular Nestorian doctrine, would logically rule out any absolute necessity for the connexion. A relation between Christ and God which was essential to the being of God seems to be ruled out or, if not, to be obscured. Christ is only man indwelt by God to the utmost degree.

Of somewhat different character is the Apollinarian heresy, which denied to Christ a rational soul and held that in Christ the place of the rational soul was taken by the Logos. Christ was thus not a perfect man but a sort of flesh-clothed logos.

These heresies with regard to the person of Christ are instructive because they show how difficult a task these old theologians set themselves when they sought to explain the mode of the Incarnation. They should also encourage us to a wider and deeper sympathy with Muslims who seek an explanation of these things. With regard to the two terms which may be considered to cover a great deal which is held in the Nestorian School, namely, "union" and "indwelling", it is interesting to find that when the Muslim theological books speak of the tenets which Christians hold with regard to the Incarnation, these two ideas are expressed. For the first of these the term "*ittiḥād*" is used and for the second "*ḥulūl*". The latter word has become almost the technical expression for "incarnation" in Islam, but one may be permitted to question whether the word truly represents the Christian doctrine.[1]

Whether there was any heresy to justify the charge of tritheism is very doubtful, but a misunderstanding of the Trinity might account for that. John Philoponus (early sixth century), an Aristotelian of Alexandria, was called John the Tritheist, but he was also stigmatized as an atheist. He was a Monophysite and is known in Islam as Yaḥyā an Naḥwī. Any really tritheistic sects must have been very obscure and have left no remains.

(*c*) *Pelagianism*. Though it might seem to be out of place to discuss Pelagianism in relation to a religion which so strongly emphasizes the

[1] For a full discussion see Vol. II.

dominant will of God, it will be seen that influences can be traced not only where there is agreement but also where there is opposition. One of the matters of debate in the early days of Islam was the question of the freedom of the will and the relation of the divine will to man's actions. The ground for this debate had already been prepared in Christianity, and since Pelagianism influenced Nestorianism and the Eastern Church in general, there gradually grew up the broad distinction of Christianity acknowledging freewill and Islam accepting predestination, which does justice neither to Christianity nor to Islam and brings two doctrines into opposition which are not necessarily contradictories.

The doctrine of the Church was that man has freewill. Augustine is in no doubt about it though he was the opponent of Pelagius. "God foresees the power of the will also. Therefore this power is not taken from me by God's prescience; on the contrary it belongs to me the more surely."[1] But the general opinion is that the will has been corrupted by the fall and for the enfeebled will the aid of God is needed through His grace manifested in Christ by the agency of the Holy Spirit. Pelagius questioned this corruption and set himself to combat a belief in hereditary sinfulness which to his mind led to antinomianism. Man had naturally the power to do right. Now the strange thing is that in Islam original sin is denied. It is not questioned that man is weak, but natural ability to do right is presupposed *so far as any actions can be referred to man at all.* There is no supernatural endowment to do right, and grace is the working of God as He wills in the particular human life. Islam really presents a paradox here. On the one hand, rejecting the original corruption of man by the fall, it would imply a position somewhat akin to Pelagianism, and on the other hand, holding with such extraordinary tenacity to the dominant will of God, it can be classed as predestinarianism. Furthermore, the principle of the Pelagian Coelestius that the Law brings men to the Kingdom of God even as the Gospel, is in harmony with the presumption that prevails throughout Islam that without any particular plan of salvation such as Christianity preaches, it is possible for men to obey the Law and attain to the righteousness which is by the Law.

When we examine the way in which love is attributed to God in the Qur'ān it becomes at once evident that it is predominantly a reward to the meritorious, and although Pelagius formally refused to acknowledge that his belief was that God's grace is given in proportion to man's merits and worthiness, nevertheless this principle seems implicit in his system.

It is possible that the ramifications of the Pelagian heresy were very wide in the East. Marius Mercator considered that the real author of Pelagianism was Theodore of Mopsuestia, and there is no doubt that

[1] *De Libero Arbitrio,* III, viii.

there was a very real and definite association of Pelagianism and Nestorianism. The School of Antioch made much of Christ's possession of freewill, and in the subsequent inquiry as to what constituted human nature the common attribute of freedom was easily deduced. The Antiochene theology became familiar to Pelagius through Rufinus of Syria and finally Pelagius settled in Palestine.

Before leaving the question of Pelagianism in relation to Islam two matters should be mentioned. One of the questions at issue was the justice of God. Could the idea of inherited sinfulness be reconciled with this? The question of God's justice in relation to man's freedom was raised by the Mu'tazilites at a very early date. The second matter is that it was a principle of Pelagianism that ability limits obligation. This, too, became one of the classical matters of debate, the Ash'arites holding that there was obligation beyond ability and the Mu'tazilites that this was not the case.

(*d*) *Iconoclasm.* Though this is hardly to be classed as a heresy it is convenient to mention here the movement against the worship of images which came to a head in the Byzantine Empire during the reign of the Emperor Leo the Isaurian at the beginning of the eighth century. Some have seen in this movement a result of the rise of Islam and its uncompromising opposition to anything which savoured of polytheism. One would rather see in this movement something parallel to Islam and due to the same forces which were at work to emphasize monotheism. The Paulicians were inconoclasts before the time of Leo, and there is on record the rebuke of Gregory I (590–604) in his letter to Serenus of Marseilles,[1] showing that protests against the use of images were common before the Iconoclastic movement proper. That the edict of Leo in A.D. 725 was prompted in some part by a previous persecution of Christians for worshipping images by Yazīd II in A.D. 722 is quite likely,[2] but it must not be thought that this was in any degree the beginning of opposition to image worship in Christianity, and if it was regarded as political wisdom to seek to conciliate the Muslims by the edict, Leo was not doing something which was unsupported by powerful opinion in the Church which had been formed quite apart from political considerations, although there were equally influential leaders of the Church who favoured image worship, e.g., the Damascene.[3]

(v) JOHN OF DAMASCUS. Perhaps no individual Christian thinker is so important in a comparative study of Islamic and Christian theology as John of Damascus. His works belong to the years of Islam's infancy—he died before the middle of the eighth century. He wrote

[1] *Patrologia Latina* (Migne), lxxvii. 1027.

[2] *Vide* Assemani ii. 105. For a long and valuable statement on the subject see Browne: *Eclipse of Christianity in Asia,* pp. 74 ff.

[3] *De Imaginibus*, iii. *Patrol. Graeca,* xciv. 1376.

in the environment of early Islam. He knew Islam well, being the son of a Christian official at the court of the Umayyad Caliphs and himself engaged in similar service as a layman before he became a priest. In his book on the heresies he shows an acquaintance with the Qur'ān, and he is indeed one of the earliest witnesses we have outside Islam for the existence and part of the contents of the Qur'ān. A good deal of what he wrote is extant, and though there may be a doubt about some of the books which bear his name, it is fairly certain that if they did not come from his pen, they came from the pen of his disciple Theodore Abu Qurra. The works important for our study are his *Dialectica*, his *De Haeresibus* and *De Fide Orthodoxa*, which form a trilogy, and his dialogues known as *Disputatio Christiani et Saraceni* and *Disputatio Saraceni et Christiani*. These two dialogues will be referred to again when we come to speak of the Apologists. When the different doctrines come to be considered at the close of this section we shall have occasion to quote from his treatise on dogmatics which is called *De Fide Orthodoxa*. Strictly speaking his *Dialectica* could form the introduction to our later section on the comparative scholasticism of Islam and Christianity, but as in that section it is more convenient to confine the discussion to mediæval Christian Scholasticism we must take notice of the *Dialectica* here.

It has already been remarked that the dialectic theology (called by Muslims *Kalām*) was not the invention of Muslim theologians and that there were schools of dialectical theology in Christianity for many centuries before Islam. In the Damascene's *Dialectia* we have a scheme of dialectic to be applied to theology so complete in its details as to compare favourably with any later introduction to *Kalām*. In this we find sixty-eight "*capita philosophica*" which are explained according to the terminology and methodology of Aristotle. Starting with an article on knowledge he proceeds to define philosophy and then turns to a discussion of being, substance and accident. Then follows a number of logical *capita*, definition, genus, species, individua, differentia, accidents, properties, predication univocal and equivocal all being dealt with. Other subjects are the ten predicamenta, substance, nature, form, hypostasis, person, enhypostasis, anhypostasis, the classification of being and substance (οὐσία—*jawhar*), quantity (ποσόν—*kam*), relation (πρός τι—*iḍāfa*), quality (ποιόν—*kaif*), activity and passivity (ποιεῖν & πασχεῖν—*fi'l* and *infi'āl*), position (κεῖσθαι—*waḍ'*), place (ποῦ—*'ayn*—where), time (ποτέ—*matā*—when), acquired character (possession, ἔχειν—*malaka*), etc. He concludes with six definitions of philosophy and an article on the four dialectical methods.[1]

It is this scheme which appears again and again as the method of the dialectical theology in Islam.[2] It is the Aristotelian method which

[1] Migne: *Patrologia Graeca*, xciv. 525 ff.
[2] Cf. Ijī: *Mawáqif* and *vide infra*, Vol II.

the Muslims found so congenial and which they developed till they gave it back to Europe in the Middle Ages. And thus we come full circle from Christian dialectic in pre-Islamic days to the mediæval scholasticism through the Muslim system.

In his *De Haeresibus*, John speaks of the Muslims as Ishmaelites or alternatively Hagarites, and explains their name Saracen from the words of Hagar, " Sara sent me away empty ". Thus they are Σάρρας κενούς. Formerly they were idolaters, but in the reign of Heraclius " Mamed " arose, instructed in all probability by an Arian monk. " Mamed " claimed to have received a book from Heaven. John avers that the Qur'ān teaches that God is One, the Creator, neither begotten nor begetting (Sura cxii. 3); that Christ is a word of God and His Spirit (Sura iv. 169), but a creature and a servant, born without seed from Mary, the sister of Moses and Aaron; the Word and the Spirit came into Mary and she bore Jesus, a Prophet and Servant of God; the Jews unlawfully purposed to crucify Him, and, apprehending Him, they crucified Him only in appearance for Christ was really not crucified nor did He die, but God took Him to Heaven for love of Him. When Christ came to Heaven God asked Him whether He said He was the Son of God and God, and He denied it. " Men, the sinners, wrote that I said this." John then goes on to ask what were the credentials of the Prophet and how His revelation came? The answer which he puts into the mouth of the Muslims is that revelation came upon Him while he was asleep. John ridicules this. He refers to the fact that Muslims called the Christians " Associators ", i.e., those who joined partners with God (*mushrikūn*—ἑταιριστάς). When the Christians assert that the Sonship of Christ was delivered to them by the prophets and the Scripture, they (the Muslims) say that this is what the Christians read into the Scripture. He then proceeds to ask why Christians should be called Associators if the Qur'ān refers to Christ as Word of God and Spirit? For these are inseparable from God. " It would be better for you (Muslims) to say that He has a partner than to mutilate Him. . . . When you call us Associators we call you Mutilators (κόπτας)."

John then goes on to ask why Christians should be blamed for bowing before the Cross, when Muslims kiss the Black Stone which still bears the traces of an engraved figure and is an idol? There is then an attack on the character of Muhammad and some criticism of the contents of the Qur'ān.

Nothing very much is added to our knowledge of Islam by this brief notice.[1] It is interesting because it shows a knowledge of the Qur'ān and because the reply to the Muslim charge of " joining partners with God " is repeated again and again, in the polemic which was used against Islam. There it is said that the Muslim idea which separates

[1] For *De Haeresibus* see Migne: *Pat. Graec.*, Vol. xciv, 764 ff.

from God that which is essential to His being and life, namely, Word and Spirit, is a mutilation of God. We also find the attack on the character of Muhammad repeated in the later apologists.

(vi) THE APOLOGISTS. In addition to John of Damascus, early apologists for Christianity against Islam are John's disciple Theodore Abu Qurra (ninth century) who was Bishop of Harrān, 'Abdul Masīh b. Isḥāq al Kindī (tenth century according to Massignon and ninth according to Muir), Yaḥyā b. 'Adī the Jacobite (d. 974), Ḥunayn b. Isḥāq the Nestorian (d. 873), Timothy the Nestorian Catholicus (780–823), Cyriacus, the Jacobite Patriarch of Antioch (793–817), Abū 'Alī 'Isā b. Isḥāq b. Zur'a the Jacobite (d. 1007) and Eliyyā the Nestorian Metropolitan of Nisibis (1008–1049).[1] Of these we may choose John, Theodore, Timothy and Al Kindī as representative. John of Damascus is apparently more concerned to give instruction to Christians than anything else. He is on the whole on the defensive. Theodore follows his master. Timothy adopts a conciliatory tone and Al Kindī is distinctly on the offensive, having been promised immunity so that he may speak his mind freely. The Muslim riposte is provided by the book by 'Alī Tabarī.[2]

It should be observed in the first place that the pre-Islamic apologists should not be neglected when we seek to understand the lines of which the polemic against Islam was conducted. One should particularly notice Aphraates of Edessa [3] (fourth century), Chrysostom [4] (347–407), and Gregentius [5] who was Bishop of Zafār, the capital of the Himyarites in South Arabia (end of fifth or beginning of sixth century).

John of Damascus in his *Disputatio* starts with a question about the terms Word and Spirit used in the Qur'ān for Christ. He advises the Christian whom he is instructing to ask whether these were created or uncreated. If the reply is that they were uncreated he should hail this as agreement and if not he should further inquire who created them ? If the Muslim is compelled to answer that God Himself created them the Christian should retort that in this case before God created them He had neither Word nor Spirit. If the Muslim shifts the question to whether the " words " of God are created or not the answer must be that the Christian believes in one word.[6] The next question suggested is the difference between figurative and literal interpreta-

[1] For these Browne : *Eclipse of Christianity in Asia*, Capp. vi and viii should be consulted. Sbath : *Vingt Traités philosophiques et apologétiques d'auteurs arabes chrétiens* (Arabic), Cheikho : *Vingt Traités théologiques d'auteurs arabes chrétiennes* (Arabic) and *Trois Traités anciens de polémique et de théologie chrétiennes* (Arabic), Muir : *Apology of Al Kindy*, S.P.C.K., *Studia Sinaitica* vii and viii contain a great deal of material for this study. See also MSS. 70 of Bibliothéque Nationale (Paris) discussed by Guillaume in *Moslem World Quarterly* for January, 1925.

[2] Mingana : *Kitáb ad Dīn wad Daula*, ed. and trans. (Manchester, 1923–4).

[3] *Patrologia Syriaca*, Vol. i (His *Homilies* were written 336–345).

[4] *Pat. Graeca* (Migne), xlviii. 813 ff.

[5] ibid., lxxxvi. 621 ff.

[6] Cf. Shahrastānī : *Nihaya* on the subject Allah's Speech is One. Cap. xiii.

tion of scripture. "Literalness has reference to the fixed meaning of a thing while figurative interpretation involves a secondary meaning." The illustrations which are given of this are: "The sea saw and fled", but the sea has no eyes, and "The earth which hath opened her mouth to receive thy brother's blood". Here "mouth" is used metaphorically. The next question put into the mouth of the "Saracen" is "How did God come into a woman's womb?" The reply is that the Qur'ān says that God first cleansed Mary and the Spirit and Word of God came down upon her, and the Gospel says: "The Holy Ghost shall come upon thee and the power of the Most High shall overshadow thee." Thus there is agreement in the two! But ascent and descent are not to be taken literally, for how can He descend and ascend Who holds all in His hands? Then if the Muslim asks: "If God was Christ, how did He eat, drink, sleep, suffer crucifixion, and die?" the Christian should reply that God created from the body of the holy Virgin a complete, living and intelligent man. He was truly the Word, but the Word of God did not eat, drink, sleep, nor was He crucified nor did He die. It was the assumed flesh which was crucified. The Word after the assumption of the flesh was anhypostatic—impersonal—and there was no fourth person added to the Trinity after the ineffable union. The reply to the question: "Did He whom you call God die?" is in the negative.

There follows a section of the dialogue dealing with the question of the creation of evil. A worm forms in a wound. Who created it? Is God the cause of evil? asks the Muslim. No. Then what caused evil? It is by our own foolhardiness and the wiles of the Devil. In reply to the question how this could be, the Christian answers that it is by freewill, to which the Muslim retorts: "Have you freewill and are you able to do whatever you please?" The Christian replies that he has been formed with freewill by God. Then the question proceeds to whether evil is by God's command, for then "according to you God will turn out to be unrighteous which he is not"; for if God commands the fornicator to commit fornication and the thief to steal and the murderer to commit murder then all of these are worthy of praise, for they have done God's will. To this the Muslim objects that God forms the unborn child in the womb and so the fruit of fornication is formed by God and God would become a partner with the fornicator and the adulterer. To this extraordinary idea the reply is given: "We in no wise find that Scripture says that after the first week (of creation) God formed or created anything." He made man in the first week and commanded him to beget and to be begotten. . . . "Because man had life he made seed to develop in his own life." In procreation "I use my own freewill and it comes to pass in answer to God's first command". The Saracen then asks how it could be said by God of Jeremiah "In the womb I knew thee"? The ground is then shifted somewhat and, probably with some actual experience to guide him, John suggests that the Muslim might ask whether those who do God's will are good or evil, having in mind a further question as to whether Christ suffered willingly or by the will of God at the hand of the Jews. In reply the Damascene describes God's action towards the committing of evil as permissive—God's will is patience and forbearance, i.e., He forbears when man sins and does not compel him. In Migne there follows an appendix from Theodore Abū Qurra which contains an argument for Christianity from the miracles of Christ of which a list is given.

Theodore Abū Qurra follows his master in the main. In his debate in the court of Ma'mūn we find that the questions raised are, whether circumcision is to be observed, and whether Christ is coequal with God, to which Theodore replies with quotations from the Qur'ān (Suras iii. 52 and iv. 169). The disputants agree that Christ is Word and Spirit. Theodore wants Hāshimī with whom he was debating to agree that Christ was Creator and not created—relying on the idea that the Word was the executive of God in creation. Another antagonist quotes to the Christian advocate the words : "I ascend to My Father and your Father, to My God and your God." Theodore has no direct reply to this but proceeds to argue for the incarnation. He also puts a poser as to the meaning of Sura v. 116. If God knew this why did He ask Jesus ? Someone interjects that if Christ is God then He is dead. The answer to this is given by Sura iii. 48 and the opponents agree. Theodore then says that the Qur'ān is right when it says that Christ was like Adam but that it also calls Christ "Spirit" and "Word of God". A Jew intrudes into the debate at this point and asserts that Christians crucify their God and worship the wood on which He was crucified. In defence of the veneration of the Cross, Theodore reminds the Muslims that they kiss the black stone which reminds us of what is said by John of Damascus in *De Haeresibus*.[1] The argument again returns to the description of Christ as Spirit and Word, and an objector asks : "If Christ is Spirit and Word in the sense of the executive of God in creation and providence, was this at an end when the Word came down upon Mary ?" Was God without His Word and Spirit when Christ was on earth ? Theodore answers that this would be tantamount to attributing temporal and spatial limitations to God. The Word of God was both in heaven and on earth. There follows the question whether Christ was crucified willingly or not. If the former, then the Jews were not to blame for what they did, and if the latter, then Christ is not omnipotent. There is also the question of the freedom of the will.

The Nestorian Patriarch Mar Timothy I was a man of great zeal and energy. The extant apology is to be found in both Syriac and Arabic.

[1] *Vide supra*, p. 65.

It consists of two days' conversation with the Caliph Mahdī. We shall refer to the contents of this in the summary of the subjects of debate. Timothy's apology is remarkable for many concessions which he makes. In reply to the Caliph's question as to what he had to say about Muhammad he said, Muhammad walked in the path of the prophets, taught the unity of God, drove men from bad works and brought them near to good works, separated men from idolatry and polytheism, and taught about "God, His Word and His Spirit". "Who will not praise, honour and exalt the one who not only fought for God in words, but showed his zeal for Him by the sword?"[1] As Abraham had turned his face from idols and from his kinsfolk so Muhammad did. There is more than a hint of political compromise in his words, but on the whole the apology is clear and rather fuller than some others we possess.

Al Kindī as well as Theodore Abū Qurra mentions as a Muslim protagonist Muhammad b. 'Abd Ullāh al Hāshimī. Sometimes this Al Kindī is confused with Abū Yūsuf b. Isḥāq al Kindī, the philosopher, who was apparently a Muslim, for he wrote a treatise against the Trinity. The lines which the apologist Al Kindī follows are far more in the nature of an attack on Islam than a defence of Christianity. In the first section of the book he examines the question of the Trinity, mentions the fact that there is a mistake in thinking that there is a female element in the Trinity and advances the usual arguments. He then examines the claim of Muhammad to be a prophet. He takes incidents from the life of Muhammad as throwing light on the Prophet's character. He then takes up the question of what is the evidence for a divine mission. Prophecy is one and this consists of revelation of the past accredited by miracle, and revelation of the future accredited by the fulfilment. He then asks what prophecies Muhammad gave of future events? Is there any record of miracles performed by Muhammad? These the Prophet disavowed in Sura xvii. 61. He says that the Muslim victories should not be reckoned as miracles, and quotes Deut. ix. 4–5. He then turns to the Christian argument for the truth of Christ from the miracles He performed.

There follows a discussion of the Qur'ān as a proof of the mission of Muhammad, and he examines its matter and its style. He condemns Holy War and the laws concerning women. He further goes on to a critical examination of the collection and text of the Qur'ān. This is the first extant record of such an attempt being made. He accuses Al Ḥajjāj of corrupting the Qur'ān and points to contradictions in it. He gives instances of foreign words in the Qur'ān, and criticizes the doctrine of the abrogation of one text in the Qur'ān by another. Other subjects he deals with are the question of the intercession of Muhammad on the Last Day, the Christian's adoration of the Cross,

[1] Mingana: *op. cit.*, p. 61.

the prophecies of the Old Testament, the question as to whether the Scriptures have been corrupted, etc.

In support of Christianity he sets forth answers to Muslim objections to the Trinity, and then goes on to give an account of Christ, His Annunciation and Birth, His ministry and teaching, His death and resurrection. He speaks of the spread of the Gospel throughout the earth and finally deals with the question why the followers of Christ no longer work miracles.

As said previously the counterblast from the Muslim side is provided for in the work of ʻAlī Ṭabarī. A brief outline of the contents of this book may be given. The Message which Muhammad brought was that which all the prophets had given, namely the Unity of God. This is the faith of Abraham. Ṭabari gives an outline of the religious laws of Islam and concludes: "These are messages and points which demonstrate that the man who laid them down was sound, steadfast, pious, devout, and was not a plagiarist, an appropriator of other's rights nor one making light of things and lacking gravity." He also asserts that miracles were performed by Muhammad, the Night Journey, Lahab was miraculously eaten by a lion at the word of the prophet. "Walīd b. Mug͟hīra met him and the Prophet made a sign to a wound he had in the sole of his foot and it broke out and killed him. Then Aswad b. ʻAbd Yag͟hūt͟h met him and the Prophet made a sign to his belly; and he became dropsical and died". A camel and a calf spoke to him and a wolf gave testimony of his prophethood. Trees walked at his command. He miraculously provided water.

From the miracles of Muhammad he turns to consider the prophecies attributed to him, but has not much to say on this score. In consideration of whether the Qur'ān is a sign of the Prophet's mission, he points out that Muhammad was an unlettered man and yet produced the Qur'ān. A comparison of the Old Testament with the Qur'ān is for the disparagement of the former. It deals generally with "genealogies of the Israelites, their exodus from Egypt, their camping and striking camp and the names of the places where they halted. It contains also lofty laws and maxims which dazzle the mind and which man's intellectual capacity and power are unable to compass. But what the Qur'ān says of the historical events is as a reminder of the favours of God, as edification, warning and admonition". The Gospel, while containing good maxims of morality and excellent parables, is deficient in laws, prescriptions and history. The Book of Psalms contains historical events, praises and hymns of great beauty, but it also is deficient in laws. There has been no book like the Qur'ān "since man began to write on parchment".

Muhammad's triumph is also a sign of his prophetic mission. His victory is from God and not from the Devil. His companions were just and righteous men. Four chapters follow on the asceticism of

Abū Bakr, 'Umar b. ul Khaṭṭāb, 'Alī, 'Umar b. 'Abd ul 'Azīz, 'Abdullāh b. Umar, etc. Whence the writer proceeds to examine the prophecies concerning Muhammad which it is alleged are to be found in the prophets of the Old Testament and in the words of Christ. In David such passages as Psa. xlv. 2–5 ; xlviii. 1–2 and l. 2–3, in which praise and praised might be translated *ḥamd* and *maḥmūd*, the reference is claimed to be to Muhammad and similarly in Isaiah (ii. 12–13, etc.) and other places. The sign of prophethood is on his shoulder (Isa. ix. 6). In Isa. xxi. 1–14, the South means Yaman. Thus he goes on through Hosea, Micah, Habakkuk, Zephaniah, Zechariah, Jeremiah, Ezekiel and Daniel. From the New Testament he advances the promise of the Paraclete as a promise of Muhammad. Christ referred to the Muslim dispensation when he commanded his disciples to sell their garments and buy swords. Gal. iv. 22–26 and its obscure allegory of Hagar and Mount Sinai in Arabia is also pressed into service. In a later chapter he argues against those who quarrel with the Prophet, saying that he changed the rules of Moses and the Gospel.

(vii) THE CHIEF POINTS AT ISSUE IN THE APOLOGISTS. We must now come to consider the main points at issue according to the Apologists. In his introduction to Mingana's edition of Timothy's *Apology*, Rendel Harris draws attention to the indebtedness of the Christian Apologists who debated with the Muslims to those who had previously debated with the Jews. Cyprian's *Book of Testimonies* undoubtedly formed a source book for later Christian apologists.

There is much in the Apologists with which we cannot find ourselves in whole-hearted agreement. Take, for instance, Justin Martyr, in whom we have a most inadequate description of Christianity. He holds that Christianity is true doctrine opposed to pagan ideas. It is a doctrine of virtue and rewards and punishments, and the whole is set before us as a new philosophy attested by revelation. "Christ is the *logos* of whom the whole human race partakes, and those who live according to reason are Christians even though they were considered to be atheists."[1] The *logos* of Justin is Philo's rather than the "Word made flesh" of the Gospel. "God begot Himself, a beginning before all creation, a certain rational power which is called Holy Spirit, Glory of the Lord,[2] and at other times Son and Wisdom, Angel, God, Lord and *Logos*." Christ is in some sort a creature, for He was begotten by an act of the Father's will. The personal distinction between the Son and the Father is not eternal. God is the transcendent, and He is only revealed in and through intermediate being, i.e., the *logos*. It might be similarly said that Clement's explanation of the Trinity seems more akin to a doctrine of emanation than to a Trinity of coequal, consubstantial persons. It is distressing to find in the apologists

[1] *Apol.* i, 46, 2.
[2] Cf. Ibn Miskawaih : *Barz ul Bārī*, p. 137, *infra*.

hesitancy where there should be none, and a marked absence of the preaching of the saving grace of God. Christopher Dawson [1] has most acutely said: "Theology in the West found its centre and principle of organization in the doctrine of Grace, the sacraments are conceived primarily as Means of Grace, and the Christian Life is the Life of Grace. In the East the theology is the doctrine of the Consubstantial Word. The sacraments are conceived as mysteries of illumination and the Christian life is seen as a process of deification by which humanity is assimilated to the immortal nature of the Divine Word." Those words have a wider application, and they should always be borne in mind as a key to many a problem which confronts us in this study. No wiser words could sum up the position.

We shall group the subjects which will make clear the method and mind of the apologists under seven headings: The Person and Incarnation of Christ, The Trinity, God's Being and Attributes, The Crucifixion of Christ, Scripture, Muhammad, Miracles and Signs.

(*a*) *The Person and Incarnation of Jesus Christ.* Cyprian starts with this subject in the Second Part of his *Liber Testimoniorum.* Christ the Son of God is also begotten in the flesh. The Jews (if we are to trust Pseudo-Chrysostom) [2] were not above suggesting unworthy ideas of the paternity of God. The Caliph Mahdī asks outright at the commencement of his conversation with Timothy [3] whether he believes that God married a woman from whom He begot a Son, and Timothy replies that this is blasphemy. For physical reasons the Caliph also suggests that Timothy believes in a "hollow" God, with a disgusting insinuation.[4] The Caliph wants to know also how begetting can be without genital organs.[5] The answer of Timothy is that God is incorporeal and that He begets as He creates without instruments. But sometimes language used by Christians was not altogether free from ambiguity. An example from a later period (perhaps) is in the *Dialogue of Papiscus and Philo*,[6] where in exposition of the words of Psa. ii. 7, "This day have I begotten thee", it says "'I have begotten thee' refers to the begetting in the flesh". In answer to the question, What is Christ? Timothy gives the answer that He is the Word-God who appeared in the flesh for the salvation of the world, "As light is born of the sun and word of the soul,[7] so also Christ who is the Word is born of God high above the times and before all the worlds. As to

[1] *Mediæval Religion*, p. 36.
[2] Migne: *Pat. Graec.* xlviii, 1075–1080.
[3] Mingana: *op. cit.*, p. 17.
[4] Mingana: *op. cit.*, p. 78.
[5] Mingana: *op. cit.*, 21 f.
[6] *Ed.* A. C. McGiffert, 1889.
[7] Cf. also *Discourse on the Triune Nature of God* (MS. 154) in *Studia Sinaitica*, vii–viii. "We do not say that God begat the Word as any man begets; God forbid . . . but as the Sun begets rays, as the mind begets the word, and as the fire begets heat; none of these things existed before what was begotten of them."

His birth from Mary, He is born without the seals of virginity being broken, even as Eve was born from Adam without fracture, and fruit is born from trees without breaking them." In response to the question of the Caliph, how the eternal could be born in time ? he replies that it was not in eternity that Christ was born of Mary. The Caliph thereupon considers that this makes Christ two beings, but, standing on his orthodoxy, Timothy says: "No, not two beings but two natures." One nature belongs to the Word and the other to that which is from Mary. In reply to a further inquiry as to how two could be one and one two ? Timothy gives an illustration from man, who consists of body and soul and is therefore two but is yet one individual and one composite, and from speech since "the tongue and the word are one with the sound in which they are clothed". There is here a very stumbling attempt to explain the union, and throughout these arguments we find a similar failure to realize in what consists the true union of the human and the divine in Christ and a most imperfect conception of human nature. Too often the idea emerges that the humanity is rather an appearance than a reality; we have already noted the naïve idea of Gregory of Nyssa that Christ by assuming a human form deceived the Devil into thinking he had only a human being to deal with, whereas this was not so. We find the same idea in Gregentius.[1] In his discussion with Herban, the Jew, he says: "God sent His Logos, who is united with a man in the womb of the Virgin and who defeats the demons and dies and rescues men from Hades. Then he ascends and sends his disciples forth. If Christ had appeared in all this as God, the Devil might have been excused for thinking that he had not been dealt with fairly."[2] Behind this is an idea that human nature is such a low and mean thing that the Son of God could not have been contaminated by any connection with it except in some manner which suppressed the humanity or, it may be, elevated it into something beyond humanity. Browne[3] quotes Jāḥiẓ as declaring that there was an affinity between the Christians and the Manichaeans or Mazdakians (*zandaqa*) in the way they regard the body and teach virginity.

Beside these points there are the difficulties raised with regard to the divinity of Christ. The Christians call a human being God. It is surprising how often we find John xx. 17 quoted by opponents. Thus the Jew Herban quotes this to Gregentius: "I go to My Father and your Father, to My God and to your God." How could Christ use these words if He were the Son of God ? It has already been noticed in the Qur'ān. In Gregentius we have it used in pre-Islamic times and in the Qur'ān there is an echo of this, and later we find it in Theodore

[1] Migne: *Patrol. Graec.* lxxxvi, 621–784.
[2] See also Theodore Abu Qurra in Cheikho: *Vingt Traités*, pp. 116–117.
[3] *Eclipse of Christianity in Asia*, p. 69.

and in Timothy [1] and in other apologists. It seems to have been a standard argument. It is also asked why did Christ pray? [2] Did He need worship and prayer? Timothy asks another question in reply: "Did Christ sin?" The Caliph is shocked at such a suggestion, and Timothy then says that Christ prayed not as one in need nor as a sinner. He worshipped and prayed in order to teach these things to His disciples. His disciples would not have yielded to His teaching if He had not put it into practice. It is interesting to note that when Muhammad's prayers for forgiveness in the Qur'ān are advanced by Christians as proof of his need for forgiveness, a similar reply to that of Timothy on behalf of Christ is given by Muslims on behalf of Muhammad. Another text advanced against the Christian by Al Mahdī is Matt. xix. 17: "Why callest thou Me good?" [3] Was Christ disclaiming goodness? And was He differentiating Himself from God? Timothy replies with John x. 11, where Christ calls Himself the Good Shepherd. The Caliph seems to be well informed for at one point he proceeds to inquire whether the prophets of old have not called Christ a servant.[4] The reply given to this is in the affirmative, but that Christ did not lose His sonship by His service any more than the Caliph's son when he went in obedience to fight at Constantinople against the Byzantines. The prophets also called Christ a servant because He was believed to be so by the Jews. The Sonship of Christ also causes some difficulty, and this is true to the present day. It is not so much that Christ is spoken of as a servant, but that He is spoken of as the Son of God. We find the same points raised in Cyprian and in Aphraates in his seventeenth Homily. There the Jews object: "You worship and serve a man who was begotten and a human being who was crucified. You call a human being God and though God has no son, you say of this Jesus who was crucified that He is God's Son." To this Aphraates replies that Moses was called Son of God and quotes: "I have made thee a god to Pharaoh" (Exod. vii. 1). This reminds us of the Quranic passage in which it is asserted that the Jews call Ezra the Son of God. Aphraates continues, that God bestows this title on whom He pleases, which is hardly to be interpreted as incarnation. With regard to the appeal to the testimony of the prophets, it may here be remarked that in addition to those passages which are clearly of a Messianic character, the strangest passages are advanced in support of the person of Christ. If we are disposed to smile at the way 'Alī Ṭabarī deals with the Old Testament in search of prophecies for Muhammad, it is well for us to see to what strange allegorizing the early Christian apologists resorted. Thus the seals of the lion's den are a type of the

[1] Mingana: *op. cit.* 20.
[2] *Ibid.*, 29–31.
[3] *Ibid.*, 53.
[4] *Ibid.*, 83 ff.

Virginity of Mary.[1] In Psa. cx. 2 the "rod" is the cross. From Hab. iii. 3 we find the exposition that "Paran", the dark-shaded mountain of the LXX, means that Christ was hid within the Virgin. Jesus on the cross is seen in Deut. xxviii. 66 ff. In Isa. xxix. 11 the sealed book is the Virgin.[2]

(*b*) *The Holy Trinity.* The Caliph Al Mahdī accuses Timothy of tri-theism and the Patriarch says that while he believes in Father, Son and Holy Spirit, he still believes in one God.[3] He illustrates this by saying that the Caliph and his word and his spirit are not distinguishable and neither are the light and heat and the sun three suns but one sun. The Caliph wants to know whether the Word and the Spirit are separable from God, and the reply, which we find also in Epiphanius, is that if this were so then God would cease to be rational and living. As source and fount of wisdom God imparts wisdom by His Word, and as the source of life to all living beings He imparts life by means of His Word and Spirit. The Caliph wants to know where in the Scripture it is said that the Word and Spirit are eternally with God, and the following passages are given: Psa. xxxiii. 6; Psa. lvi. 10; Psa. civ. 5; Psa. cxix. 89; Isa. xl. 8; John i. 1 and 4; John xvii. 5 and Matt. xxviii. 19. Later on in the debate[4] the Patriarch strongly insists that he believes in the Unity of God "I do not believe in three different Godheads". The question is taken up as to the distinction between the persons of the Trinity.[5] The difference between the Son and the Spirit is that the former is "begotten" and the latter "proceeds". The first person is "unbegotten", but otherwise there is no difference in the relations of the three. God is not corporeal and not composite and so it is unfitting to speak of Him having members or being susceptible to dissection. Reason comes out of the soul without cleavage and without organs. "Why", asks the Caliph, "did not all three become incarnate if they are not separable one from another? If Father and Spirit did not put on a human body with the Son how can they be inseparable by distance and space?" This inquiry is prompted by the statement of Timothy that just as the whole of the taste and the whole of the scent is from the whole of the apple, and yet scent is not taste nor taste scent, so, too, the persons of the Trinity being uncircumscribed are not separate one from another and not mixed and confused with one another but "separated in their persons in a united way and united in their nature in a separate way". The Patriarch's answer to the question of the Caliph is that the word of the Caliph clothes itself with the papyrus on which it is written while his soul and mind cannot be said to do so. The Word-God clothed

[1] *Studia Sinaitica*, vii–viii, *loc. cit.*
[2] Gregentius: *op. cit.*
[3] Mingana: *op. cit.*, 22 ff.
[4] Mingana: *op. cit.*, p. 62.
[5] *Ibid.*, 25 ff.

Himself with a body from among us without having been separated one whit from the Father or the Spirit.

On the second day of the debate Timothy launches out into a mathematical argument which is weird and wonderful.[1] " One is the cause of three . . . because this number one is the cause of number two and the number two of the number three. This is how one is the cause of three as I said. . . . On the other hand the number three is caused by the number two and this number two by the number one, the number three is therefore the cause of the number one." The Caliph observes that in this case the number four would be the cause of the number five and so on, and then the question of one Godhead would resolve itself into many. To this Timothy replies that there is always a time to stop (though why it should be so conveniently three he does not explain in a way which was likely to convince his opponent); number three is perfect and complete, all other numbers being simply added to one another by means of that complete and perfect number, " as it is said ". This is certainly poles apart from the Christian conception of the Trinity, but it did not seem to strike the learned Patriarch in that way. To do him justice it should be said that he seems to sense that this mathematical reasoning is somewhat out of place. When the Caliph says that neither " three " nor " two " can be predicated of God, he retorts that neither then can " one " be said of Him, and it may be that he was leading up to this by the nonsense—for so it seems to us—in his previous remarks. " There being no number in God, we should not have applied it to Him. As, however, we do apply this number, i.e., one, to God without any reference to the beginning of an arithmetical number, we apply to Him also the number three without any implication of multiplication or division of gods, but with a particular reference to the Word and the Spirit of God." The Caliph insists that the number one is applied to God in Scripture, and Timothy says that so also a number implying plurality, e.g., the plural in Gen. i. 26, the triple Holy in Isa. vi. 3, " The Lord God and His Spirit " in Isa. xlviii. 16 and also Psa. xxx. 6. In the Qur'ān he points to the use of the plural in Suras xix. 17 and xxi. 91. The Caliph replies that these are plurals of majesty or God is addressing the angels. Timothy asks what honour could accrue to God from such a device ? and says it would be dishonourable for it to refer to angels, for they are created and could not be thus associated with the Creator. Timothy then goes on to make the astounding statement that the triple letters which stand at the head of some of the Suras of the Qur'ān are mystical symbols of the Trinity. The Caliph asks if this were so then why should not the Prophet have affirmed it plainly ? Timothy says that the reason was that because the Arabs were polytheists they would be likely to mistake this for polytheism,

[1] Mingana : *op. cit.*, 63 ff.

and it was for this same reason that Muhammad preached so strongly the unity of God.

Timothy later[1] advances what may be called philosophical proof for the Trinity. If God is a perceiver and knower from all eternity He must have an object for this perception and knowledge. But in eternity there was no created being with God, so, if there were no being at all with Him whom He might perceive and know, how could He be called a perceiver and knower in a divine and eternal sense ? The Caliph answers, very fittingly, that God perceived and knew Himself. Timothy then goes on to say that if God is all a perceiver, uncircumscribed so that He does not perceive and know with one part and be perceived and known with another part then how can He perceive Himself ? The meaning seems to be that if there is no differentiation within the Godhead then how could this be possible. Asked for further explanation, the Patriarch says that God was perceiving and knowing His Word and His Spirit from everlasting, and perceived and knew His creatures as not existing then but going to exist in the future. These are not parts set at a distance one from another so that one perceives and the other is perceived, because the Father is in the Son and the Son in the Spirit without any break or interval or confusion, just as the soul is in the reason and the reason in the mind without any break or confusion. The Caliph then says that since God perceived the creatures before they came to exist an eternal perceiver does not involve the eternity of the object perceived. To this quite sound argument the Patriarch says that an infinite perceiver requires an infinite object of perception ; so as well as the creature, He perceived the Spirit and the Word who are eternal. Al Mahdi is not convinced, and says that this only proves that the Word and the Spirit are creatures, to which Timothy retorts that if this is so, by what instruments did God create the heavens and the earth ? having either forgotten that he said previously that God needed no instruments, or perhaps to show that if there were need of instruments to create and these instruments were themselves created then other instruments would be needed to create those instruments and so on *ad infinitum.*

This is a very fair example of the manner in which the question of the Trinity was approached by these apologists. When we may safely assume that being a Nestorian the Patriarch has entered into the heritage of the School of Antioch, where exegetical and historical study was emphasized, and that he can yet present the Trinity in the manner we have seen, what could be expected from another school which did not concern itself so deeply with sound exegesis ? The Trinity is debated like a metaphysical puzzle and not in its divine significance for our salvation.

This may be seen also in the illustrations given : the sphere of the

[1] Mingana : *op. cit.,* 73 ff.

sun and its rays and heat; the eye with its pupil and the light in the eye; soul, body and spirit (note the order); root, branches and fruit; mouth, tongue and word.[1] These are the triads which are supposed to illuminate the understanding when we consider the problem of the Blessed and Holy Trinity.

(c) *God, His Being and Attributes.* It is natural that in such debates as we have described the matters dealt with concerning the Godhead should be in definite relation to the questions of the Incarnation or the Trinity. Alongside rather crude suggestions we find a repudiation of anthropomorphism to which both sides pay lip service but which fails to check them in certain unworthy ideas about God. Thus the Caliph Mahdi protests to Timothy, "You will not go very far with God in your bodily comparisons and similes",[2] which is rather unfair because he has just made the suggestion himself that Christians believe in a "hollow" God. The Patriarch boldly replies that he makes use of bodily metaphors because he is a bodily man. Earlier[3] in the debate the Caliph had said that it is never allowable to draw a demonstration from creatures for the Creator. The remark is prompted by the subject under discussion and the question of what Fatherhood, Filiation and Procession mean when applied to God. Timothy affirms that these are not applied to God in the same way as they are applied to humanity, but in a "divine way which the mind cannot comprehend", but on the other hand he says plainly that if it were not permissible to draw a proof of God from creatures then we should be in complete ignorance of God because what we say of God is deducted from natural things. The Caliph cannot see this and asserts with some justice that kingship, life, power, greatness, honour, wisdom, sight, knowledge and justice belong really and naturally and eternally to God and only belong to creatures in an "unnatural", imperfect and temporal manner. On this both the debators are agreed, and Timothy himself deprecates the lowering of God to a comparison with creatures, for "He has no comparison with created beings at all". Soon we shall see the debates which took place on *tashbīh* and *ta'ṭīl* in the Muslim theological schools. Meanwhile in answer to the implied question how man is to have any knowledge of God, it is interesting to note what another apologist says: "We ought to know that we understand nothing about the power of God nor His Majesty by speech, by figures, nor by word, but by faith and piety and the fear of God and purity of spirit."[4] When we come to sum up the theological results of the whole period we shall have an opportunity of observing what the Damascene has to say on this important subject. It will suffice to say here that neither Christian

[1] *Studia Sinaitica*, vii–viii, *loc. cit.*
[2] Mingana: *op. cit.*, 79.
[3] *Ibid.*, p. 70.
[4] *Studia Sinaitica*, vii–viii., *loc. cit.*

nor Muslim has a monopoly of ideas on this subject either way. Different schools of thought are to be found in both religions.

(*d*) *The Death and Crucifixion of Jesus Christ.* "Can God die?" was a question asked of Christians by both Muslims and Jews. And, of course, no Christian held that it was possible for God to die. But on the other hand there were those who seemed to assert with the divinity of Christ that God could die.[1] The Caliph Mahdī drew the attention of Timothy to this. We have already mentioned in another place how Justinian was responsible for the formula: "God was crucified for us". The Nestorian Patriarch repudiates such a notion on behalf of his own church, but says that the Jacobites and Malkites (the orthodox Byzantines) hold that God died in the flesh. This is no doubt an error on his part. Before this statement, however, he has taken something off the edge of this remark by saying: "If Christ has been called by the prophets God and Lord and if it has been said by some people that God suffered and died in the flesh, it is clear that it is the human nature of the Word-God which he took from us which suffered and died, because in no book in the prophets or the Gospel do we find that God Himself died in the flesh, though we do find that the Son and Jesus Christ died in the flesh. The expression that 'God suffered in the flesh' is not correct."

The Muslim quotes the denial of the crucifixion to be found in the Qur'ān (Sura iv. 156) and almost invariably the Christian replies with Suras xix. 34 and iii. 48. This is true even to the present day, and it cannot be said that these two sets of texts from the Qur'ān have been satisfactorily explained. In any case to appeal to the Qur'ān against the Qur'ān is a most unsatisfactory proceeding. In answer to a question about the prophecies concerning the crucifixion of Christ, Timothy (and most others) quote Psa. xxii. 16–18; Isa. liii. 5; Lam. iii. 4 and 30, etc.; Daniel ix. 26; Zech. xiii. 7 and Jer. xi. 19. When Al Mahdi presses the text that God made a similitude and it is to this to which the Scripture refers, Timothy asks whether God was a deceiver, and if this was the case then the disciples of Christ were not to be blamed if they reported what God intended them to see. If Satan was the deceiver, who gave him the power over the disciples? The Caliph urges that it was dishonourable for Christ to die by crucifixion but Timothy reminds him that other prophets had been slain as the Qur'ān itself says.[2]

At this point the question is raised as to whether Christ was slain willingly or not. This seems to have been a point at issue for a long time. It may be that in the earlier arguments with the Jews they had said that if Christ died a voluntary death then they were not to blame.

[1] Mingana: *Apology of Timothy*, pp. 86 f. See also Clement of Alex.: *Protrept.* x, 106, 4 and *Acts of Philip*, 74.

[2] Mingana: *Apology of Timothy*, pp. 40 ff.

Mahdi makes the same point. Theodore of Mopsuestia has a question and answer on the subject in his *Synopsis of Christian Faith*: "Did our Lord die willingly or forcibly? If He died willingly, He agreed with His murderers, who in this case would not deserve the pain of death, but are all the more to be rewarded because they have accomplished His will." The answer is: "He did not die forcibly, and He was not weaker than His murderers, who murdered Him because they hated Him and His sender. He died by God's tacit permission, which preserves the freewill of man. If He had saved Himself from the Cross He would have coerced His freewill and required that it should not accomplish His desire. He did not coerce His freewill, but He tacitly permitted the act of His crucifixion, and, though able to save Himself from the Cross, He did not do so in order to safeguard His freewill and act spontaneously."[1] Timothy follows this argument closely in his reply to Al Mahdī. Theodore Abū Qurra also says practically the same and we find similar arguments as to whether Christ could save Himself, in the debate of Gregentius and Herban. It will be noted that the debate about the crucifixion is concerned with a metaphysical problem and is related to ideas about the Divine Being and attributes and not to any question of atonement or soteriology.

(*e*) *Scripture.* In the *Apology of Timothy* after a question as to why Christians do not observe the rite of circumcision (also reminiscent of the earlier apologists to the Jews), the Caliph Mahdī says that if Christ abolished the Law He was the enemy of the Law.[2] Timothy says that the light of the stars is abolished by the light of the sun, but the sun is not therefore its enemy. It should be noted that here again a subject raised by the apologists to the Jews is taken up with the Muslim. The Caliph asks Timothy whether he believes that the Qur'ān is from God, and Timothy says it is not for him to say, but that the former scriptures were confirmed by miracles. When God wished to abrogate the Mosaic law he confirmed this by miracles, and since this is so similarly He should have confirmed the abrogation of the Gospel by miracles also. This is a very interesting statement indeed, for apparently Timothy has no knowledge of any miracles performed by Muhammad, and the Caliph does not enlighten him on the subject. If the Caliph knew of any miracles reported of Muhammad would he have let this pass? Another point is the use of the idea of abrogation in relation to the Scriptures of a former dispensation. The Muslim doctrine of abrogation is of the Qur'ān by the Qur'ān. Were the Christians the first to talk of the abrogation of the Old Testament by the New and were they followed by the Muslims claiming that the Qur'ān abrogated the Gospel?

The next subject for discussion is whether the Scriptures have been

[1] See Mingana's edition.
[2] *Apology of Timothy*, pp. 27 ff.

corrupted or whether the Scriptures in the hands of the Christians are the genuine Gospel. The Muslim assumption is that this Gospel is a book given to Jesus. Thus Al Mahdī asks the questions: "Who gave you the Gospel and was it given before the Ascension?" The point of this is clear. If it was given before the Ascension and it can be proved that the Scriptures in the hands of the Christians were written after the Ascension then the books in the hands of the Christians cannot be the genuine Gospel. To this question Timothy, knowing what the implication is, replies very well. He says that the Gospel was given before the Ascension, "as the Gospel is the narrative of the Economy of the works and words of Jesus Christ and as the works of Christ were done and His concrete words delivered to us before His Ascension", and further if the Gospel is the preaching of the Kingdom of Heaven it certainly came before the Ascension. But the Caliph is not prepared to let it go at that and asks whether the Gospel was not written in parts by Matthew, Mark, Luke and John? to which the reply is that they wrote and transmitted what they heard and saw and learned from Christ and what the Spirit had brought to their minds. When the Caliph again suggests that the "*Furqān*" has abrogated the "*Injīl*" as the Gospel abrogated Moses, the Patriarch says that changes of the law of Moses had been predicted in Jer. xxxi. 32–34 and Joel ii. 28–30.[1]

More particularly with regard to the corruption of the Scripture. Al Mahdī says that there were many prophecies of Muhammad in the Scriptures, but the books have been corrupted.[2] Timothy replies that if this is the case then where is the uncorrupted copy whereby it may be known that the books in the hands of the Christians have been corrupted? What had the Christian to gain from such a proceeding? From the Gospel all the doctrines of the faith were taken; how could they suffer it to be corrupted? Though there were prophecies of Christ in the Jewish Scriptures, the Jews had not attempted to change their wording. Even if Christians had been able to corrupt the books which they had in their hands how could they do this with books held by the Jews with whom they were in conflict. Finally, if the Christians had changed the books in any way they would have altered those things which, according to some people, were undignified in the Christian faith and so an embarrassment, e.g., Christ's growth in wisdom, His eating and drinking, His fatigue, His anger and lack of omniscience, His prayers, His passion and crucifixion and burial. While in general there is a good deal to say for Timothy's argument, when we look at the things which he says were considered to be undignified and unworthy we cannot help but express our utter amazement! Surely Timothy could not mean that he had any sympathy with such a view. If he did he implies a greater condemnation for the Christianity

[1] *Apology of Timothy*, pp. 47 ff.
[2] *Ibid.*, pp. 35 and 55 ff.

of his day. The Cross was indeed to be a stumbling block to the Jew and foolishness to the Greek, but that it should be considered an embarrassment to the Christian is not understandable at all. The Cross is the glory of Christ, and Timothy elsewhere says as much. It is true that he ascribes these ideas to others, but it almost seems as if he thought that it would have been much better if the object of his advocacy had been someone who did not eat and drink and had not suffered fatigue and death. It does seem as if these early writers and theologians found the true humanity of Christ an embarrassment to them. It is not that he is not prepared to defend the Cross. He worships the Cross because it is the cause of life,[1] and it is only fitting that the medium by which God showed His love to all should be the medium through which all show their love to God, but there seems to be an embarrassment about the Person on the Cross.

(*f*) *Muhammad.* Little can be added to what has already been indicated in the preceding pages on the person of Muhammad in the pages of the apologists. Prophecies of his advent are sought in the former Scriptures and the suggestion is made that just as the Jews rejected Christ so the Christians have rejected Muhammad. The usual reply is to quote copiously from the Old Testament, prophecies of Christ similar to those found in Cyprian, and to state that there is no prophecy of Muhammad at all to be found either there or in the New Testament. From the Muslim side are usually advanced Deut. xviii. 18 and the question of the Jews to Jesus "Art Thou that Prophet?" The question of the Paraclete is always raised. To this question the Patriarch Timothy replies that if Muhammad were the Paraclete he would be the Spirit of God and incorporeal and invisible. The Paraclete searches the deep things of God, but Muhammad confesses ignorance (Sura vi. 50). The Paraclete wrought miracles through the disciples but Muhammad not a single miracle through his. Since David said that by the Spirit of God all the powers were created this would mean that Muhammad would have to be a Creator.[2] Some attack the character of Muhammad and some, like Timothy, are conciliatory.

(*g*) *Signs and Miracles to procure Faith.* Generally speaking, too much stress is placed on miracles as proof of the truth of religion and the mission of the prophets. True, sometimes the good works and piety of Christians are advanced as a proof, but even here there is a tendency to supplement this by appeal to mysterious powers. Sometimes it is suggested that miracles are needed to "overpower" men's opposition. The very word which is used for miracles in the Arabic (*mu'jiza*) means something which renders impotent.[3] In the *Dispute* of Gre-

[1] *Apology of Timothy*, 39.
[2] *Ibid.*, 32 ff. 50, 55.
[3] Cf. Ḥunayn b. Isḥāq in Cheikho: *Vingt Traités*, p. 144; also *Risála* of Al Kindī quoted by Browne: *op. cit.*, p. 85 and for Theodore Abū Qurra, Sbath: *Vingt Traités*, p. 81.

gentius and Herban we find that the whole controversy ends with the conversion of Herban after a miraculous appearance of our Lord in answer to the prayers of the Archbishop. The Jews were blinded by the vision, but their sight was restored by baptism. Timothy does indeed close his conversation with the Caliph with a description of the pearl of great price which shines of itself and is known by its lustre when it is found, but unfortunately too little is made of the self-authenticating truth. The appeal to piety is often accompanied by claims to powers acquired by asceticism which make strange reading. Apparently the more violence a man could do to his nature the more pious he was esteemed.

Part of the appeal to signs is seen in the climax that success is the hallmark of truth. In the earlier days the Christians pointed to the forlorn state of the Jews as the sign that God had forsaken them. Thus we find Aphraates [1] asking: "Do you think that God is with you though you are dispersed among the nations?" The Jew in this case is ready with his reply, quoting Lev. xxvi. 44: "And yet for all that, when they be in the land of their enemies, I will not reject them, neither will I abhor them, to destroy them utterly, and to break my covenant with them: for I am the Lord their God." Chrysostom [2] makes the same appeal to the evidence of success. "The very tomb of His slain body, small and constricted as it is, is more reverenced than the palaces of Kings." The Gospel has been preached even in the British Isles. Understandable as this is for poor frail human beings who look on outward things, is it not somewhat presumptuous for the followers of the "despised and rejected of men"?

How might the Muslim retort now as he well could do that since the conquests of the armies of Islam had laid low a mighty empire, God's blessing was upon Islam, and the truth of Islam was proved. Even the Nestorian Patriarch anticipates this.

[1] *Patrol. Syr.*, Vol. i, *Homily* xvii.

[2] See in his proof that Christ is God to Jews and Greeks in *Patrologia Graeca*, xlviii, 813 ff.

SECTION TWO

THE INTRODUCTION OF PHILOSOPHY INTO ISLAM

A. THE TRANSLATORS AND THEIR WORK

We have shown in an earlier section that the Christian Church in the East had developed philosophical schools and that theology had been treated in the philosophical manner. We have now to answer the question as to how Islam became acquainted with the philosophical sources, with Plato, Aristotle and the Neoplatonists, which, having served their purpose in philosophizing Christian theology, were to be set to the same task in Islam. Who were the early teachers of Islam in this particular province? It is here that we shall see the beginnings of those philosophical schools which, famous as the "Arabian Philosophy", were destined at the period of their highest development, to achieve something which would lend Islam an unique influence in the Middle Ages and refashion the Aristotelian Scholastic of Europe.

It is remarkable how in Islam's earlier formative period, that religion took gifts which the Christian Church offered, and later at her zenith returned to Christian scholars of the Middle Ages what she owed. The return was made with an accumulated interest of doubtful value to Christianity as such but as a stimulus to thought in the renaissance doubtless an enrichment.

Let it be understood that the philosophy with which we are primarily concerned here is the Hellenistic. That there were other influences at work is quite certain, but a great deal of research must be undertaken if these are to be properly analysed and adequately presented. For the most part that research remains to be done. It includes inquiry into the Persian, Zoroastrian, Mazdian, and Indo-Buddhist philosophies, and it can hardly be undertaken here.

The first centre of philosophical culture which we should notice is Harrān in Mesopotamia. Mas'ūdī [1] connects Greek philosophy with Harrān, and in mentioning this speaks of Platonist, Pythagorean and Aristotelian doctrines. We have in this area the evidences of a pre-Islamic culture that resulted in an eclectic system which, on the one hand, displays elements akin to Eastern solar cults and the Light myth, illuminism and Persian dualism and an emanational scheme of First Cause, Intellect, Soul, Matter and the World, all of which gradations are thought of as interacting [2] and, on the other hand, a paganism which recalls the reaction against Christianity in Egypt. Orpheus, Hermes, Apollonius of Tyana (Bulīnus) with Agathodaemon and

[1] *Prairies d'Or*, iv, 64–66.
[2] See traces of this in Miskawaih, *infra*.

Pythagoras were their prophets. These wrought miracles and taught men the mysteries. The many-sided Hermetic literature has its reflection in Harrān. Added to all this is Neoplatonism, which it is not always easy to differentiate in that setting from older—perhaps Indian—emanation systems. The synthesis, if it can be dignified by such a term, is already complete before it comes to us. An identification which the Harranians made between Hermes and Seth, and Agathodaemon and Enoch hints at some sort of Gnosticism.[1] Some of the later pantheistic notions of Islam may have had their origin in this school. But the occult and mystical were not the only interests of the Harranians. We find notable Aristotelians among them. The *Fihrist* mentions one Abū Rūh, the Sabian, as a translator of the *Physics*, and Ṭhābit b. Qurra summarized the *Hermeneutics* and commented on part of the *Physics* with the commentary of Porphyry.

Nor was the Sabian left untouched by Christianity. Not far away were Edessa and Rasain. From the former city we read of Jacob of Edessa, and it is there we find the Syrian compilations of the pseudepigrapha of Pythagoras, Socrates, Plutarch and Dionysius. If ever the Greek literature apart from the philosophy had a chance to make some impact upon the East, it might have done so from that city. Theophilus of Edessa (d. 785) translated the *Iliad* and the *Odyssey* of Homer into Syriac. Theophilus was the court astronomer of the Caliph Mahdī (775–785) and he translated the *Sophistica* of Aristotle into Syriac. Jacob was born just within the Muslim era and studied in Alexandria and other centres. His *Enchiridion* was a treatise on philosophical terms and some people credit him with the invention of the vowel system in Syriac.[2]

Another centre whence the Greek learning spread into the Middle East was Persia. There we find both Neoplatonist and Nestorian exiles. Erdmann[3] has said: "When Justinian, in the year 529, closed the schools of philosophy through anxiety for the Christian doctrine, he did not realize that if he had let them continue, the anti-Christian philosophy would not have been in the least dangerous, because it would have perished of itself, but being compelled to emigrate toward the Orient, it would, centuries afterwards, exercise an influence upon Christian thought more powerful than he had ever feared." While this puts rather too much emphasis on one particular episode in the infiltration of the Hellenistic philosophy into the Middle East, there can be no doubt that the exile of the Neoplatonist philosophers to which he refers and their taking refuge with Anushirwān <u>Kh</u>usrū (*c.* A.D. 530) was an event fraught with important consequences for the development of thought in Persia. There were translations of

[1] See Shahrastānī: *Al Milal wa'n Nihal* (Cureton), pp. 203 ff.
[2] For fuller details, see Wright: *Short History of Syriac Lit.*, p. 149.
[3] *History of Philosophy*, Vol. i, p. 253.

Greek philosophical works into Pahlawi before the Muslim era. And while Persia is ordinarily associated with the dualism of Zoroastrianism it should be remembered that there were monistic schools of thought there influenced by Indian and Buddhistic thought. Such schools would find something congenial in the Neoplatonist emphasis on the transcendent One and something to fortify them in their monistic leanings. However little or much the exile of Simplicius, Damascius, and their companions may have accomplished directly, some of the attractiveness of Neoplatonism for the great mystical poets of Persia may be due to an early familiarization of the Persians with Neoplatonist doctrine. Add to this the reinforcement of such influences from the Christians of the Nestorian Church and the subsequent Persian influence in the Muslim empire at Baghdad, and we may find that a great deal of the favour extended to Greek thought in the 'Abbasid Caliphate was fostered by Persians.

Of the names we have mentioned, by far the most important for us is Simplicius, whose commentaries we find mentioned again and again in the translations and the source literature for " Arabian " philosophy. In Simplicius we have an example of the synthesis of Aristotelianism and Neoplatonism. He belongs to the school of Porphyry. We find that he wrote commentaries on Aristotle's *De Coelo, De Anima*, the *Physics*, the *Categories*, etc.

Let it not be supposed for a moment that these last remnants of the Academy were the sole agents in bringing the philosophy of Greece to Islam. Their name is legion. High and low took part in it. The Muslim could learn the Greek knowledge from his fellow-citizens. Mansūr (750–775) made a direct appeal to the Byzantine Emperor to send him mathematical works. From the beginning of his reign Christians were the chief medium for the transmission of Greek learning and science. Until the tenth century they remained in the ascendancy as scribes, doctors and translators.[1] From that period they begin to decline, having lost touch with the source of their inspiration. The general level of culture of the Christians up to that time was high, though they did not produce any man of outstanding and original genius such as Al Fārābī, Ibn Sīnā and Al Bīrūnī.

Before the advent of Islam we have in Persia the Nestorian Schools and therefore the Aristotelianism which the school of Antioch favoured. Of the great scholars of that period may be mentioned Paulus Persa, who is also called Paul of Nisibis (530–580 ?). He is credited with a Logic which he dedicated to Khusrū. He is for many reasons a most important personage. He stands in the line of direct influence upon Junilius Africanus and Cassiodorus. The debt of the former to Paul

[1] In the time of Ibn Miskawaih we have evidence that there was a great colony of *Greeks* in Baghdād. They appealed to the Syrian Patriarch to appoint a metropolitan for them. See Browne : *Eclipse of Christianity in Asia*, p. 57.

is obvious from his *Institutia Regularia* which is the precursor of *De Institutione divinarum Literarum* written by Cassiodorus. Here we have examples of the principles of exegesis which Paul taught. In him we find those problems discussed which afterwards agitated the schools of Islam, e.g., whether there was creation *ex nihilo* or an eternal primary matter. We should also note his theories in opposition to dualism and his discussion of the formula "God possesses contrary qualities" devised in the interests of a severe monism. To save dualism and the opposition of two principles, one of evil and one of good, one of light and the other of darkness, there were those who would predicate both light and darkness of the One Principle, sacrificing a unity of internal harmony for an external and arithmetical unity.[1] It should be noted that Paul of Persia wrote in Syriac, but most of these Syrians seem to have been bilingual.

We now come to those Christian translators who were the direct means of bringing the works of the Greek philosophical writers to the Muslims. These are quite well known by Muslim writers. Some of them, though Christians, have been claimed as Muslim philosophers. Thus Shahrastānī says that among the Muslim philosophers are Ḥunayn b. Isḥāq, Yaḥyā b. 'Adī, etc.[2] The *Fihrist* of Nadīm[3] is constantly referring to these writers who sometimes were mere scribes, but sometimes collectors of manuscripts, translators and commentators. Some of them must have been men of great intellectual ability though not, perhaps, original thinkers. They probably added little to the tradition which they received. They seem to have exercised care in their work, and even when it was merely of a scribal character they took the trouble to record the state of the manuscript they used and, when opportunity offered, corrected these manuscripts by the use of better ones which came to hand.[4] Nadīm is writing in A.D. 987, and in addition to him we have evidence from Mas'ūdī (d. 956) and Bīrūnī (late tenth century), and from bibliographers and writers of biographical sketches like Ibn Khallikān. Ibn Miskawaih will be given, in evidence of the material assimilated, in a short translation, to which notes have been added.

A Jacobite commentator of whom we frequently hear in Muslim circles is Yaḥyā Naḥwī, John the Grammarian also known as Philoponus. There seems to be some uncertainty about his date. Some accounts would make him contemporary with Muhammad and some much later in the time of Mu'taṣim (b. 795). We may dismiss as apocryphal the story that he tried to preserve the library at Alexandria from the Muslim invaders. Indeed we may take it for granted that he

[1] Cf. Land: *Anecdota Syriaca*, iv (Leyden, 1870).
[2] *Kitāb ul Milal wa'n Nihal*, ii. 348.
[3] The main account is to be found in pp. 331–370 of my copy published in Cairo (n.d.).
[4] *Fihrist*, p. 352.

was not then alive, but lived in the sixth century. It is possible that he was a disciple of Ammonius the Neoplatonist. The *Fihrist*[1] refers to his works in refutation of Proclus,[2] Aristotle and Galen. Whatever he wrote in refutation of Aristotle did not prevent him from writing commentaries on the *Categories*, the *Prior Analytics*, the *Posterior Analytics* and the *Physics*. His book against Proclus was on the subject of the eternity of the world and it was translated into Arabic.[3]

A famous family of translators was that of Ḥunayn b. Isḥāq (809–73). He was a physician in the court of the Caliphs Mutawakkil and Wāthiq bi'llāh. He travelled in the Byzantine empire and there studied Greek, and he brought back with him many manuscripts. He was most prolific in his translation work, which included Euclid[4] as well as the Philosophers. His interest in medical matters and in meteorology is referred to by Mas'ūdī.[5] His translations include the *Laws* of Plato,[6] the *Republic* and the *Timaeus*. His translations of Aristotle are the *Categories, Generation and Corruption*, the whole of *De Anima*, parts of the *Prior and Posterior Analytics*, and the *Hermeneutics*. With his translation of the *Categories* he included the commentary of Porphyry. He amended Ibn Biṭrīq's translation of *De Coelo et Mundi* and epitomized the *Hermeneutics*. Most of his translations seem to have been into Syriac and it is even said that he translated the *Prior Analytics* into Syriac from an Arabic version by Theodore, but this may be a mistake. He and his son Isḥāq and his nephew seem to have formed a school of translators in Baghdad, and we often find it recorded that Ḥunayn did a certain translation into Syriac and that Isḥāq[7] translated it into Arabic. The Translations attributed to the latter are Aristotle's *Rhetoric, De Anima*,[8] the *Ethics* (with Porphyry's commentary), the whole of the *Post Analytics* into Syriac, Mattā b. Yūnus turning it into Arabic, the *Hermeneutics* into Arabic from the Syriac of his father, the *Topica* into Syriac, whence it was done into Arabic by Yaḥyā b. 'Adī, and the commentaries of Themistius and Alexander of Aphrodisias on the same. He is also credited with a translation of Plato's *Sophist* with the commentary of Olympiodorus. Aristotle's *Metaphysica, De Anima, Generation and Corruption* and *Hermeneutics* he translated with Alexander's commentaries.

Mattā b. Yūnus,[9] sometimes called Abū Bishr Mattā b. Yūnus al Qannai was a translator and commentator. Among his translations

[1] P. 356.
[2] See Al Bīrūnī's *India* (Sachau's trans.), i. 36, etc.
[3] Steinschneider: *Die Arabischen Uebersetzungen aus dem Griechischen*, p. 93.
[4] Ibn Khallikān: (De Slane) i. 478.
[5] *Prairies d'Or*, iv. 180 ff.
[6] *Fihrist*, 343.
[7] See *Fihrist*, 344, 352, etc. Isḥāq died 910 A.D. See also Ibn Khallikān: (De Slane) i. 187.
[8] See Mas'ūdī: *Prairies d'Or*, iv. 61.
[9] *Fihrist* and Brockelmann, i. 207. He died 940.

were the *Sophistics* of Aristotle into Syriac, the *Poetics* from Syriac into Arabic, several parts of *De Coelo et Mundi* and the commentary of Alexander on *De Generatione et Corruptione*. He commented on the *Categories*, parts of the *Prior Analytics*, the *Post Analytics*, and the first part of the *Topics*, and wrote a super-commentary on the commentary of Themistius on the *Poetics*.

Abū Zakariyā Yaḥyā b. ʿAdī al Manṭiqī (d. 974),[1] is credited with a translation of Plato's *Laws* [2] and Aristotle's *Poetics* which "is said to contain Themistius also". He translated Ḥunayn's Syriac translation of the *Physics* into Arabic. He also turned the *Sophistics* in the Syriac version of Theophilus into Arabic, and corrected a translation of the *Timaeus*. He seems to have done a good deal of emendation, the *Phaedrus*, the *Physics* of Abū Rūḥ, the Sabian, Mattā's translation of Alexander's commentary on *Generation and Corruption* and the commentary of Themistius on *De Coelo et Mundi* all passing through his hands. He also did some work with Alexander's commentary on the *Topics*.

Yaḥyā b. Biṭrīq [3] (f. ninth century) is said to have translated the *Timaeus*, and Aristotle's *Meteorology* and an abridgement of the *De Anima*. He was also responsible for a version of the *Book of Animals* and *De Coelo et Mundi* which Ḥunayn amended. Qusṭā b. Lūqā is attributed with a translation of a book by Plato on the principles of geometry. He turned the Syriac of Ḥunayn's translation of the *Physics* into Arabic. Beside these Nadīm says that he translated commentaries of Alexander Aphrodisias on the *Physics* and *Generation and Corruption* and Yaḥyā Naḥwī on the former work. ʿAbd ul Masīḥ b. ʿAbdullāh Nāʿima al Ḥimṣī is mostly famous for a translation of the so-called *Theology of Aristotle* into Syriac and a translation of the *Sophistics*. We read of one Abu'l-Khayr al Ḥasan al Khammār (late tenth century) as the author of a harmony of Christianity and Philosophy. Others whom we may briefly name are Abū ʿAlī ʿIsā b. Isḥāq b. Zurʿa (d. 1008),[4] and several who are merely names, a certain Basīl who is said to have translated the *Physics* with the commentary of Porphyry, Stephen of Alexandria who summarized the *Hermeneutics* and whose work on the *Categories* is also mentioned in the *Fihrist*, one Theodore or Theodorus who, according to the same, translated the *Prior Analytics* into Arabic, and perhaps most surprising of all, a book by Gregory of Nyssa on the *Nature of Man*,[5] is mentioned by Nadīm. In contrast to the very extensive list of Christian translators, we find very few Muslims engaged in this task, but the day was shortly to

[1] *Fihrist*, 369 and Brockelmann, i. 207.
[2] *Fihrist*, 344.
[3] Brockelmann, i. 203.
[4] Brockelmann, i. 208.
[5] *Fihrist*, 357.

come when they would use the material provided for them and, bringing fresh minds to the work, accomplish a new synthesis which became familiar to Christians after an interval of centuries.

It would be as well here to summarize the results in order to form some idea of the material available at this time and which forms the bulk of the source literature for the later philosophy of Islam.

Of Plato[1] we find the following works known and translated at least into Syriac if not into Arabic. *Laches*, *Charmides*, the two called *Alcibiades*, *Euthydemus*, *Gorgias*, *Ion*, *Protagoras*, *Euthyphro*, *Crito*, *Theaetetus*, *Cratylus*, *Sophist*, *Timaeus*,[2] *Parmenides*, *Phaedrus*, *Meno*, *Menexenus*, *Thaion* (?), the two called *Hippias*, *Phaedo*,[3] *Clitopho*, *Republic*, *Laws*,[4] *Apology of Socrates*,[5] *Theages*, *Politicus*; and *Minos*, *Hipparchus*, *Athleticus* (?) and a book on the principles of geometry attributed to Plato. Of commentaries on Plato we have reference to those by Proclus on *Phaedo*, *Gorgias*, part of the *Republic*,[6] and *Timaeus* and that of Olympiodorus (fifth century) on *Sophist*.[7]

For Aristotle[8] the list is also quite comprehensive. We find *Categories*, *Hermeneutics*, *Prior Analytics*, *Apodeictics* (the name for the *Posterior Analytics* in the Muslim writers, following Galen and Alexander of Aphrodisias), *Topics*, *Rhetoric*, *Poetics*, *Physics*,[9] *De Coelo et Mundi*, *De Generatione et Corruptione*, *De Anima*, the *Ethics* and the *Metaphysics*.[10] The commentaries known are: Nicolaus,[11] Simplicius particularly on *Physics*, *De Anima*, *Categories* and *De Coelo et Mundi*, Damascius (perhaps), Themistius[12] (so extensively mentioned that it is futile to particularize), Alexander[13] of Aphrodisias (also most extensively used), Olympiodorus on *De Anima*,[14] Porphyry on *Prior Analytics*, *Categories*, *Ethics* and his *Isagoge*.[15]

The Neoplatonists known include the following: Proclus who, in the *Fihrist*[16] is given his full name Diadochus Proclus and to whom is attributed, beside the commentaries mentioned, books on Pythagoras, his *Elements of Theology*, and a shorter *Elements* which we believe is otherwise unknown. He is also mentioned and quoted in Al Bīrūnī's

[1] Mas'ūdī: *Prairies d'Or*, iii. 134 and 362–3 and *Fihrist*, 344 f.
[2] Mas'ūdī: *op. cit.*, iii. 363. Al Bīrūnī: *India* (Sachau's trans.), i. 35, etc.
[3] Al Bīrūnī: *op. cit.*, i. 65, ii. 166. He quotes it in i. 85–6.
[4] Al Bīrūnī: *op. cit.*, i. 123, 385, etc.
[5] Referred to by Ibn Abī Usaybi'a cf. Al Bīrūnī: *op. cit.*, ii. 171.
[6] Baumstark: *Geschichte der Syr. Lit.*, p. 231.
[7] Quoted by Ibn Sīnā, cf. also *Fihrist*, 344.
[8] Mas'ūdī: *op. cit.*, ii.250 and *Fihrist*, 353, etc.
[9] Al Bīrūnī: *op. cit.*, quotes i. 320.
[10] Mas'ūdī: *op. cit.*, ii. 250.
[11] *Fihrist*, 355.
[12] Mas'ūdī: *op. cit.*, iv. 61, and *Fihrist*, 357, etc., also Al Bīrūnī, *passim*.
[13] Mas'ūdī: *op. cit.*, iv. 61, and *Fihrist*, 353, 357, etc.
[14] *Fihrist*, 352.
[15] Mas'ūdī: *op. cit.*, iii. 68, etc.
[16] P. 353.

India.[1] Porphyry is well known.[2] Simplicius we have already had occasion to mention. Beside these there are Ammonius [3] and Iamblichus and some less important names. Pseudo-Dionysius seems to have been known but not by name so far as we have learned. His disciple and devotee Maximus (580–662) is mentioned.[4] Plotinus is known through the misnamed *Theology of Aristotle* which contains some of the material to be found in the *Enneads.* This book is to-day obtainable in cheap form in the East. Its exordium runs: "The book of Aristotle the Philosopher called in Greek the *Athūlūjīya* (*theologia*). It is the statement on Divinity with the commentary of Porphyry the Syrian and ʻAbd ul Masīḥ b. ʻAbdullāh Nāʼima al Ḥimṣī [5] and Abū Yūsuf Yaʻqūb b. Isḥāq al Kindī amended it for Aḥmad b. al Muʻtaṣim." The *Elements of Theology* was known in an abridgement or rather translation of parts of that book into Arabic. This Arabic compilation became, when translated into Latin, the *Liber de Causis,* which we find quoted so much in the mediæval scholastics. It is rather interesting to see that Al Bīrūnī refers a book of this name to Apollonius of Tyana.[6]

Among other famous Greeks of whom we find some notice in the early bibliographers we may instance Galen and Hippocrates,[7] Plutarch,[8] Pythagoras,[9] and Socrates,[10] and Homer is quoted by Al Bīrūnī.[11] Hermes is known apparently only as an astrologer.[12]

On the whole, we find that Aristotle takes the chief place and that he is acclaimed as the philosopher *par excellence,* but there does not seem to have been any standard of judgment available to the Muslims, alongside the works which were copied and translated for them, whereby they might be able to distinguish Aristotle from Plato or the Neoplatonists. It seems to be assumed that, except in minor points, all taught the same, that is the truth. Their very Aristotle comes to them for the most part at the hands of Neoplatonists, and of his commentators Themistius and Alexander are plainly preferred, but the former seems to have been more in favour than the latter, particularly with Shahrastānī, and Ibn Sīnā before him. Subjects which we find rooted and integral in the later theology have their origins in Aristotle, e.g., the denial of infinite series, or the impossibility of infinite causes

[1] I, 57.
[2] *Fihrist,* 354, 357, etc. Al Bīrūnī: *India* (*ed. cit.*) i. 43. Masʻūdī: *op. cit.* iii. 68, iv. 8.
[3] *Fihrist,* 355 and Al Bīrūnī: *op. cit.,* i. 85.
[4] Reference lost.
[5] In the Arabic of this name there is a *tashdid* written in my copy cf. Emessa.
[6] *Fihrist,* 373; see Al Bīrūnī: *op. cit.,* i. 40.
[7] Al Bīrūnī: *op. cit.,* i. 95, 123, 222, 35 and ii. 168, etc. Masʻūdī: *op. cit.,* iii. 134, etc.
[8] *Fihrist,* 342 and 355.
[9] *Ibid.,* 342.
[10] *Ibid.,* 342.
[11] *Op. cit.,* i. 42, 98 and 231.
[12] *Fihrist,* 373.

and effects, the argument from the First Mover[1] (though some reject this), his definitions in the *Metaphysics*, the division of form and matter, the classification of the possible and the necessary. There is an acquaintance with elements to be found in Aristotle, Plato and the Neoplatonists with regard to the Soul, and all are forced into a strange juxtaposition which hardly becomes a synthesis. Thus we have the division of the soul as rational, concupiscible and irascible, which is Galenist Aristotelianism, joined with ideas contained in the *Phaedo*,[2] and such conceptions as the pre-existence of the soul and transmigration (raised as a question to be refuted). The mystical idea of union with the One[3] reflects Neoplatonism. Al Fārābī uses arguments for the existence of God which have their origin in the *Timaeus*.

In his *Fields of Gold*,[4] Mas'ūdī gives us glimpses of the debates which took place on the nature of the Soul, on the spheres, meteorology, the properties and measurement of figures, disposition and nature, relation and aggregation, the syllogism, composition, physics in general, metaphysics, substance, accident, etc. The discussion still goes on.

It is a dangerous proceeding to try to reconstruct the body of knowledge available to these early Muslims. It is just as easy to underestimate their knowledge as to overestimate it. We have not only the lists of books to go by, but the sudden budding genius of the early Muslim writers on philosophy. No one can doubt the genius of Al Bīrūnī, and there are the less scientific but more purely philosophical Al Kindī, Al Fārābī and Ibn Sīnā. There was a stimulus of an unique order behind their work, and it is not to be accounted for by a mere smattering of knowledge about books but of real and commendable study of them. The pity is that they had not more than they possessed and more to make their critical judgment sounder, but even as it was they were able to accomplish a great deal.

So that the reader may form some sort of independent judgment on the subjects which at this early period were discussed by the philosophizing theologians we here append a translation of the Shorter Theology of Ibn Miskawaih called *Al Fawz ul Asghar*. With this we have given footnotes which are not to be taken as indicating the immediate source so much as parallel ideas to be found in early writers which illustrate the general body of ideas current at this period. Nothing in the nature of dogmatism about the sources is intended. If sometimes we have been betrayed into a categorical statement which appears to conflict with this warning we crave forgiveness. We are here very seldom travelling in the region of absolute certainty.

Ibn Miskawaih died an old man in A.D. 1030. He was said to be a

[1] Al Bīrūnī: *op. cit.*, i. 320.
[2] *Ibid.*, i. 65 f, and Mas'ūdī: *op. cit.*, i. 19.
[3] Al Bīrūnī: *op. cit.*, i. 85.
[4] *Op. cit.*, i. 19–20.

convert from Zoroastrianism to Islam, but if the work of a modern writer[1] contains genuine material for his life and work, it seems possible that he had some association with Harrān, for his works are said to have contained an account of Thales, Hermes Trismegistus and Agathodaemon. In the account given in Yāqūt's *Dictionary of Famous Men*[2] we find him a devotee of Yaḥyā b. 'Adī and in the service of Abu'l Khayr al Ḥasan al Khammār, the Christian, already mentioned as the author of a harmony of Christianity and philosophy. Mention is made of his study of the *Isagoge* and the *Categories*. Not much is known of his life, but his great work *Tajārib ul Umam* (*The Experiences of the Nations*) has been published in facsimile,[3] and *Al Fawz al Asghar* was published in Beirut.

B.

AL FAWZ UL ASGHAR

THE SHORTER THEOLOGY OF IBN MISKAWAIH

PART I. GOD

CAP. I. THE PROOF FOR THE EXISTENCE OF AN ARTIFICER

In one respect this question is very easy and in another it is very hard. On the one hand the quest of this supreme goal transcends our customary ends and purposes, while on the other hand there is nothing so clear and evident, because the essence of the Exalted Truth is most luminous and bright. Thus the proof of the Creator is exceedingly easy in respect of His Essence, but in respect to the impotency and infirmity of human intelligence it is extraordinarily difficult. A philosopher has made this clear by an excellent illustration of the bat which is incapable of seeing the sun. In the same way, man's reason fails to perceive the essence of God.[4]

Wherefore sages and rational philosophers have endured great pains and mortifications to achieve this honourable quest and, becoming inured to the hardships of the task, have gradually progressed to that measure of contemplation of the Creator which is within the compass of the creature. And in truth, there is no other way to the knowledge of God except these mortifications and gradual advances.

[1] Muhammad Bāqir: *Rawdat ul Jannāt*, 70.
[2] Vol. 2, 88.
[3] Gibb Memorial Series No. 7 (Old Series).
[4] Arist: *Metaphysica*, Bk. *a* 993a, 30 ff. It is interesting to note that the opening words and the illustration of the bat almost translate Aristotle. But in Aristotle the subject of inquiry which is in "one way easy and another way hard" is Truth. Here there is a tacit acceptance of the identification of the Creator of the Universe with the Truth.

Many men have thought that the philosophers have selfishly hidden this matter and have not allowed these things to be revealed to the common people. But this is not so. The fact is that the intellects of common people are quite incapable of grasping this subject, as the illustration mentioned above shows. These points should be considered in the pursuit of this lofty goal, so that gradually advancing from the low to the high, the difficulties encountered in traversing the stages of this hard journey may be borne with patience and fortitude, so that haply success may be achieved as we will hereinafter briefly explain, indicating its principles and rules.

The truth is, that the reason our intellects fall short in grasping divine and spiritual things is that man is the ultimate stage of physical existence, and after reaching the human creation elemental compositions come to an end. Thus the manifold veils and material compositions have become a veil to the intellect, that bright substance. These veils of matter prevent the intellect from perceiving intellectual things. For simple elements, when they proceed from their primary state to the intermixture of multiplicity, come as far as the human composition and then stop. Because it is impossible for the composition and dissolution of things actually produced to be infinite or without an end. So then, if in this composition man should desire to perceive the simple elements, it is only by reversing the process and dissolving (or reducing to its simple elements) what has been composed and what has resulted in this final human composite, that one could perhaps arrive at the (other) extreme of the simple elements. For in reference to man, pure elements are at the opposite extreme, and so the perception of them is hard and troublesome for him. A certain philosopher in a book called *Sam'u'l Kiyān* [1] has said most cogently that

[1] *Sam'u'l Kiyān* or *Sam'uṭ Ṭabī'ī* was the title given to Arabic translations of Aristotle's *Physics*. In *Kashf uẓ Ẓunūn*, however, it is said that the book called *Sam'u'l Kiyān* is by Alexander of Aphrodisias (fl. 200 B.C.) and is an abbreviation of Aristotle's *Physics*. There are eight matters discussed in it. On the first Abū Rūḥ Ṣafā'ī has commented and Yaḥyā b. 'Adī (Jacobite Christian d. A.D. 974, cf. *Brockelmann*, i. 207) amended this commentary. The second was translated into Syriac by Ḥunayn b. Isḥāq (d. A.D. 809, cf. *Brockelmann*, i. 205 f.) and Yaḥyā b. 'Adī translated it from the Syriac into Arabic. The fourth was expounded in three articles by Yaḥyā b. 'Adī. The fifth was the subject of a commentary by Qusṭā b. Lūqā (d. A.D. 835, cf. *Brockelmann*, i. 204). The seventh was translated by the latter. Porphyry expounded the first four articles. The commentary of Themistius was translated from Syriac into Arabic by Abū Bishr b. Mattā (d. A.D. 940, cf. *Brock*., i., p. 207). Abū Aḥmad b. Kirmast (?) commented on this. Thābit b. Qurra (d. A.D. 836, cf. *Brock*., i. 217) commented on part of the first article. Abū Ibrāhīm b. aṣ Ṣalt translated the first article. Abu'l Faraj Qudāma b. Ja'far (d. A.D. 922, cf. *Brock*., i. 228) also commented on parts of the first article. Nemistius expounded the whole book, but as it was not clear, Yaḥyā Naḥwī (John the Grammarian) commented on it and this he did from the Greek into the Arabic in a work of ten volumes (cf. *Fihrist*, p. 356, where it is said that John was a Jacobite Christian). Cf. also Finlay's *History of the Byzantine Empire*, Pt. I, Cap. III, Sect. ii; and Cap. IV, Sect. i (Dent, 132 f. and 191 ff.). For further information in regard to Aristotle in Islam, the article by De Boer in the *Encyclopædia of Islam*. Vol. i, 432 ff. *Arisṭūṭālīs* should be consulted.

the parts of human nature at the time of composition were in their lowest stage, and after natural composition came to their final stage. Or, to put it in another way, those parts or elements which were at that time nearest are now farthest away, and if you consider this in relation to the human composite, they become still more remote.

From this explanation it can be estimated, when man has such a difficulty in reaching the perception of things which are nearest to him in the universe of bodies and which are parts of his own composition, how exceedingly difficult it must be for man to understand those divine things and abstract substances, when from that universe of light he is estranged and separated in every way and by the utmost distance!

Bearing in mind all these difficulties, it is essential that when we attempt this supreme quest, namely, to traverse the universe of the abstract, we should first of all strive to attain to a knowledge of physical things (*ṭabʿīyāt*)[1] and then laboriously proceed gradually, and with patience and fortitude to that supreme goal. Otherwise there is no way to achieve our object.

Plato says that the one who desires success in any important purpose must courageously endure the difficulties and hardships which confront him. That great philosopher so said because when man seeks knowledge of the realities of things, he must patiently and perseveringly consider the causes and origins of the universe and bear the difficulties which present themselves in the course of his inquiries and then at last he will reach the primary source before which there is no other; and this is the supreme achievement.

Let it be understood that man may learn the natures or realities of things in two ways. The first is by way of the five senses, i.e., by the animal power (*quwwa ḥaiwānīya*) which is shared by man and animal alike.[2] The second is peculiar to man and is that which gives him superiority over all animals, and this is by means of the intellect. But it is not possible for man to perceive by the intellect alone without the assistance of sense until he exercise prolonged endeavour and hard labour. For we have the external senses from our birth, and our rational soul never comes to a time throughout our whole life when we can dispense with the aid of the senses and the phantasies (*awhām*)[3] in perceiving and understanding. Therefore, when we decide to give our attention to any intellectual matter, because it is customary or a matter of habit with us for our phantasy to present sensible forms, the result is that no intellectual matter comes to our mind in its pure

[1] John of Damascus: *De Fide Orthod.*, Bk. I, Cap. III (*P.G.*, 94, 796) proceeds on the assumption that the Creator is known through the Creation and this is the basis of most Scholastic inquiry (cf. Peter Lombard: *Libr. IV Sententiarum*, Vol. i, Bk. I, Distinct. iii, Cap. I, and Bonaventura: *Commentaria Quatuor Libros Sententiarum Magistri Petri Lombardi, ad loc.*).

[2] Cf. John of Damascus: *De Fide Orthod.*, Bk. II, XII (*P.G.*, 94,925).

[3] Cf. *op. cit.*, Bk. II, Cap. XVII (*P.G.*, 94, 933). *Wahm* is the Aristotelian *phantasma* which is not exactly imagination but rather presentation. Cf. also *Timaeus*, 71.

form without the inclusion of some sensible form. So consider, that when you aim at understanding the intellect, or the rational soul, or any other immaterial things, unless you form an idea of some corporeal form with which you are familiar and draw an analogy from that for the spiritual, there is no other way for you to understand them.[1] This is the case with all those spiritual things which are beyond the universe of bodies and which we cannot perfectly understand in any way. E.g., when we think that beyond all the universe of bodies there is either a vacuum or a plenum,[2] powerful proof and rational argument clearly inform us that there can be neither a vacuum nor a plenum. This cannot be taken in by our mind because in the universe of bodies we have become accustomed to think that everywhere there must be either emptiness or fullness, and this in spite of sound reason proving conclusively that there is neither, and that we have the proofs before us.

The reason is that we are not habituated to perceiving intellectual matters and are most intimately acquainted with things of sense. But in spite of all this, when we engage in such hard endeavour that, contrary to our wont and nature, we succeed in concentrating our attention on intellectual matters and abstractions, and so far as it is possible, give up using the external senses, and think about intellectual things so much that at last we form the habit and become inured to the toil, then the eyes are opened and it is learned how superior intellectual things are to the things of sense.

Moreover, it then begins to dawn upon our minds that in comparison to sensible things intellectual things are as an ornament of solid gold is to gilt. For all sensible things are subject to continual flux and alteration and nothing remains in the same state even for a short time. The reason for this is that no sensibles are devoid of matter, and in matter there is always less or more, intensity and weakness, and susceptibility to alternating movement and rest. So, at the time of perception, we are assured in ourselves that we have grasped the sensible thing in every respect, but then after a short time some change or other takes place and in the real thing there is some divergence from our mental picture of it. Let us fix this subject in the mind by an illustration: The eye sees something in a certain condition. It is certain that that thing will occur at another time in another condition because matter must change. Someone sees Zayd to-day and finds him in a certain stable condition, but because Zayd's natural heat is always acting upon his original moisture, some part is dissolved in the form of vapours, and by food and air there is something being substituted from one moment to another. And this increase and decrease is going on in the body continually. So it needs must be that when

[1] Cf. John of Damascus: *De Fide Orthod.*, Bk. I, Cap. II (*P.G.*, 94, 792).
[2] A favourite matter of discussion. Cf. Arist. *Metaphys.*, 1009 a 25 ff.

Zayd is seen again, he will be different from what was sensibly perceived at first, although the sight may not be able to discern this with exactitude. But the intellect understands quite well that variations in the universe of bodies keep occurring and must so occur.

This is the case with sensibles, but in intelligibles there is never any change and alteration, or movement and rest, but they are eternal and everlasting and remain in one condition. So to those people who, after great toil and endeavour, begin to understand the intelligibles, this world of sensibles comes to be regarded as but an ornament of gilt and the world of spiritual things as the genuine jewel.[1]

On account of these things Plato called this universe the world of sophistry,[2] and sages and philosophers have always considered this world to be the lowest and most inferior, and have never deigned to turn their attention to it, but, considering intellectual things most honourable, have continually occupied themselves in the quest of the same.

It will be plain from what has been said that when we proceed from the understanding of the things of sense to the understanding of the universe of spiritual things, we have to exact excessive toil from our nature, and to bid farewell to all those forms which dwell in our mind the creation of our sense-perception, and which are the cause of error and uncertainty in our perception of the genuinely intellectual; and we have to cut ourselves off from all those phantasies which are obtained through the senses. But this severance of relations is a most difficult task, for how hard it is to dissociate ourselves from something which has always been habitual to us, and to achieve a separation from the notions of ordinary people! This severance is more difficult than the actual knowing, because at such a time it is as if a man were to cut himself off from his former existence and choose another. But God's elect servants undertake this toil because the delights of this supreme knowledge pass not away and its end is exceedingly blissful and pleasant. By the boon of this knowledge one walks in eternal realms and perpetual bounties fall to one's lot, ultimately coming to dwell in Paradise, there to commune with the celestial hierarchy and to be graced by blessed nearness to the Creator. May He be praised and magnified!

[1] Cf. Arist. *Metaph.* 999b and 1036a 3 ff. It should, however, be observed that it is not merely the instability of sense, but the changeability of matter which hinders correct knowledge. For the intelligibles, one must abstract from sense-impressions because we are not observing the same thing twice. It is interesting to note that Abū Rashīd Sa'īd an Nīsapūrī was a contemporary of Ibn Miskawaih, and his *Kitáb ul Masá'il* contains a complete atomistic theory. Ibn Miskawaih is no atomist, but in this passage he is considered by some Muslims to point that way. Cf. also Plotinus: *Enneads*, I, viii. 5, "What we incorrectly call reality in the world of sense."

[2] I.e., illusion, cf. Plotinus: *Enneads*, I, iii. 5, "Untruth and sophism it knows, not *directly*, not of its own nature, but merely as something produced outside itself, something which it recognizes to be foreign to the verities laid up in itself."

This is the subject which we will explain as we proceed. And because our quest is exceeding difficult, several stages have been set, firstly, the lower knowledge, secondly, the intermediate knowledge, and lastly, the supreme knowledge. Thus from the lowest knowledge, which is most fitting to our habit and nature, we will proceed gradually from the beginning, so that no stage may be left out. And when one stage has been properly traversed and its ideas completely mastered, then the second will be begun.[1]

By this gradual process I have reached the goal; for that person alone can be called a philosopher who begins with the exact sciences [2] (*'ulūm riyāḍīya*, i.e., mathematics, etc.) and proceeds step by step, and after acquiring logic, which is the instrument of philosophy, acquires knowledge of the natural sciences and attains to philosophical method. Otherwise a man is only entitled to be called according to the science he serves. For instance, the one who knows the exact sciences will be called a mathematician, the one who knows the world of the stars an astronomer, another will be a physician, another a logician, another a grammarian, etc. None of these can be called a philosopher. But he who gradually acquires all the sciences and reaches the ultimate and final stage can be called by the honourable title of philosopher.[3]

CAP. II. DESCRIBING HOW ALL THE PHILOSOPHERS OF OLD HAVE UNANIMOUSLY AGREED ON THE DOCTRINE OF THE ARTIFICER OF THE UNIVERSE [4]

Of those people who, according to the last chapter, are entitled to be called philosophers, i.e., those who, according to what has been said, have studied divine things after gradual advances and laborious

[1] The curious blend of mystical fervour and serious philosophical discipline is characteristic of Plotinus. In this and the previous paragraphs there is a distinctly religious tone, and in the succeeding paragraph we descend to a simple statement of philosophical method.

For the stages mentioned it is interesting to compare Bonaventura's *Itinerarium Mentis in Deum*, Capp. I and II. In Cap. I we have three grades: (1) We must pass through the vestiges which are corporeal, temporal and external to us. This is to be led into God's Way. (2) We must enter into our own minds which are the image of God, eternal and spiritual and within. This is to enter God's Truth. (3) We must rise on high to the eternal and purely spiritual which transcends us, by contemplating the First Principle. This is to rejoice in the knowledge of God and in reverence for His Majesty. The first corresponds to the sensible and corporeal external to us, the second refers to sense by the agency of the soul, and the third refers to the mind or intellect. In Cap. II Bonaventura discusses how all created things of this sensible world lead the mind of the contemplative and wise to the eternal God.

[2] Cf. Plotinus: *Enneads*, I, i. 3 f., "Mathematics will be prescribed to train him to abstract thought. . . . After mathematics he must be put through a course of dialectic, etc."

[3] Arist. *Metaph.*, 1004a, 34. "It is the function of the philosopher to be able to investigate all things."

[4] This is a very sweeping statement. It reminds us that Christians and Muslims alike have accepted theistic arguments from polytheists.

endeavours, not one has differed with respect to the affirmation of the Artificer of the Universe. Neither has any one of them denied that the qualities ascribed to man, so far as human power goes, are found to the limit of perfection in the Creator, may His Name be honoured! that is to say, benevolence and goodness, power and wisdom. Originally all these attributes are of that hallowed Majesty and for us men they are merely borrowed.[1]

In proof of this assertion we set forth the statement of the Philosopher Porphyry. "One of those matters which according to reason are self-evident or axiomatic (*badīhī*) is the doctrine of the Maker, and all the truth-loving and right-thinking philosophers of Greece accept the self-evident character of this. And those people who do not hold that the proof of the Maker is self-evident[2] are, in my opinion, not worthy to be mentioned, and are not entitled to be included in the company of the Philosophers. By their refractoriness they have committed many errors and they have been forced to accept things which are contrary to observation (or contemplation, i.e., *mushāhada*) and the self-evident. It is as though they said that the proof of the Artificer was not self-evident, but this statement of theirs was not based on any universal rule, neither did this idea come to their mind without reflection and study, which is the rule for the self-evident. But the reason for this false idea was that they did not choose for themselves any genuine highway and were not bound by any universal rule. For this reason when they became mutually contradictory they were at last confused and, contrary to sound reason, began to say things without

[1] Cf. John of Damascus: *De Fide Orthod.*, Bk. I, Cap. XII. Speaking of the divine names, he says, "Some have an affirmative signification as indicating that He is the *cause* of all things. For as the cause of all that is and of all essence He is called both Ens and Essence; and as the cause of reason and wisdom. . . . He is called rational and wise, and similarly . . . living, powerful, etc." (*P.G.*, 94, 845 f.).

[2] First to speak of the laborious method by which this knowledge of the divine is acquired, and then to follow on with an assertion that this knowledge is self-evident, or of an intuitional character is seemingly contradictory. We might think that *badīhī* had been used in a loose way, but that this is not so is made clear by what follows in the text.

Of knowledge which is *badīhī* it may be said that it is that the acquisition of which does not depend on speculation (*naẓar*) and it is equivalent to *ḍarūrī*, i.e., necessary. It sometimes, however, seems to convey the sense that the knowledge so described is conclusive or carries conviction, after due thought has been exercised. It may be that it is used in this manner in the text.

It should be noted that a few lines further on, "*mushāhada*" is used. There is more than a hint of direct apprehension here also, and the term is used by the Sufis for "contemplation".

It may be that a reconciliation can be suggested in the Neoplatonist manner supported by what Porphyry says in his *Life of Plotinus*. There in respect to one by whom the philosophical discipline is taught we have the record of the climax—which Plotinus achieved four times—in which there was this direct mystical apprehension, "not by inherent fitness but by ineffable act". But even then the intuitive cannot be that which is self-evident or axiomatic and the basis of all knowledge, but only mystical intuition, not the possession of man as a thinking being, but the prerogative of the few elect, prepared by bodily and intellectual discipline.

foundation. I do not like to argue with such people and, moreover, I have no wish to address people whose intellects are confined within the limits of natural phenomena until they have cultivated their intellects with labour and toil and have become accustomed to understanding the truth."

See how emphatic and fervent is this declaration of the philosopher Porphyry, from which it appears that no philosopher who was sound in his thinking has denied the proof for the Artificer.

If you consider, it will be plain that the agreement of every rational person with regard to the Real Artificer is necessary and inevitable. For those men, who by means of toil and labour purify their reason and achieve abstraction from sensible things and from phantasy, arrive most assuredly at the conclusion to which people of wisdom and insight have arrived, and will come to say what the most eminent philosophers and prophets have already said. Behold, all the leaders of the past have instructed the whole world in the doctrine of the Unity and have shown the way to justice and righteousness; they have bound the common people to political and social laws by the Divine command, and taught the elect the methods of reasoning and discrimination. For just as physicians of the body heal men, so the prophets are the spiritual physicians of men and heal the human soul. We see that it is necessary to use force with some sick people when curing them and sometimes even to beat them, for the sick person does not understand the benefit of the medicine which the physician wishes to give him and so hesitates to drink it. So they have to be made to take it by force. Physicians often do not fully explain to sick people the reason why they forbid them to eat some food which they long for and why they prescribe the use of unpalatable food and medicine.

The reason for this is that, in the first place, there are many difficulties in the way, and again, neither is the time sufficient nor does the necessity demand it. Many patients have not the wit to understand these fine points. Thus there is little use and a great deal of labour in explaining the reason for every method of treatment. Many patients have been seen who when they have been cured by the labour and remedies of the physician, begin to resort to subterfuges to get what they fancy to eat, and begin to adopt some régime of their own although it may be ever so harmful.

This is exactly the condition of the spiritually sick, to whom the respected philosophers and prophets explain when they come in quest of the truth, that they should sever their connections with the vile habits and conditions of this world of bodies, and from senses and phantasies, and consider the abstractions of the reason and use profound speculation. It is then that the knowledge of the truth in quest will be obtained, and complete health and real ease become the lot of their soul.

But because this method is difficult, ignorant and unfortunate people have resorted to forced interpretations of the commandments of the Lawgiver (i.e., *tā'wīl*). For one thing there is ease and repose in this because who would be plunged into the irksomeness of labour and leave all the delights of the world ? Secondly, they think that by the aid of these interpretations they may gain the respect of the common people and become founders of a regular school. So in accordance with their wishes, they make a new interpretation and produce a new school and taunt and slander one another. For the conditions and desires of people are very various and so conflict of opinions is most rife, and things have even come to such a pass that the real reason for conflicting schools is that one is at enmity with the other.

Later we will briefly set forth proofs from which it will be learned that the person who thinks justly will admit the Unity of God and the existence of the Artificer of the Universe. And it will also be learned that the people who have explained these things to us were themselves believers in the same.

CAP. III. THAT THE EXISTENCE OF THE ARTIFICER CAN BE PROVED FROM MOTION AND THAT OF ALL THINGS MOTION IS THE FITTEST FOR THIS PROOF

It has been explained in the first chapter that because we have physical bodies, our states are in accordance with them and so the nearest and most closely related to us of all those things from which we can argue are those selfsame physical bodies which we perceive by the five senses. A more detailed statement of this is that each separate power of sense perceives those things which are appropriate to it in the following manner : Each sense has a particular balance [1] bestowed on it and so when the effect of anything external falls upon it, and the external thing is in a condition repugnant to it, then the sensitive power becomes aware of it. This is called perception or sensation (*idrāk* and *iḥsās*).

This abstruse theory should be fixed in the mind by an illustration. By means of the moisture which is granted to the power of tasting it perceives that other moisture which is in general repugnant to its own. And the power of hearing, by its own balanced air, senses that repugnant air which comes to it. Likewise the power of touch has given to it an earthy balance, by which it can perceive anything pertaining to its own class and repugnant to it. And the power of sight by its fiery rays senses other external fiery rays, and so also by similar analogy in the case of the power of smelling. But in this latter there is a slight difference, for the power of smelling is composite, because this power perceives vapours, and vapours are composed of air and water.

[1] "Sense is a ratio." Arist. *De Anima*, iii. 2, 3.

It seems fitting that here the method of the perception by one sense should be explained in detail, so that the analogy may be drawn for the other powers.

The air which remains in the cavity of the ear has an equilibrium which is suitable for the receiving of other air. So when any external air moves that original air, man learns something and the name for this is " perception " and " sensation ". Similarly for that moisture which is put into the tongue.

Now we wish to prove that every natural body must have a movement which is proper to it.[1] For body may have two conditions. It can either be actually (*bi'l fi'l*) existing or it can be potentially existing (*bi'l quwwa*).[2] And the identity and subsistence of the body is by that form which is proper to it. And that proper form is something from which the essence or reality of any body is made. That which is essence is nature (*ṭabī'a*) and the nature [3] of a body is the cause of its particular movement. It is its nature which moves the body towards its final perfection, and makes it perfect. It is plain that the end of everything is suitable and convenient to it.[4] And just as everything that moves must move towards its end, in the same way, it should be understood that when every mover moves, it must have a desire and attraction towards its end. Further, it is plain that whatever is desired and sought is the cause of the one who desires and seeks. But it is essential that every cause should be prior in nature (*bi'ṭ ṭab'*) to its effect. Thus it is proved that it pertains to all physical bodies to move and [5] it is also necessary for them to have a mover which is their cause. Thus to prove the existence of the First Maker and Real Cause from movement is clearer and plainer than anything else, because movement is proved to be necessary for all bodies.

Here by way of introduction the kinds of movement are described, the consequence of which will be seen in the following chapter. The movement of physical bodies is of six kinds: 1. The movement of generation. 2. The movement of corruption. 3. The movement of augmentation. 4. The movement of diminution. 5. The movement of alteration. 6. The movement of transposition, i.e., change of place.[6] For movement is a sort of change and it is clear that a body may change in three cases, namely, in its state, its place or its substance and essence.[7]

Now change of place will be by the change and movement of the whole place or only change of a part of it. The name for the change

[1] Arist. *Metaph.*, 1069a, 30 ff.
[2] *Op. cit.*, 1069b, 15 ff. and 1071a, 4 ff.
[3] *Op. cit.*, 1070a, 11 ff.
[4] *Op. cit.*, 1072b, 1 ff.
[5] *Op. cit.*, 1072b, 10.
[6] Arist. *Categ.*, xiv. 15a, 13 ff.
[7] It should be noted that Al Ghazzālī in *Maqāsid ul Falāsifa* excludes substance and includes position (cf. iii. 236).

of the whole is straight movement, and partial movement is called rotary or circular movement. In the latter also there are two forms. There is movement from the centre to the circumference, this is called growth, i.e., augmentation (*namw—αὔξησις*). When there is movement from the circumference towards the centre this is called diminution or withering (*idmiḥlāl* and *dhabūl*).

That body which changes in condition has also two states. In one the condition changes but the essence continues, and in the other the substance changes along with the condition (*kayfiya*). The former is called alteration—*istiḥāla*—and the latter is corruption (*fasād*). In this latter case when we consider that substance into the form of which the body is altered after change of condition and substance, then this is called the movement of generation (*kawn*).[1]

CAP. IV. THAT THE MOVER OF EVERYTHING MOVED IS SOME OTHER THING AND THIS WHICH IS THE MOVER OF ALL THINGS IS NOT ITSELF MOVED

In this chapter it is purposed to prove two things. Firstly, everything moved (of whatever sort of movement as mentioned above) must have a mover,[2] and beside that which is moved there must be something else different from it. Secondly, that which is the mover of all things is not itself moved, but is the perfecter (*mutammim*) of those things or the cause of their motion.

The first assertion is proved in the following manner: Every body which moves must have something or other to move it. Then a moved body is in one of two conditions, either it is animal or not-animal. If it is animal and some person asserts that its motion is essential and not *ab alio,* then we say that if we should sever one of the nobler members of the body of that animal, then by essential movement that animal ought to continue to move and its severed member also (because a part is in nature and quiddity similar to the whole of which it forms a part). Howbeit this is not so (but the whole ceases to move through the severance of the member). Thus it would seem that the movement of an animal body is not by its essence, but it must have some mover distinct from it. And if the thing moved is not animal then it must be either vegetable or mineral. In the case of the vegetable the same argument applies as for an animal, because in this also is the movement of augmentation or growth, etc., of the same kind.

However, there still remains the inanimate (*jamād*) with regard to which it may be said that this must be either one of the elements or

[1] The argument from motion is based on Arist. *Physics*, Bk. VIII, and *Metaphysics*, Bk. λ. John of Damascus uses the argument in *De Fide Orthod.*, Bk. I, Cap. III (*P.G.*, 94, 793 f.).

[2] Arist. *Metaph.*, 1073a, 2 ff. and 25. The argument from motor cause is in Plato: *Laws*, Bk. X, but this is for the World Soul created by God.

a thing composed of elements. If it is a simple element then on the supposition of essential movement, it follows that it should, after coming to its centre and proper place, continue to move, and not to come to rest, because according to the supposition its motion is by its essence. And if it stops at its centre, then it follows that like an animal it can stop wherever it wishes as well as at its centre and when it wishes it can keep moving. But this is contrary to observation and to what is self-evident, because all elements continue to move until they reach their proper place and, reaching their centre, come to rest.[1]

Therefore it is proved that the motion of elements and inanimate things is not by their essence (but by some mover other than their essence). If any one should say that the elements continue to seek or desire their centre, and their motion is by reason of this their quest and desire for their proper place and that the object of their quest is their mover, even then we have found what we sought to prove, namely, that the object of their quest is without question other than that which seeks and is moved.

We may explain this subject in another way. The motion of animals is for two reasons, either it likes something and so desires it and therefore runs towards it, or it feels repugnance to it and so it runs away from it. Thus it is plainly seen that what it likes or what it dislikes is the cause of its motion and is certainly other than the animal which is moved.[2]

And now to consider this mover, whether it possesses any sort of motion or not. If it does, then in accordance with the previous argument it must itself have some mover. Then we should consider this mover too, and apply the same rule. Thus, perforce, it must be admitted that we should come at last to some mover which has no sort of motion. Otherwise an infinite series would be involved which is impossible. So this is what it was sought to demonstrate.

By this argument it is also proved that that mover (which is not moved) cannot be body, for we have proved that every body must possess motion. Thus it is learned that this mover is the first cause and cause of causes of the existence of all things, and by this every existing substance comes to be in the world of phenomena.

By this exposition it is also proved that the existence found in all things is accidental,[3] and in the Creator of being and place it is essential.[4] Because all philosophers agree that what is found accidentally in anything must be found *per se* in something else. For that which is

[1] For the general questions involved see Arist. *Physics*, viii. 4 and 5, 254b–256a. 13 ff. Proclus: *El. Theol.*, Prop. xiv. Plato: *Laws*, 895A 6–B2. *Phædrus*, 245C, Aristotle asserts that the light and heavy elements are not moved by themselves. Ibn Sīnā took the other view; cf. *An Najāt*, 26.

[2] I.e., the soul is the cause of the movement of animals; cf. *De Anima*, i. 2, 404b, 6 ff., and iii. 10, 433a.

[3] Cf. Arist., *Anal. Poster.*, ii. 7, 92b.

[4] The Unmoved Mover is identified with God in *Metaph.*, λ, 7–9.

accidental to anything is an effect and every effect is motion, of which there must be an effective cause and a mover. And this chain of effective cause and effect must terminate at an effective cause which itself does not suffer the effect of anything, but is effective cause *per se*. Therefore it follows that the First Originator and Eternal Creator's existence must be essential, for He did not obtain that existence from anything else. Howbeit, from that Holy Essence existence was conferred on the things of the whole universe, and all existing things appear entirely by the beneficence of His existence.

When from the foregoing exposition it is proved that existence is essential for the Creator, i.e., that Holy Essence necessitates existence, then no one can imagine Him to be non-existent, because on account of the existence being essential, the idea of the essence is necessarily accompanied by the idea of existence. This is what is called the " Necessary of Existence " (*Wājib ul Wujūd*).[1]

That which is Necessary of Existence must be permanent of existence also.[2] And that which is permanently existent is eternal (*azalī*, i.e., eternal in past or pre-eternal). Thus when it has been learned that the Creator is necessary of existence and eternal, no sort of existence or perfection can be conceived which is not found most perfect and complete in that Holy Essence. For the Fountain of Grace bestowed existence on all existences and the perfections of all things are due to It. That Holy Essence has the highest degree of existence, and all created things obtain their existence from It. Therefore the existence of created things is of an inferior order.

One other argument is advanced for the assertion that for everything moved a mover other than itself is necessary. Everything moved moves either naturally or not naturally. If the former is the case, then it is plain that its nature has made it move, and its nature is other than the thing moved, as the theory of the movement of the nature has been proved in Physics. And if the movement is not natural then it must be either voluntary or compulsory. In the case of the voluntary it is clear that that thing for which there is the will, is the cause of movement and undoubtedly the cause is other than what is moved. And if the movement is by compulsion or aversion, nevertheless the compelling mover is other than the thing moved. Now if that mover is itself moved we can continue the inquiry until the series concludes at a

[1] Cf. Arist. *Metaph.*, 1072b, 10 f. The " self-constituted " of Proclus (*Elements of Theology*, Propp. 40 ff.) must not be overlooked in considering the sources of the concept of the *Wājib ul Wujūd* as properly applied to God. Cf. also *El. Theol.*, Prop. 9, where Proclus advances the conception of the self-sufficient in existence.

[2] Cf. Proclus: *El. Theol.*, Prop. 46. " The self-constituted is imperishable."

Additional note on the " Necessary of Existence ". The identity of Essence and Existence in the Divine Being was deemed equally important also to maintain the pure oneness or simplicity of the Creator. Otherwise the difficulty would arise discussed in *Parmenides*, 142b ff. It would have to be said that the One *has* being and this would imply a plurality.

mover that is not itself moved and is the foremost of all movers (*primum movens*). That is the Essence of the Necessary.

Another argument is put forward that every body has a nature and if there is nature there must be movement because movement is the demonstration and indication of nature. So it is not possible that that which is the *primum movens* should be moved, because if it were moved, then it would be necessary to hold that it had a mover, and if another mover were discovered then it would cease to be prior, although we assumed that it was the *primum movens*. So that is contrary to the hypothesis. By this argument it is also proved that the *primum movens* has no body, because a body must be moved and in the case of it being moved (in its turn) the above arguments may be set forth.

CAP. V. THAT THE ESSENCE OF THE CREATOR IS ONE

The argument for the oneness is that if the Lord of the Universe and the Real Agent were more than one, then it would follow that there would be composite cause (*sabab murakkab*) because all would participate in being agents, and would be different in their essences. And it is necessary that that thing by which there is a difference must be other than that thing which is a cause of participation (*ishtirāk*). Thus every agent must be composite of its own essential substance and some additional property. Composition is itself motion, for composition is an effect for which it is plain there must be an effective cause. It would therefore follow that for a composite agent there must be another agent and such a series might be carried to infinity. So it is necessary that this series should terminate at an agent which is single. Otherwise an impossible series will be involved.

In this argument, the doubt may be expressed : How may multiple and varied acts proceed from one agent (i.e., a simple agent) especially when such acts are mutually contradictory ? For from a simple one only a simple act can proceed, i.e., from the one which is in all respects and all senses one only one act can proceed.[1] The reply to

[1] The principle " *Al wāḥid lā yaṣdiru ' anhu illa'l wāḥid* " nothing proceeds from the One except the One, is hard to trace to its origin. In Plotinus : *Enneads*, VI, v. 9 we find something which approximates " Plurality cannot be got out of unity unless it is first put into it." If we note the thirtieth and thirty-fifth propositions in Proclus' *Elements of Theology* we might come to the conclusion that if it be held that everything which is immediately produced by any principle both remains in the cause which produces it and proceeds from it, then if the one is to be guarded from plurality it must have one effect. Ibn Sīnā uses the principle, and he and Ibn Miskawaih were contemporaries. I have had no access to *De Causis* and wonder whether the expression is found there. Al Fārābī may have used it. The difficulty is that such a principle can hardly be regarded, in the sense in which it is usually interpreted, as pure Neoplatonism. The usual interpretation given is a straight line of unitary procession. This is manifestly not in accord with the Procline view (see *El. Theol.*, Prop. 21), where there are henads consequent upon the Primal One, intelligences consequent upon the Primal Intelligence (which is spoken of as single—ἐξ ἑνός νοῦ) and souls consequent upon the primal soul, etc. And while, according to Prop. 62, that which is nearest to the One will have fewer members than that which is

this doubt is that there are four cases in which the one agent can do many and diverse acts. Firstly, when it is a composite agent and in it are several parts or several powers. Secondly, when that agent acts on different materials, i.e., when the things acted upon are many. Thirdly, when the acts of the agent are by means of different instruments. Fourthly, from a simple agent many acts proceed but not directly from the essence of that agent,[1] but by means of other things which are intermediaries in the procession of act. An illustration of the first kind is man, who does some acts at the demand of the concupiscible power, others at the demand of the irascible power, and others by reason of intellect. So it is as though man were composed of several diverse powers and for this reason many acts proceed from him. An illustration of the second kind is a carpenter who cuts by means of an adze and makes holes with a drill. The illustration of the third may be found in fire which melts iron, and hardens earth, i.e., one agent has different effects in different materials.

remote from It, It will nevertheless be a manifold. It is even explicitly stated in the end of Prop. 5, " From the One Itself, every manifold proceeds." On the other hand, if the quotation from Porphyry later on in this chapter is correct the principle may have been in some way derived from Aristotle.

It should be noted that in these early writers the distinction between Platonist, Aristotelian and Neoplatonist, is not observed and plainly not understood in many cases. The outstanding instance of this is the attribution of a Neoplatonist book to Aristotle, *The Theology of Aristotle.* In *Metaphysica,* 1074a, 36 ff. Aristotle says: " So the unmovable mover is one both in definition and in number; so, too, therefore, is that which is moved always and continuously; therefore there is one heaven alone." Stated in concise terms, this means that God is one and the object he sets in motion is one.

Another difficulty arises in this way: it is quite clear that it was regarded as possible to refer to the manifold as one. The very word " universe " testifies to this. So, bearing this in mind, " nothing proceeds from the One save one " might be interpreted along the lines indicated in Pseudo-Dionysius (*Div. Nom.,* Cap. XIII, 2). " Without the One there can be no Multiplicity; yet contrariwise the One can exist without the Multiplicity just as the Unit exists before all multiplied number. And if all things be conceived as being ultimately unified with each other, then all things taken as a whole are One."

It will be seen that this is quite different from saying that from an Unity only one unit proceeds, which is the turn given to this aphorism when it is used in the Arabic.

The argument runs thus: The One cannot possess diverse powers, it cannot work by diverse means, because this would involve their prior existence; who wrought these effects? He could not work with diverse materials for this, too, would involve the prior existence of materials. Therefore the many cannot flow from the creative act of the One. The only possibility left is that there should proceed One from One, and by a gradual descent from the higher to the lower, from the subtle to the gross, we might at last make a new beginning in the contrary direction from the primordial elements, from the inferior to the superior. In the main this follows the lines laid down by Al Fārābī.

This is no place to debate the whole matter, but a further reference for the whole subject of the Many and the One should be made to Plato's *Parmenides,* particularly Taylor's edition.

The influence of the idea of unitary procession may be seen in the Alexandrian Trinity which is not a trinity of coequal persons but a succession similar to the schemes of emanation under the influence of Neoplatonism.

Finally, cf. *Enneads,* III, ii. 2. The One gives birth to the second by Its essence.

[1] Cf. *Enneads,* III, ii. 2. The ground of the second is the *essence* of the One.

The example of the fourth—viz., that the agent does some things himself and causes others to proceed accidentally by the intermediary of other things—is ice which by itself makes cold and by intermediary and accidentally causes heat, the manner of this being that ice causes the contraction of the pores by cold and so less heat is given off from the body and it gets hotter. So ice does not make heat by its essence but by means of some other thing.

Now the matter to be considered is, which of these four is valid in the case of the first agent ? It is clear that it is not possible to find several powers in the prime agent because in this way plurality and composition will be entailed in the essence of the agent, and that we have already seen to be false. It is also not possible that it should cause acts to happen by means of manifold instruments, because those instruments must either be effects or not. If so many instruments are held to be acted upon, then how is it possible that so many things can proceed from one agent ? For " Nothing proceeds from the one save one " is an agreed principle. And in the second case, it would follow that an effect would be found without an effective cause, and this also is impossible. And it is also not possible that the acts should be manifold on account of the number of materials, because in this case also, we might ask whether these materials are effects (i.e., acted upon) or not and in both cases the same impossibility is involved as before.

So there is no other possibility remaining than that from the single agent some acts properly proceed by essence and some by the medium of others.[1] This view was first adopted by Aristotle as Porphyry

[1] It will be noted that in order to provide accidental causation for the First Agent, it has been necessary for Ibn Miskawaih to adopt the idea of *media*, by which more acts than one may proceed from the simply One. But the same question which he asks about the instruments and materials, namely, whether they are to be regarded as objects of the divine act or not, may be asked about the *media* which are postulated for accidental causation, with the same unsatisfactory results. He seems to be quite unaware of this difficulty. Why ? The rest of the argument runs smoothly enough. We should also have to ask the question whether we can with any propriety speak of accidental causation in relation to the first cause ?

It is hard to see how this theory of " accidental causation " saves the First Cause from being committed to the use of those instruments which it was thought would involve numerous effects from the One or a multiplicity in the nature of the One. The only difference which is discernible is that now the intermediaries by which accidental causality proceeds from the One are not His direct creation. The scheme seems to us to break down badly here. The criticism might be expressed as follows :

The One cannot produce many directly, but the many must exist. What the One cannot do directly He can do by intermediary. Therefore He creates One out of His Oneness. This One has power which the Primal One does not possess, namely to produce many. Whence has the Second this power ? Has it this power of itself ? Then it has something which is not derived from the One. Therefore in a certain respect it is independent of the one and has something by its own essence. If there is something which exists independent of the One and which has something by its own essence, then the One cannot be the Primal Source of all. If, however, the potentiality to multiplicity in the Second is derived from the One, then in what sense can it be said that from the One only one proceeds ? It would have to be said that from the One

says: "Plato holds that from the Creator the abstract form of every existing thing proceeds, and by means of it He perceives what exists. There is, however, the objection to this view of Plato that it involves the procession of many things from the simply One. Therefore this theory of Plato, of a number of exemplars (*ta'addud ul amthāl*) is refuted and the view of Aristotle mentioned is correct."[1]

From this explanation it is clear that the Creator is One and that He is the First Agent. All the points in this section are quoted from Porphyry.

CAP. VI. THAT THE CREATOR DOES NOT POSSESS A BODY[2]

From the foregoing expositions it has been made clear that body must have composition, plurality, and movement, and it is not possible for any of these things to be found in the Holy Essence of the Primal One.

Composition cannot be attributed to that Holy Essence because composition is an effect, and for every effect there must be an effective cause, because effect is a relative matter (which can never be found without another; even the understanding of them is not possible without the idea of two things). So it is impossible that there should be found in the Essence of the First Effective Cause something for which another effective cause is necessary. There remains multiplicity which is the contrary to oneness and which cannot be found in the Essence of the One. Similarly, motion must depend on some other mover as we have already proved. Therefore this cannot be predicated of the Essence of the Creator. Secondly, motion is itself an effect and effect is itself motion (thus neither motion nor effect can be found in the Essence of the Primal One).

That God has not a body may be proved from the following logical argument. We have already proved that the *primum movens* is not moved, and the converse of a universal negative must be a universal negative. Therefore the converse of this will be, "No moved thing is the *primum movens*". With this we join another proved proposition,

proceeds that which has oneness and multiplicity, or one which has a potentiality to multitude, and such an one cannot be absolutely one.

If it is said that the Second has plurality only by reason of relations, namely, its derivation from the Primal One, and its own necessitation *ab alio*, its own existence *per se*, and its potentiality towards posterior plurality, then it may be urged that there must be similar relations conceived of the Primal One, as the later Sufis thought when they differentiated *aḥadīya, huwīya* and *anīya* in the One.

Further, on the general question, this is an emanational system, and is not the same as deliberate creation by will. This was clearly seen by the orthodox theologians, and is expressed in the differentiation between the concept of "cause by necessity of nature" and the free agent (*mūjib* and *qādir mukhtār*).

[1] The reference is, of course, to Plato's doctrine of Ideas and to Aristotle's objection to the same.

[2] John of Damascus: *De Fide Orthod.*, Bk. I, Cap. IV (*P.G.*, 94, 797). "It is evident that He is incorporeal, for how could that possess body which is infinite, boundless, formless, intangible, and invisible, in short, simple and not compound?"

namely, "Every body is moved". The last mentioned of these two propositions forms the minor and the first mentioned the major; so exclude the middle and the conclusion will be found, "No body can be the *primum movens*", and the converse of this is "The *primum movens* cannot be body", and this was the assertion with which this chapter started.[1]

CAP. VII. THAT GOD IS ETERNAL [2]

Eternity is that time (*sic*) which is without beginning. The first argument is that we have proved that existence is essential for the First Author, and that Primary Origin, God, is Necessary of Existence. Thus it is also proved that God is eternal because this is the meaning of the word.

The second argument is that it has already been proved that the *primum movens* is not moved, and it is also plain that everything moved and generated, i.e., everything which has come into the world of contingent or potential existence, is temporal or has been originated (*muḥaddath*). It is therefore clear that an essence which is not originated is also not generated (*mutakawwan*). For generation or "becoming" (*takawwun*) cannot be without movement. Thus, that essence which is not created or generated and originated must have nothing prior to it and must therefore be eternal. If the aforementioned proved propositions are set in order (of the syllogism) they will yield the required result.

We would now draw the reader's attention to an abstruse question. To those persons who have studied with thoughtful attention what we have already explained, it will be quite clear that the Creator is One and Simple in His Essence and in His Attributes. From all the material things which surround us His Essence is entirely free. No multiplicity of any sort, in any mode or manner whatever can be mixed with His oneness. The conclusion is that His Holy Essence cannot be like anything which we can conceive (i.e., of which we can form an image). But the difficulty is, how can man, weak in expression and faltering in tongue, in any way declare and explain that pure and uncontaminated Essence, and how indicate His Essence and Attributes so that people may understand?

What other form can this take than that such words should be used for this lofty subject, as mortal man employs with his tongue of flesh,

[1] John of Damascus: *De Fide Orthod.*, Bk. I, Cap. IV (*P.G.*, 94, 797). "If some say that the body is immaterial in the same way as the fifth body (Arist. *De Coelo* i. 3 and *Meteor*. i. 3, 339b–ether) of which Greek philosophers speak (which body is an impossibility) it will be wholly subject to motion like the heaven, but the *Primum Movens* is not moved."

[2] That God is eternal is held, of course, by John of Damascus: *De Fide Orthod.*, Bk. I, Cap. VIII (*P.G.* 94, 816). "God whose nature and existence are above time", and Bk. I, Cap. II (*P.G.*, 94, 792). "God is without beginning, without end, eternal and everlasting, uncreated, unchangeable, invariable, simple, uncompounded, incorporeal," etc.

and that the Attributes found in contingent and frail creatures should be used metaphorically for the Essence of the Necessary of Existence. What better method can we adopt than this ? [1]

So in such circumstances it is appropriate that we should make use of the very best words available for the Essence of the Necessary, e.g., when we have two terms of opposite meanings before us, it is necessary for us to employ the one which we find to be better and superior in reference to the Creator who transcends all attributes and names. For instance, existing and non-existing, powerful and impotent, knowing and ignorant, the better of all such opposite terms should be used.

In addition, it is also most fitting and necessary that we should look extensively at all terms and, after complete search and scrutiny, use for the Creator only those terms which the Lawgiver used in the Law, and which the common people and the elect alike are accustomed to use for this sacred subject.[2] Having understood this, when man applies such epithets to the Essence of the Necessary, it should be believed that the Holy Essence is superior to all these attributes because He Himself created these attributes. Thus the Creator will be in every respect more honourable and excellent than creatures.[3]

Now it should be understood that it is not possible for the knowledge of any person to comprehend the Essence of the Creator in any way, or to recognize anything in it, because that Holy Essence is distinct from all those existing things with which man is acquainted, and God Most High is the Author and Creator of them all. On the basis of this proposition, we will in the following chapter prove that no argument concerning the Creator can be put forward in the mode of affirmation, but the argument advanced will be by way of negation and privation.

CAP. VIII. THAT THE CREATOR CAN BE APPREHENDED BY THE METHOD OF NEGATION AND NOT BY THE WAY OF AFFIRMATION [4]

People who are acquainted with the rules of Logic know that in those arguments in which something is proved by affirmation the pro-

[1] See *De Fide Orthod.*, Bk. I, Cap. II (*P.G.*, 94, 792). "Many of the things relating to God, therefore, that are but dimly understood, cannot be put into suitable terms, but in regard to things above us we cannot do other than express ourselves according to our limited capacity."

[2] See *De Fide Orthod.*, Bk. I, Cap. II (*P.G.*, 94, 793). "It is not within our capacity to say anything about God, or even to think of Him, beyond the things which have been divinely revealed to us whether by word or manifestation, by the divine oracles of the Old Testament or of the New."

[3] Here we have the exaggerated transcendence prepared for in Philo, Clement of Alexandria and Plotinus ; cf. *De Fide Orthod.*, Bk. I, Cap. II (*P.G.*, 94, 793). "Neither do we know nor can we tell what the essence of God is." See also Bk. I, Cap. IV (*P.G.*, 94, 797). "It is clear that there is a God, but what He is in His Essence and Nature, is absolutely incomprehensible and unknowable." The whole subject is dealt with in fuller detail in a later chapter, see Vol. II.

[4] For the *via negativa* see Pseudo-Dionysius : *Divine Names*, v. 3, and the *Mystical Theology*, *passim*. John of Damascus owes much to him and asserts the *via negativa*.

positions which are essential for the proof must be affirmative. And the propositions which are essential to anything must be such that if they are found, then that thing will also be found, and if those propositions are not found, then that thing will also not be found. Now it is clear that the Holy Essence of God is pure and free from all such connections because it is prior to all existing things, as we have already proved, and is their Author and Creator. Thus anything which might be included in primary propositions about Him and might be prior to His Essence cannot be found in Him.[1] He is also One, and there can be nothing found in Him, i.e., in His Essence, because this would be contrary to His oneness. Neither is any attribute of His essential, i.e., included in His Essence, because His Essence is not composite. Neither is any attribute of His non-essential, i.e., not of His Essence, and attributed to it metaphorically. In such circumstances for that most holy Majesty no direct or positive demonstration (*burhān mustaqīm*) can be set up, i.e., it is not possible that we should prove anything of It affirmatively. Nevertheless, for this purpose *argumentatio ex absurdo* (*burhān k͟hilfī*) can be employed, the method of which is to show that the contradictory of a certain thing is absurd and so that thing is proved.

In this method the negation and inapplicability of ideas to the Holy Essence has to be established, e.g., that God is not a body, not moved, not manifold, not created, or that it is not possible that the chain of causes in the universe should not end at a single cause. Thus it is proved that for the explanation of divine things the most fitting is negative proof.

There is another point which ought to be mentioned, namely, that when a man wishes to explain anything about the Creator, he can only use those words and expressions which are found in the universe and are employed in relation to the various species and individuals of the universe. Because if those familiar words and expressions are not used for this supreme purpose, then where shall other new terms be found?

It is plain also how lofty and transcendent that pure Essence is above all likeness to the things which exist in the world. The most eminent thing in the world has nothing common in any point with the Supreme Majesty so that a likeness may be drawn (or a simile given) and therefore we are compelled when speaking of the divine majesty and describing His attributes, to adopt only the negative and are forced

quite plainly in *De Fide Orthod.*, Bk. I, Cap. IV (*P.G.*, 94, 797). "It gives no idea of the essence of God to declare that He is unbegotten, without beginning, changeless and imperishable and possessed of such qualities as we are wont to ascribe to God and His environment. For these do not indicate what He is but what He is not." Cf. Plotinus: *Enneads* VI, viii. 11.

[1] The meaning seems to be that we cannot make positive affirmations about God as though they were universal propositions constituting the prior specification of the genus God and with which this particular must comply. For God is not in a genus and is prior to all that could be said about Him.

to use expressions like the following: "He is not so", or "He is so but not quite so but better than this".[1] Thus, for instance, we say that God Most Honoured and Glorious is not intelligence, or we say "He is knowing but not knowing like the knowing of the people of the world", or "He is powerful but not like those who possess power in this world", and similarly with other expressions.[2]

CAP. IX. THAT ALL THINGS EXIST BY MEANS OF THE HONOURED AND GLORIOUS CREATOR [3]

We have already explained that existence is found in all things accidentally, but in the Essence of the Creator essentially. And by this we proved that the Holy Essence is eternal and that all things have their being from Him. In this respect all things are inferior to His Essence (i.e., defective in comparison with It), for the effect cannot possibly be equal to the cause. Also we have mentioned that some things obtain existence from the Necessary without any medium. Now we describe how the first existence bestowed on anything by the Necessary Existence is the First Intelligence, another name for which is the Active Intellect (*'Aql Fa''āl*). This is the reason why the existence of the First Intelligence is perfect and will survive for ever, and why it is always in one condition without change or alteration, because the overflowing bounty of the Real Outpourer [4] at all times and for

[1] In this there is a slight hesitation in expressing the idea that terms may be used of God *in sensu eminentiori*, cf. *De Fide Orthod.*, I, Cap. XII (*P.G.*, 94, 845) on the divine names. "Of the divine names some have a negative signification and indicate that He is super-essential, and such are 'non-essential', 'timeless', 'beginningless', 'invisible'; not that God is inferior to anything or lacking in anything, but that He is pre-eminently separated from all that is. . . . Some again have an affirmative signification, as indicating that He is the cause of all things. For as the cause of all that is and of all essence, He is called both Being and Essence, and as the cause of all reason and wisdom and the rational and the wise, He is called both reason and rational and wisdom and wise. . . . Similarly power and powerful, etc." For the twofold division, i.e., *via negativa* and *in sensu eminentiori*, cf. Sanūsī's *Catechism* in Wensinck: *Muslim Creed*, Chapter IX.

[2] *De Fide Orthod.*, I, Cap. IV (*P.G.*, 94, 800). "It is impossible to explain what He is in His essence and it is more fitting for us to discourse about His absolute separation from all things." "For He does not belong to the category of existing things; not that He has no existence but that He is above all existing things, nay even above existence itself."

[3] In this chapter we have a thorough Neoplatonist scheme. The Grades of existence in Plotinus are the One, the Intellectual Principle, the Soul, etc. Here we have God, the First Intelligence or Active Intellect, the Soul, the Spheres, our Bodies. In Al Fārābī there is a slight difference: the One, the All, the Spirit of the Spheres, the Heavenly Bodies, Reason active in Man, the Soul, Form, Matter. The vocabulary is distinctly Neoplatonist. For degrees of causality which formed a useful basis for effecting a modification of the emanational theories towards the theory of deliberate creation see Proclus: *Elements of Theology*, propp. 56 ff. It should also be borne in mind that the Pseudo-Aristotelian *Theology* is the basis of much of the doctrine in Ibn Miskawaih.

[4] Here is an example of Neoplatonist terminology. *Fayḍ* and words from the same root represent the Greek ὑπερερρύη and ἐξερρύη of Plotinus, i.e., "He overflowed." There is the familiar term *ṣudūr*—procession πρόοδος while *naẓar wa 'alam* corresponds to θεωρία and πρᾶξις.

The Active Intellect is the Aristotelian νοῦς ποιητικ

ever continues to flow upon it. For this reason the Intelligence is everlastingly existent and is more complete and perfect than all other existences beside. Although, as compared with the Essence of the Creator, it is quite defective, because in no case can the effect equal the cause, as we have explained.

After this, by the medium of the First Reason came about the existence of the Soul (*nafs*), and because the soul, in respect to being an effect, is inferior in existence to reason, therefore it is dependent on motion for the requirements of its perfection and likeness to its cause. It is always occupied in movement and alteration. But when compared with natural bodies you will find that the Soul is in the perfect and supreme degree.

After the soul and by its medium, the spheres come to exist, because the spheres by comparison with the soul are of inferior existence, i.e., less perfect, because they are dependent on a movement which is in the power of the body, i.e., movement in place. Now because the bounty of the cause of the sphere flows for ever, and never rests nor pauses, therefore the circular movement was ordained for the sphere (movement in which there is no rest and in which the whole does not change but only the part) which by the Divine command is cause of its perfection in the manner He wills.

After the creation of all these creatures by the medium of the spheres and the heavenly bodies, the accidental existence of our bodies appeared. And because the cause of the existence and creation of our bodies, namely, the spheres and the heavenly bodies, was transient (*fānī*) and even so unstable that they never continue so much as a moment in one state, therefore the existence we obtained from them was extremely prone to change, and weak and imperfect; indeed such an existence is one in which there is movement and time also, which is continually changing and once was not, at one time existing and at another time not existing.

From this explanation it will be clear that all existing things came to exist by the bounty and goodness of the Creator, and that the order of the Universe is set up by Him. His Power and Might encompass all creatures.

When the First Cause has this sort of connection with the whole universe, we should consider that if the Creator were for a single moment to withdraw His bounty from the creation, the whole world in that very moment would cease to exist.[1] For if you compare substances

[1] This is significant in view of what has been said with regard to a simple effect from a simple cause. As in Philo the Divine Providence contradicts the utter transcendence. John of Damascus also provides for the effect of the Creator in the process as well as in the initial act, in the latter part of his chapter in *De Fide Orthodoxa* (Bk. I, Cap. III (*P.G.*, 94, 796)), " The very continuity of the Creation, its preservation and government, teach us that there exists a deity who supports and preserves and always provides for His Universe," etc.

with accidents, you will find that substance subsists *per se* and accepts various and indeed contrary accidents. But on the accidents becoming non-existent or privated the substances do not become non-existent; on the contrary, accidents are imperfect and weak.

Similarly when we compare the substances of the world with their Creator and Fount of Origin, we cannot call these substances self-subsistent, but, like accidents, it may be said of them that they are transient and not subsisting. And if the Creator were assumed to withdraw His bounty from these substances for a moment, they would cease to be in the twinkling of an eye.

Here another abstruse question is explained. It has been proved that every composite substance is composed of primary matter and form.[1] Form is laid over primary matter by means of composition, and composition is itself a sort of movement, the mover of which is something other than its own essence, as we have already proved. It has also been proved in its place in theology (?) that form is never without primary matter, and primary matter is never found without form. So it seems that both depend on an author to bring them into existence at some time. And for them a composer is necessary who at the time of creation may join the two and create them jointly. It has already been explained that composition is movement, for which, by reason of the impossibility of infinite series (*tasalsul*), a mover is necessary which is not itself moved. Thus that first mover is singular and eternal.

Secondly, it should be understood that in addition to the primary matter, there is a secondary matter[2] which in bodies has the potentiality to different forms and is found in all physical forms and bodies. And nature embraces and encompasses that second matter. Nature is a God-given power which pervades all bodies and prompts them to obtain perfection. And because impotence and weariness can never in any case be joined to nature, because the bounty of the abstract divine power keeps reaching it always, therefore bodies are in continual motion and are continually engaged in the perfecting of their imperfection. This second matter is body itself.

[1] For the Aristotelian theory see *Physics*, i. 7. Cf. *Metaph.* Z, 3, 1029a, 1–3; Z, 10, 1035a, 2; H, 1, 1042a, 26 ff.; λ, 3, 1070a, 9 ff.; λ, 4, 1070b, 13–14. The division of substance is into four kinds: *al hayūli*—ἡυῦ λη, *ṣūra*—form, *jism*—body, *al ʻaql ul mufāriq*—separate intelligence, according to Al Ghazzālī in *Maqāsid ul Falāsifa* (ii. 82). With regard to matter and form Al Ghazzālī in *op. cit.*, ii. 85–86, says that there are three theories: (1) That body is composed of indivisible atoms—indivisible in thought and in actuality; (2) that body is not composite at all; and (3) that it is compounded of matter and form.

[2] The same term *hayūlī* is used. The mention of "second matter" is very interesting. In Al Fārābī it is quite clear that primary matter is considered to be incorporeal. There it is mere passivity. This second matter is corporeal matter or the form of corporeality, which is more primitive than the four elements. Reference should be made to the commentary of Simplicius on the *Physics*. He affirms the incorporeality of first matter. Corporeal form in Al Fārābī is length, breadth and depth.

CAP. X. THAT GOD MADE ALL THINGS BUT DID NOT MAKE THEM OF ANY OTHER THING [1]

People who are not accustomed or practised in the study of speculative matters think that nothing can be made without some other thing. This is because they see that one man is produced from another and one horse from another horse and similarly all animals, beasts or birds are produced from one another.[2] This idea spread to such an extent that Galen became an exponent of the view, but Alexander wrote a book devoted to the refutation of this theory and proved that contingent things which came into existence were not made from anything else. We will explain this subject briefly but clearly. The reality of change and alteration, death and life, mortality and immortality (disappearance and survival), which come and go in all created things in the universe, is simply that their form goes on altering and the matter which is the subject and suppositum of them does not change at all. For the philosophers have clearly explained that in bodies form is subordinate to a positive thing which is not mutable (presumably "in itself" *Trans.*) and which keeps assuming one form after another.[3] Thus all shapes and material forms (*ṣuwar hayūlānī*) are contained (*ḥulūl*) in bodies or found in them and the form [4] which is the bearer (*ḥāmil*) of those forms keeps on changing its condition (*kayfīya*) and its form. That body itself, which should be called the second matter, does not change.

Now consider that for the body which has changed from one form and adopted another, there are three possibilities: Firstly, the first form may survive in the body and it adopts a second form; secondly, that prior form may change into another body; thirdly, the prior form may completely disappear and become non-existent. The first possibility cannot be, because diverse forms and mutually contrary shapes cannot be gathered together in a single body. The second possibility cannot be correct by the following argument: Change of place is in bodies, and forms are accidents. Their change of place and

[1] It is interesting to find Ibn Miskawaih committed to the doctrine of creation *ex nihilo* in conjunction with his emanational theories. We may note here that the *ex nihilo nihil fit* principle, which is Aristotelian, does not necessitate anything eternal and external to the Divine Creator from which creation should take place.

[2] Heraclitus was one of the early philosophers who considered that matter was organically living and self-producing and it is hard to think that Galen could have done anything more than emphasize natural production which is in no way contrary to *creatio ex nihilo*.

[3] Here we have second matter again. With this should be compared what Ibn Sīnā says in *An Najāt*, viz., that second matter is not mutable but the form changes. Cf. Al Ghazzālī: *Maqāsid ul Falāsifa*, iii. 239.

[4] It has to be remembered that this second matter is corporeal form, i.e., the first form which matter assumes. "Assumes new forms" is rather loose. It implies an activity of the *suppositum* in acquiring new forms, and such activity must be conceived as motion or change, whereas it is said that the *suppositum* is immutable. The whole is rather loosely expressed, and it may be that we have not the original clarity of Ibn Miskawaih in this passage.

alteration, like accidents, is by means of their substances and the bodies which support them. They cannot alter themselves. This doctrine has been proved in its proper place in divine philosophy and is not dealt with here for considerations of space.

Thus, perforce, the third possibility remains and thus, when a body adopts a new form, the prior form disappears, passing from a state of existence into a state of non-existence. And when in the first form there is admitted to be existence after non-existence, it must be admitted also in regard to the second form which is now joined (to the body) that it has just come into existence from non-existence, for it has already been shown to be false that the second form was previously in this body or that it was in some other body and transferred from that into this. Therefore it is proved that all created and mutable things, namely, forms and lines, and images and shapes, and all accidents and conditions, are not produced from something but come into existence from non-existence.

What the philosopher Galen says, to wit, that every existence is produced from another existence, is utterly mistaken and its falsity is obvious. For if God Most High had brought something into existence from something already existing, there would be no meaning in beginning (*ibdā'*), because the meaning of *ibdā'* is "creation of a thing not out of anything" (*ījād ush shay'i lā min shay'in*), otherwise creation *ex nihilo*; Galen's statement would involve the existence of something before the beginning.

In connection with this theory, if we carefully consider those matters which are most near to our mind, i.e., things pertaining to the universe of bodies, then what we aim at will be more easily proved, namely, that everything has come into existence from non-existence and that things were previously not existing.

The illustration of this is that every animal is produced from what is not living. Animals are produced from semen and semen leaves its original form and successively adopting various forms becomes animal. In the same manner semen is produced from blood, blood from food, food from plants, plants from elements, elements from simple elements, and simple elements from primary matter and form. That is to say, this semen was formerly in these forms. And because primary matter and form were the first existences and are never found separate from one another, their dissolution or disseverance (*inḥilāl*) is not possible in the case of any existing thing. But perforce it has to be admitted that these came into existence from non-existence. In this way it is proved that the final terms of the dissolution of every body is non-existence. And this is what we had to prove.[1]

[1] Cf. Arist.: *Metaph.*, 1072b, 30 ff. In this chapter Miskawaih faces the problem of emanationism *versus* creationism. His doctrine is throughout emanational, but he seems conscious of difficulties, though he can hardly be said to have faced them

PART II. THE SOUL AND ITS STATES

CAP. I. ON THE EXISTENCE OF THE SOUL AND THAT THE SOUL IS NEITHER BODY NOR ACCIDENT

To discover the truth concerning the soul, what its quiddity and what sort of existence it has, and whether after separation from the body it survives or not, and if it survives in what manner is an exceedingly difficult task. And because our primary aim and the scriptural creed, i.e., judgment and the hereafter, and other religious doctrines, cannot possibly be established without proof that the Soul exists, and that it is manifestly not a body, nor an accident, nor a disposition (*mizāj*) but a substance subsisting *per se* and free from death and mortality, it is necessary for this subject to be discussed.

It is plain that a body can accept a form when it leaves its former form and is entirely separated from it, e.g., silver can take the form of a ring when it completely leaves the form of a button, or a seal can be impressed on wax when the previous impression has been completely obliterated from it. This is the case with all bodies, and this is so obvious that it does not seem necessary to give any special proof of it. Therefore when we see something with which it is not the case as explained of bodies, but which takes diverse and manifold forms even while the previous form has not disappeared or become erased from it, then it must be admitted that this thing cannot be a body.[1]

adequately, e.g., " From one only one can proceed " is enunciated as a first principle, then an account of manifold effects is interpreted as accidental and by mediation, and lastly, the causal activity of the first cause is implied in all the causes, even if it is not explicitly stated. What then becomes of the (numerical) unity of the causal activity or effect, if the first cause is effective in all secondary causes ?

How an immaterial, simple and immutable being can be a Creator is a problem which has not been solved. It can, in some relations, be expressed as the problem of the One and the Many. It can lead a philosopher like Spinoza to deny creation altogether.

The God who is Creator must possess infinite potencies and not one potency. The oneness of God may be the focussing of all potencies in one point. But a God conceived to be with only one potency would inevitably point to pantheism. The world of multiplicity would be but seeming, and would have no real existence ; and the manifold being denied, we should have to deny the validity of every thought which was based upon the hypothesis of the manifold.

[1] Cf. Arist. : *De Anima*, iii. 4, 429a, 27 ff. " It was a good idea to call the soul the place of forms, though this description holds good only for the intellectual soul." This is still further amplified in iii. 8, 431b, 27 ff. " Within the soul the faculties of knowledge and sensation are potentially these objects, the one what is knowable and the other what is sensible. They must be either the things themselves or their forms. The former alternative is, of course, not possible. It is not the stone which is present in the soul but its form. It follows that the soul is analogous to the hand ; for as the hand is the tool of tools, so the mind is the form of forms, and sense the form of sensibles." Cf. also Proclus : *Elements of Theology*, Prop. 195. " Every soul is all things, the sensibles after the manner of an exemplar and the intelligibles after the manner of a similitude. . . . It possesses as images the intelligible principles and has received their forms."

The incorporeality of the soul is derived from Aristotelian and Neoplatonist sources and is significant. Orthodox Islam has not yet made up its mind as to whether the

And when it is learned that its condition is such that the more forms it takes, the more its power to accept forms increases, until there is no end to its potentiality and power, then our conviction is strengthened that this is not a body. This is exactly the case with the perceiving soul, which when it perceives some matter and has well grasped what is perceived and known, then the power of knowing other things comes to it without the first perception being lost, and this to such a degree that the more it obtains the multifarious forms of what is intellectually conceived, the more this power of perception increases, so that in the end it takes whatever intellectual conceptions and ideas are offered to it. And the interesting thing is that far from the former conceptions disappearing, the power of understanding continues to grow more powerful.

Again it is conceded and quite obvious that man is distinguished from all other creatures in the world by this very power of understanding.[1] Otherwise in form and shape, in body and strength, there is no reason for this superiority. For when it is said that a certain person is superior in humanity to such and such a person, no one means that he is goodly in face and form, but that in him the power of intellect is greater, and so it is said that he has a high degree of humanity. This human quality is sometimes called the rational soul (*nafs nāṭiqa*), sometimes the intellectual power, sometimes the discerning power, and many other (names) which may be used at will.

We advance another argument for the soul not being a body.[2] All the members, external and internal, small and great, of all animals (of whom man is one) are made for a purpose, and each member is the instrument for such special purpose as cannot be achieved except by means of such an instrument. So when all the members are reckoned to be instruments, it is then necessary that there should be someone to use them, e.g., the carpenter and the builder and others use tools. If any one should think that one member uses another member, this would be quite unreasonable, for that member proposed as the user

soul is incorporeal or not (cf. Levonian : *Studies in the Relationship of Islam and Christianity*, Cap. IV).

Proclus states categorically that " every soul is an incorporeal substance and separable from body ". *El. Theol.*, Prop. 186. John of Damascus maintains the antithesis of body and soul in *De Fide Orth.*, Bk. II, Cap. XII (*P.G.*, 94, 924). " The soul is a living essence, simple, incorporeal, invisible in its proper nature to bodily eyes, immortal, reasoning and intelligent, formless, making use of an organized body, being the source of its powers of life, growth, sensation and generation."

[1] *De Fide Orthod.*, Bk. II, Cap. XII (*P.G.*, 94, 925 f.). " The bond of union between man and inanimate things is the body, . . . and the bond between man and plants consists, in addition to these things, in their power of nourishment, growth and seeding. Finally, above and beyond these connections, man is related to irrational animals by appetite. . . . Lastly, man's reason unites him to incorporeal and intelligent natures." See also Arist. *De Anima*, ii. 2, 414a, 17 ff. " The body cannot be the actuality of the soul. . . . The soul cannot be without a body, while it cannot be a body."

[2] Arist. : *De Anima*, ii. 4, 415b, 18. " All natural bodies are organs of the soul." *Ibid.*, i. 3, 407b, 25. " Each art must use its tools, each soul its body."

is itself the instrument in some work or a part of some member. And it has been conceded that all members are capable of being used in the way of tools. So it is certain that the one who employs them all must be distinct from them. Thus since the user is someone other and is not a part, it is certain that it cannot be body so that it may perfect acts by body. And it is certain also that it will not serve instead of body and will not comprise bodily instrument (i.e., will not be the place of bodily instruments). Because, by reason of its not being a body, it has no need of place.[1] It will also use equally at one time all those instruments which have been made for diverse purposes and will fulfil those purposes without any error or infirmity, so that by all the instruments a set purpose may be achieved. It is clear that all the attributes mentioned above cannot be qualities of body and all this work cannot be accomplished by bodies. Thus it is proved that the user of all these members and instruments must be some other thing different from body and in which the aforementioned qualities are found. This we call soul.

The point that the rational soul is not an accident or disposition will be explained when the difference between reason and sense is discussed. Here simply one argument is stated.

Disposition and all accidents found in body are all subordinate to body, and that which is subordinate to anything is of an inferior degree and cannot exist with the existence of that to which it is subordinate. So how can the inferior exact service from that to which it is inferior? How can it rule it as a master or lord or as the goldsmith uses his tools? And we have already explained that the soul exacts service from the body and the members of the body. Therefore it cannot be an accident or a disposition.

CAP. II. THE SOUL PERCEIVES ALL EXISTING THINGS WHETHER THEY ARE HIDDEN OR PRESENT, INTELLECTUALLY CONCEIVED OR SENSED [2]

It is clear that all existences are either compound or simple, and we see that the soul perceives all the species and individuals of composite things and the totality of simple things. Whether these are the result of the analysis of composite things or are altogether apart from such, none of them can escape the perception of the soul.

Simple things are of two sorts, material and immaterial (*hayūlānī* and *ghayr hayūlānī*). The latter are the intelligibles (*ma'qūlāt*) which exist without matter and enter the mind without reference to matter, as for instance, all universal notions (*mafhūmāt kullīya*) and intel-

[1] Cf. *De Anima*, i. 3, 406a, 16 f. "The soul has no place because it is self-moved." It has no "where" except in the divine mind. Cf. Dante: *Paradiso*, Cant. xxvii. 109 f.

[2] *De Anima*, iii. 8, 431b, 20 ff.

lectual forms (*ṣuwar dhihnīya*). And the former which proximate to matter and substance and which the phantasy apprehends (or which are presented to the mind) in the form of particulars, as in the science of mathematics the learned discuss point, line, surface and mathematical body, i.e., the three dimensions without matter, and conceived as they exist in themselves, and likewise all those things which are subordinate to body, i.e., motion, time, place and shape—in short, all conceivable things never found apart from body, it assumes to be separate from matter ; and by its phantasy (*wahm*) it sometimes thinks of them as simple and sometimes as composite, until the power of imagining them so increases, that it comes to think of the forms which it conceives in its phantasy as distinct from matter and body, to be actually existing (i.e. outside the mind, *fi'l khārij*) and considers that they have some reality by their essence outside matter and substratum. By reason of this foolish perplexity it cannot distinguish those abstracted forms from intelligibles, but comes to consider them all as intelligibles. Now it is quite clear that all perceptions are of the soul, and that it perceives composite things, and analysing them, extracts the simple elements. Then it causes these simple elements to reach the phantasy, proceeding to separate some of them from matter and substratum (i.e., from their subject) and arrange them variously. Sometimes there is some reality in actual existence (externally) corresponding to these arrangements, as for instance, when a man may form a correct idea of the form and character of a man of a foreign country whom he has not seen, etc. Or it may be that there is no reality in fact corresponding to those compositions, as for example, the fancy of the 'Anqā' (phœnix), or a flying man, or some person imagined outside the universe, or an animal with the head of an elephant and the body of a camel and the like. It is clear that outside the imagination there is nothing existing like these anywhere.[1] These are examples of the simple elements (or constituents—*basā'iṭ*) material and immaterial, which the soul perceives.

Composites are also of two kinds : elements (*istiqṣāt* or *'anāṣir*) and things composed of elements. The latter are animals, plants and inorganic things. Furthermore, within these three there are different kinds of composition and disposition. And the individuals of these numerous species are innumerable, but the soul perceives them all.

Similarly with the elements, because they are four, therefore in respect to paucity or abundance, intensity or weakness, the conditions of their composition greatly vary. This variety is either because in some composite thing one element is most powerful of the four, or two are more powerful than the remaining two, or three more powerful than the fourth, or the four may be equal in power, but a certain one of them may be more suitable to the disposition of the body, i.e., the

[1] *De Anima*, iii. 6, 430a, 26 ff.

effect or power of the element which is suitable to the nature of the body will be felt more than the others.

In short, the perception of simple elements of all these kinds and their disposition is the work of the soul. Apparently the perception of the soul is by four methods and four instruments, so that each instrument is set apart for each element.[1] And because intensity and weakness, paucity and abundance of elements are natural to bodies, the soul can by each instrument perceive the various conditions of each element. We wish therefore in the following section to discuss sufficiently yet briefly whether the soul perceives all things by one power or by several, and if by one power then in what form?

CAP. III. HOW DOES THE SOUL PERCEIVE THE VARIOUS PERCEPTIONS?

We have already shown that the soul has no parts, for partition and division are in the body, and it has been proved that the soul is not a body. Therefore the perception of the soul cannot be by means of parts. It is also clear that there cannot be as many perceivers as there are compounds. Because in respect to all compounds which are perceived there seems to be one thing which judges and discriminates. We see that there is one thing in man which judges whether a certain thing is small or large and in like manner judges in the case of colours and shapes, flavours and scents. Likewise, if several things are equal to others it judges them to be equal. If then by supposition the perceivers were various, the judgment of one perceiver on the thing perceived would not be correct according to another perceiver.[2] In regard to this matter, some people think that the soul is one but that it has manifold and various perceptions by means of several powers and various methods.[3]

Here follows the discussion of this matter. Some philosophers, just as they have thought of all the things of this existing universe as of two kinds, composite and simple, have similarly when they have looked at the instruments of perception found some to be simple and some composite. So they have judged that the power of perception and the instruments of perception which are composite perceive what is composite and those which are simple perceive simple things. They have explained this idea as follows: We have found some perceiving things to be composite and observe that they perceive composite things, as for instance, the five senses which perceive composite things, e.g., the eye, because it is composed of the power of sight (which

[1] *De Sensu*, ii. 438b.

[2] If there were one perception for length and one for colour, one would declare a thing to be, say, white and the other short and there would be no co-ordination in perception.

[3] The unity of the self. With this statement should be compared the series of questions which Aristotle puts with regard to whether it is with the whole soul that we think, perceive, move ourselves, act or are acted upon, in *De Anima*, i. 5, 411b.

is found in the organs and layers of the eye; and the power of sight cannot be perfect till all the layers of the eye are intact) perceives compositions of elements along with various dispositions. And when we study this we find that some perceivers are simple and that they perceive simple objects of perception, as for instance, the ideas and judgment of all things are obtained by thought, and it is plain that as thought is simple so these ideas and perceptions are simple. It would therefore seem that the simple perceives the simple and that it is also proved that the simple and the composite perceive what corresponds to each severally. From this argument some people hold that the simple perceives the simple and the composite the composite. But Aristotle [1] argues in this place and says that the rational soul has one power and by that power it perceives composite material things and simple immaterial things. For if the rational soul perceives sensibles by one power and intelligibles by another power, then when the senses make a mistake, how can the judgment of the reason correct the mistakes of sense?—even as one sense could not correct the mistakes of another sense. It is clear that the sense often makes mistakes in perceiving. For instance, the eye sees a big thing small from a distance, e.g., the sun appears as big as a mirror with a diameter about a span, although it is a world-illuminating globe, one hundred and sixty times bigger than the earth. Likewise, if one is moving seated in a boat, the things on the banks appear to be moving along whether they are moved or not. And under water little things appear big, and a straight stick crooked, and those shapes between which mists intervene appear of different shapes. Like the mistakes of the eye, so taste also makes mistakes, and to the sick person of a bilious disposition, sweet things taste sour, etc.

In short, the errors of sense are numerous,[2] but when the sense makes a mistake, the rational soul understands that what it perceives is not actually so. Whereupon it turns its perceptions to the real actuality and corrects the mistake. So it has been proved that if the rational soul did not perceive the intelligible and the sensible by one and the same power, then how would it know the difference between fact and not fact, between truth and error? And how could it mingle sensibles and intelligibles to form one judgment? [3]

[1] *De Anima*, iii. 3, 427a, 27 to 429a, 8.

[2] Aristotle says that sensation is always true (*Metaph.*, 1010b), but not everything that appears is true, e.g., objects at a distance.

[3] Cf. *De Somniis*, iii. 461b, 5 ff. "In every case an appearance presents itself, but what appears does not in every case seem real, unless when the deciding faculty is inhibited or does not move with its proper motion." Also 461b, 25 ff. "When the person was actually perceiving, his controlling and judging sensory faculty did not call it Koriskos (the person who appears in a dream) but prompted by this (i.e., the judging faculty) called the genuine person Koriskos."

Note also *De Anima*, ii. 5, 417b, 20 ff. "The objects which excite the sensory powers to activity, that which is seen, that which is heard, etc., are outside. The ground of this difference is that what actual sensation apprehends is individuals, while what knowledge apprehends is universals, and these are in a sense *within* the soul."

Now we will explain this with greater clearness. The rational soul perceives intelligibles by one method and sensibles by another. That is, the power of perception is one but the mode varies. For when the soul is in quest of intelligibles and wishes to perceive them, it reverts [1] to its own essence which is separated and pure from matter, and casts about as though in search of something near to itself.

And when it purposes to perceive sensibles, then it does not keep its connection with its essence but, turning its attention from its essence as though in search of something outside, seeks for some instrument which may assist it in this task and enable it to reach the object of its quest. If it finds the instrument appropriate, then it uses it and sensibly perceives external things and receives their particular forms into phantasy. And if the soul does not obtain an instrument of perception, it cannot perceive. For instance, a man born blind, because he has no instrument to perceive colours, his soul in itself has no power to perceive them. And because there has been no perception of them from outside, in the storehouse of the imagination of the blind there are no forms of colour. But this is not the case with intelligibles.[2]

The point that the soul at the time of its apprehension of intelligibles returns to its own essence ought to be fixed in the mind thus: man when he wishes to obtain some new opinion or is considering the result or consequence of something, or when he wishes to learn some difficult and abstruse matter of knowledge, puts all sensibles away from him and strives to keep the sense dormant long enough so as not to interfere with the work in hand. At that time the soul gathers all its powers and becomes intent on its own essence and obtains that sort of exhilaration and delight which a person has who reverts to his own essence. At that time with complete cheerfulness of heart he perceives the thing he sought, and he obtains more or less success in this task by that adaptation or fitness, in proportion to his pleasure and his being emptied of phantasy (for it is in the phantasy that the forms of the sensibles reside). The reason for this is that the phantasy prevents the reversion of the soul to its own essence and will not let it turn its attention towards the storehouse of intelligibles. For to the Primary Intelligence all the things of the universe are present and therefore for the quest of them there is in the soul a movement which keeps it always in motion.

Here the doubt may be mooted that when all intelligibles are present

[1] The term "reversion" recalls Proclus (*vide El. Theol.*, Propp. 81–83 and 17, etc.). Here in the act of intellection the soul reverts upon itself in contradistinction to its apprehension of sensibles when the soul is directed to that which is outside itself.

[2] The soul faces in two ways or has a duality in its acts. Cf. *Enneads*, IV, viii. 5. "Every soul has something of the lower for the purposes of the body and something of the higher for the purposes of the Divine Intellect." Cf. also *Enneads*, V, ii. 1. "The soul as looking to the Divine Order is perfect; going outside of itself in a movement which is strange to its essence, it begets an image which is sensitive and vegetative nature."

to the Reason then because of the multiplicity of the intelligibles the reason must also be multiple.[1] But such a doubt is sheer ignorance, because reason is a simple thing and the intelligibles are other, and so their presence and perception cannot entail the multiplicity of the intellect. So the soul when it wishes to perceive intelligibles, moves to its perfection and turns its attention to reason (in which all the intelligibles are present) in order that it may obtain all matters of knowledge and become perfect, and form complete unity with the intellect. This movement of the soul is called vision and thought. From what has been said it appears that the soul perceives both intelligibles and sensibles, and the only difference is in the mode of apprehension. And it is the view of Aristotle that the rational soul perceives simple elements by itself (of its own essence) and composites by means of the five senses.

People are in error in thinking that only five senses perceive things sensed and particulars, and that the soul does not perceive them but only perceives universals. The fact is that the rational soul perceives all particulars and universals by one power, although the method of perception is different. Aristotle illustrates this by saying that the rational soul perceives simple intelligibles by a straight line, i.e., directly, and without a medium, and composite sensibles by a crooked line,[2] i.e., by the medium of the senses. The Philosopher Themistius (?)[3] has explained this subject in a most excellent fashion in his book of the soul, from which we will, God willing, recapitulate something later on.

CAP. IV. WHAT IS THE DIFFERENCE BETWEEN THE ASPECT OF REASON AND THE ASPECT OF SENSE ? AND WHAT IS COMMON TO THESE TWO AND IN WHAT DO THEY DIFFER ?

The rational soul's perception of intelligibles [4] is called rational conception or intellection (*taʿaqqul*) and the perception of sensibles is called sensation (*iḥsās*). Common to both is a potentiality (*infiʿāl*), i.e., a passivity found in both,[5] to wit, when both of these are changed towards the object of their perception and obtaining it possess perfection, they have a sort of passivity and effect from what is perceived.

[1] *Enneads*, IV, ix. 3. Here Plotinus discusses how Unity and Multiplicity may exist together in the soul. The unified soul is seated in the Divine Intelligence and the divided soul is seated among bodies. Multiplicity of faculties does not destroy the essential unity of the soul.

[2] *De Anima*, iii. 4, 429b, 13 ff.

[3] Themistius' *Commentary on De Anima* ?

[4] *De Anima*, iii. 4, 429a, 13 ff. " If thinking is like perceiving it must be either a process in which the soul is acted upon by what is capable of being thought, or a process different from but analogous to that. The thinking part . . . must be potentially identical with its object without being the object. Mind must be related to what is thinkable as sense is to what is sensible."

[5] Cf. the νοῦς παθητικός of Aristotle.

For intellect and sense, until they perceive something, cannot be called reason and sense except potentially, and when they perceive then reason potential becomes reason actual and sense potential becomes sense actual.[1] For this reason we have said that the passivity and effect which falls on reason and sense by perception is their perfection, because this passivity brings their potentiality and power into existence and act (*fi'līya*). In this universe some passive things become corrupted by passivity. Thus water, when it is passive and affected by heat, neither remains itself nor does its coolness remain; both pass away and decay. But since we saw that reason and sense obtain their perfection by passivity, it is learned that the soul becomes perfect by these passivities.

We have explained that the soul by its potentiality to perception brings its power and potency into act. The proof of this is that the soul is called *hayūlānī*, i.e., pertaining to matter.[2] Just as primary matter before it adopts certain forms is empty, so the soul pictures intelligibles and sensibles and in this case when formerly it had not perceived them it was empty of them. Nevertheless it must not be assumed that the soul cannot perceive and picture all things simultaneously but pictures one particular at one time and another at another time. For if the soul had not something positive which was able to accept divers forms and to be susceptible to change from one condition to another, then how could it perceive various forms? An illustration of this is when Zayd at first does not know that the universe was created but afterwards acquires such knowledge. So if Zayd had no potentiality and power to know this, how could he acquire the knowledge? For plants and inorganic substances, etc., which have not this capacity to learn cannot perceive. Another illustration of this is the power of sight which perceives all visible objects and just as it apprehends all colours by being subject to an alteration in relation to them, or just as it receives all visible things equally by a single apprehension—because it has a uniform and single relation towards all visible things, and neither sees colours more or less than they actually occur nor sees one colour more or less than another—such is exactly the case with the soul, which uniformly perceives or apprehends all intelligibles, neither less nor more, nor contrary to fact, because its relation to all intelligibles is uniform. And as the power of sight before the apprehension of a visible thing is not identified with it but separate and apart from it, so too the soul before the apprehension

[1] *De Anima*, iii. 4, 429b, 30 ff. "The mind is in a sense potentially whatever is thinkable though actually it is nothing till it has thought."

[2] Cf. *De Anima*, ii. 2, 414a, 14–26. Aristotle does not expressly say that the soul is analogous to ὕλη. In 412a, 20 f., he even speaks of soul as substance in the sense of the form of a natural body having life in it potentially. But while it is form of natural body, in its capacity for receiving the forms of intelligibles and sensibles it is analogous to ὕλη.

of intelligibles has no intellection or perception of anything but negates them all.[1]

The condition of intellect and sense in respect to perception is like matter, for as primary matter has the capacity to receive all forms, but before the reception of forms has itself no form in it but negates all forms, and neither does it have a potentiality to a particular form, for it receives all forms equally by a single acceptance, in the same way sight, for instance, before receiving an object of sight is not a seeing thing but is the negator of all visible objects ; and similarly the soul before receiving intelligibles is not "intellected" (*shay' ma'qūl*) but negates all intelligibles.

In detail, the eye is appointed for the reception of all colours and therefore is the negator of every colour,[2] i.e., in it there is no colour, because if there were any special colour in it, it would only with difficulty receive a colour which was contrary to the colour it had, and even if it did receive it, it would not be able perfectly to perceive the contrary colour on account of its own special colour.

So also matter, since it is the substratum of all forms, has no special form of its own, but with the same kind of potentiality to all forms receives them equally one after the other, and its relation with them all is uniform and not more or less with any one of them. This then is the condition of primary matter which is the potential material of all things. For when second matter, i.e., elements before the reception of forms, is the negator of forms, primary matter which is the receptacle of all the forms, must be so in the best possible way, and is necessarily before the reception of them the negator of all forms.

This is exactly the case with all the external senses in respect to the perception of sensibles, and this is the case with the human soul or intellect's reception of the intelligibles. For if to the human intellect there were some particular form pertaining, how could it receive any other ? And if it did it would receive the form and reality suitable and agreeable to it, easily and in profusion, but anything contrary to it only with trouble and rarely, although it is clear that this is not so, for the rational soul is the negator of every form and perceives every intelligible uniformly.[3] On this account we have said that the soul is

[1] *De Anima*, iii. 4, 429a, 18 ff. "Therefore since everything is a possible object of thought, mind in order, as Anaxagoras says, to dominate, i.e., to know, must be pure from all admixture ; for the co-presence of what is alien to its nature is a hindrance and a block : It follows that it, too, like the sensitive part, can have no nature of its own, other than that of having a certain capacity."

[2] *De Anima*, ii. 7, 418b, 27 ff. "What is capable of taking on colour is what in itself is colourless, as what can take on sound is what is soundless."

[3] Ibn Miskawaih dwells on this notion of the *tabula rasa* as if it were novel to his readers as probably it was.

Cf. *De Anima*, iii. 4, 429a, 10 ff., for comparison of the intellective and sensitive in the soul.

simple,[1] for that is called composite which is compounded of matter or *subjectum* (*mawḍū'*) and form. And it has already been explained that the soul before intellection is the negator of all forms and therefore simple.

From this it is also proved that the soul is neither body nor accident, for if it had been body it would have been composite and would have possessed a particular form, whereas we have proved its composition to be false, and if it had been an accident it would have been with a material form, and would come under one of the nine *predicamenta* (*maqūlāt*) ; but we have already refuted this.

So far those matters have been mentioned which are common to intellect and sense. Now those matters will be explained in which there is a difference between intellect and sense.

It is the manner of sense that when the object of sense occurs powerfully the perception of it is weakened or by perceiving it weakness and fatigue occur. E.g., the eye cannot see intense light or a bright thing beyond its endurance, and if it does look at it, it becomes dazzled and its sight is injured. Or the power of hearing is weakened and fatigued by listening to terrific noises beyond its power. The case is the same with every sense. But this is not the condition of the human intellect, for the more it perceives powerful intelligibles in profusion and thinks about and studies forms abstracted from matter, the more perfect it is and the more it gains in power and acuteness of apprehension. And the more its power increases the more powerful it becomes in the perception of other intelligibles.

Another point in which the two are different and distinct is that sense, when it perceives any powerful sensible and then turns to the weak sensibles, is unable to perceive. Thus, for instance, the eye when it turns away after looking at the sun cannot see anything else, in contrast to reason which, after perceiving some powerful intelligible, does not become defective and weak but grows powerful and keen for further perception.[2]

The reason for this is that a sense is not separated from a body, and its perception is by means of a passive body which cannot overcome powerful things, and thus when the effect of a powerful sensible remains in it, it prevents the perception of other objects of sense.[3] But this is not the case with the intellect, because it is separate from the body

[1] That the incorporeal is simple is stated by Proclus (*El. Theol.*, Prop. 80, p. lxxviii, lines 14–15—Creuzer and Moser). He declares in Prop. 197 that the soul is immaterial and has no parts. Setting aside quantitative parts, Aristotle speaks of " parts of soul," *vide Metaph.*, vi. 10, 1035b, 18 and 1036a, 24. Cf. also *De Anima*, I, i. 402b, 1–10. The question of whether the soul is divisible is discussed. See *De Anima*, i. 5, 411a, 23 to 411b, 30, and also 413b, 10 ff. and 432a, 20 ff. *op. cit.* The Neoplatonist view is that the soul is ἀμερής.

[2] Cf. *De Anima*, iii. 4, 429a, 29 ff.

[3] *De Anima*, iii. 4, 429b, 3 ff. " The reason is that while the faculty of sensation is dependent on the body, mind is separable from it."

and survives it, as we will shortly prove, and its perception or apprehension is not by means of bodily instruments. Therefore, after the perception of powerful things it can easily perceive weak things.

In this place it has also been proved that the soul is not a material form because if it had been so, the qualities of bodily things would be found in it, whereas from our former statement the distinctness of soul from corporeality has been proved. One argument for the soul not being a material form is that it perceives by means of the intellect those things which are devoid of matter.[1] E.g., reason conceives its own essence and apprehends self-evident propositions such as that two is the half of four, etc., and it knows that between affirmation and negation there is no middle term. It forms an idea of the First Maker, and understands that outside the spheres is neither a vacuum nor a plenum, and it perceives many such things of which not one is derived from sense, because the matters mentioned are not material, neither are they found in any matter.

And the intellect in its particular perceptions is sufficient *per se* and does not depend on any instrument. The argument for this is that a person takes the aid of an instrument because that instrument can help in some task and serves his purposes in the manner required.

And if there is anything which hinders the work of that person or which, instead of helping, prevents him in his acts, and on account of which his acts are deficient or imperfect, then he does not make such a thing his instrument and is not likely to take aid from it. This is exactly the case with the rational soul. That thing which is assumed to be an instrument for it must be a hindrance and obstacle in its real task, because, as we have already explained, at the time of the apprehension of sensibles the soul reverts to its own essence and holding sense in abeyance shrinks towards itself, and by such attention can perceive intelligibles correctly. And so far as there is any participation of the instruments and senses, so far its knowledge remains imperfect. Therefore nothing can be made its instrument and neither can the soul be body or accident or material form.[2]

One difference between reason and sense is this: it is not with the reason as it is with the sense that when bodily power is stronger it is strong, and as soon as the body gets weak it becomes weak. It is plain that if reason were found in body in this fashion as in a material form, then it would certainly become weak with the weakening of the body. In confirmation of this we quote the statement of Aristotle[3]: It seems that the intellect is a substance which is found in some *body* but is not subject to corruption, for if so, the weakness and maturity of old age would certainly have its effect upon it as it does upon the

[1] Cf. *De Anima*, iii. 4, 429b, 9–430a, 9.
[2] Cf. *De Anima*, iii. 4, 429a, 26.
[3] *De Anima*, i. 4, 408b, 17 ff. Aristotle does not say "body" but "soul".

senses. For in old age a man is not able to see as in youth but in his reason there is no failure. Therefore by old age the soul does not become passive, although the state of old age may be likened to a state of intoxication or sickness. If the thought of the human soul is vitiated it is only because of something else which comes and corrupts it, otherwise in itself it remains rational and perceptive.

Abu'l Khayr in his commentary[1] says that if the human intellect decayed by the corruption of the body, then it would follow that in old age, by reason of the weakness of the body, it would become weak, although this is not so. Therefore it appears that the intellect is not corruptible and the state of the soul in old age is like intoxication and sickness. The meaning of this is that just as the intellect and discernment of the intoxicated and sleeping become less or do not exist at all, this is not the failure of the intellect but of its instruments of perception which by reason of these accidents do not work. The accidental vapours hinder perception. In the same way in the days of old age the deficiency which is accidental to intellect is not because of the weakness of the substance of the intellect but is because in the body there no longer remains the capacity for the act of the intellect. Here we quote a saying of Aristotle. It has to do with the following chapter and will be fully explained there. The Philosopher writes in the second part of his book that "from considering the intellect and the soul, it seems that both are not of the same genus but the soul is one thing and the intellect another. And it is possible that the soul may become separate from the intellect as, e.g., the eternal (*qadīm*) from that which has a beginning (*ḥādith*), or as some eternal and everlasting (*azalī wa abadī*) thing becomes separate from what is contingent and corruptible".[2]

But it is obvious that all parts of the soul are not separate as some philosophers have thought.

CAP. V. THE SOUL IS A LIVING AND ENDURING SUBSTANCE WHICH IS NOT SUBJECT TO DEATH AND MORTALITY. AND IT IS ALSO EXPLAINED THAT THE SOUL IS NOT IDENTICAL WITH LIFE BUT BESTOWS LIFE ON ALL LIVING THINGS [3]

The fact that the soul is not life has been proved from our foregoing explanations, because if the soul were life then it would be subsisting (as an accident) by a living being, which would be its subject (*mawḍūʿ*) or suppositum. And in this case it would have to be a material form, which, because it is a relative thing, would depend on its subject (the living body). Whereas we have shown that the soul is not a material

[1] The reference is in all probability to a commentary on *De Anima* by Abu'l Khayr ul Ḥasan b. ul Khammār (b. 942). See *Fihrist* of Ibn Nadīm, p. 370.

[2] *De Anima*, ii. 2, 413b, 24 ff.

[3] Cf. Proclus : *El. Theol.*, Prop. 186 and *De Anima*, ii. 2, 414a, 12.

form. Therefore the soul is not identical with life. Another argument is that the rational soul, by reason of its superiority, does not care for the delights and desires of the body and considers them mean and hinders the acquisition of them. Although it is a universal rule that nothing can oppose or obstruct that thing on which its subsistence and affirmation depends, but rather seeks it, because in the prevention of the things which constitute its essence (i.e., its *muqawwimāt*) its own corruptibility and invalidation are conceived, and in the acquirement and quest of what establishes its essence, its subsistence and its increase are in view. Thus if the soul were exactly life of the body then why should it belittle and forbid the delights and desires of the body by which the body subsists and is established ?

The third argument is that the things which are found in the body as material form and life are all subordinate to the body and those things which are subordinate to the body are under it, whereas we see and know that the soul orders the body and rules it as a lord or chief. Therefore the soul cannot be in the body as material form.[1] And therefore also the soul is not life but produces life in the body. And because the life of the body is by reason of the soul [2] it must be that the life is first for the soul and afterwards for the body. All this proves that the soul is not the form of life. We have already explained that many acts are such that they are peculiar and proper to the soul, and are separate and distinct from the body. Therefore that thing the proper acts of which are distinct from the body will certainly be itself distinct from the body, because it can have no need of the body. For this separation and dependence we have advanced the statement of the Philosopher and applied it to argument also, that the soul does not get power by the strengthening of the body and does not become weak by the weakening of the body.

The statement of the Philosopher Aristotle which we have quoted at the end of the last chapter, is his theory and the theory of many of the ancient philosophers about the parts of the soul. And by " parts of soul " is meant those modes and methods of perception which we have sufficiently explained in the third and fourth chapters. But these parts of the soul are not divisible like bodies. By these parts are meant the concupiscible soul and the irascible soul and the power of memory, etc.,[3] which all perish at the death of man. Because all these are material powers, their work is fulfilled by helping the bodily instruments, and their necessity to the soul is that the body should continue living for a long time.

The fact is that diverse acts are performed by the soul by means of diverse instruments. Therefore a name is given to each act relative

[1] Cf. *De Anima*, i. 5, 410a, 12 ff.
[2] *De Anima*, ii. 4, 415b, 7 ff.
[3] *De Anima*, i. 5, 411a, 26 ff.

to its instrument, because the particular act is always by means of one of those instruments. It should be understood thus: When the food and the blood, etc., dissolve by reason of the various motions of the body, to make up the deficiency and to ensure compensation, there are those desires from the liver from which ensue the quest for food and the urge to satisfaction. Likewise wrath and ire, which the living person has for the purpose of averting any harmful and oppugnant thing from his body, are produced from the heart and the procession of thought and reflection is by means of the parts of the brain. Thus these principal members, because they are the instruments of the soul and because by means of them the soul fulfils its purposed acts, the terminologists have devised the name "soul" for these instruments and have called them the concupiscible soul, the irascible soul and the like.[1]

But the fact is that that which makes use of these instruments namely, the rational soul, is far more honourable and eminent than all these, for it is the master and engineer and these instruments are like the tools of the machine. And because the ends and aims of these acts are the most perfect and honourable of all the purposes of wisdom, these instruments and the acts themselves are an argument for the consummate wisdom and perfect planning of their engineer.

For the rest, concerning the essence of the rational soul it has already been learned that for its proper act and essential motion it does not use any instrument, but all these instruments are injurious and a hindrance to its principal acts and essential motions, and connection with them keeps it from its principal task (i.e., holds it back from it) and this essential motion is the argument for the immortality of the soul.

We will hereinafter in some place deal with the motion of the soul in detail. Now we put forward the argument for the eternal survival of the rational soul, that it never perishes.[2] The argument is that the rational soul has a proper motion and that at the time of this motion it has no connection of any sort with bodily instruments, neither employs them. And so by reason of its being a fixed substance it does not decay with the decay of the body. And we have already explained that in the Arabic language the name for the separation of the soul from the body is death and they call every body dead when the soul is separated from it. Thus man is called dead when the

[1] The movement to pursue or avoid. Cf. *De Anima*, iii. 9, 432b, 20 ff. and *Nichomachean Ethics*, vi. 2, 1139a, 21 ff. We find the irascible and concupiscible powers frequently mentioned in the Pseudo-Aristotelian *Theology*, Cap. I and elsewhere. See also John of Damascus: *De Fide Orthod.*, II, xii (*P.G.*, 94, 928). "That which does not listen to or obey reason is the vital or pulsating faculty and the spermative or generating faculty and the vegetative or nutritive faculty; to this belong also the faculties of growth and bodily formation. For these are not under the dominion of the reason but of nature. That which listens to and obeys reason on the other hand, is divided into anger and desire."

[2] "Mind . . . this alone is immortal and eternal." *De Anima*, iii. 5, 430a, 23 ff.

rational soul is separated from him. It is the rule of the lexicographers that when they wish to describe the nature or quiddity of anything they set apart some word to signify that nature and when some other form appears, contrary to that state they devise another term. Thus for the soul's connection with the body they speak of "life" and the separation they call "death" just as there are various names for various other cases and conditions. Thus, when the original form of cloth is spoiled they call it "old", when the form of iron is spoiled they call it "rusty", and they call a fallen house "ruined". But we are bewildered and quite at a loss what name to apply to the soul when it becomes separate from the body and what term we are to devise corresponding to our use of "death" in reference to the body? [1] But if the state of the soul is similar to that of the body after the separation of the soul, then some other name should be used beside "death", e.g., annihilation or vanishing (*buṭlān*).

But we have already proved that the rational soul is neither body nor accident but a simple substance, and it has been proved in the science of Physics that a substance does not hold its contrary, and that which has no contrary is not subject to annihilation, and so the soul is not the suppositum of annihilation. Therefore its state of separation from the body cannot be called annihilation. And because the soul is not composite, it is not subject to dissolution (decomposition).

In the following chapter we will relate the statements of the ancient philosophers from which it will be learned that in addition to Aristotle, whose theory has been described, others also have held that the soul is immortal.

CAP. VI. THE THEORY OF THE ANCIENT PHILOSOPHERS AND THE ARGUMENTS BY WHICH THEY HAVE PROVED THAT THE SOUL DOES NOT DIE [2]

Plato has given three arguments for the immortality of the soul.

1. The first argument is that the soul bestows life on all those things in which life is to be found. And life must be essential to that which bestows life on all living things, i.e., its essence itself and its substance must entail life. And it is clear that that by the essentialities of which there is life cannot in any way admit the contrary of its essential quality. Therefore the soul cannot admit the contrary of life (i.e., death). The companions and disciples of Plato have described this argument in their books with great clarity. They have proved its propositions and arrangement to be correct, and with great force have all arrived at the correctness of its conclusion. When we have described the three arguments we will deal with some of them.

[1] "Set free from its present condition" says Aristotle: *De Anima*, iii. 5, 430a, 23.
[2] The argument for the immortality of the rational soul (*nafs nāṭiqa*) is the subject of the ninth chapter of Pseudo-Arist. *Theology*.

2. The second argument is that everything susceptible to corruption is so corrupted by reason of some badness in it. But there is no sort of badness and evil in the soul and so it cannot be corrupted. We should first, by way of preface describe the nature of badness and then it will be fitting to set forth this argument. Badness, i.e., to become imperfect or go bad, is akin to corruption and corruption is akin to non-existence and non-existence is akin to matter. Understand this in the following way: Wherever and in whatever things there is no matter, there can be no non-existence; and where there is no non-existence, there can be no corruption; and that thing which is not susceptible to corruption cannot be imperfect and in a state of badness. It appears that matter is the source of badness, and this matter is the fount of evil and corruption, vice and imperfection. It is from this that all corruption is produced.

The opposite of badness is goodness which approximates to immortality, and immortality is akin to existence which the Creator first created. This existence is pure good. No sort of evil or corruption or non-existence can adhere to it. In this real existence there is no sort of connection with any passivity or matter. And this existence is called First Intelligence.

In regard to this subject the account of good and evil is very long and we have perforce to content ourselves with this brevity. The one who has seen this discussion in the books of Plato and Galen or has read the book of Proclus on this particular subject will have complete familiarity with this account.

The soul is a form by which the body becomes perfect, but it is not material, and we have already related how the soul is not a material form which would be dependent on matter for its existence. Thus there is in the soul no sort of badness, and when there is no badness then there cannot be corruption, and if there is no corruption then how can there be non-existence? Thus the conclusion is that the rational soul is immortal. To abbreviate this statement and put it in the shape of formal proof, in the soul there is no badness, and that in which there is no badness is not corruptible, therefore the soul is not corruptible.[1]

[1] The second argument is more Neoplatonist than Platonist. The view that evil is non-existent and that the soul is all good is definitely Plotinian. The following references will elucidate this. *Enneads*, I, viii. 7: "Evil is from the ancient kind which we read is the underlying matter not yet brought to order by Ideal Form." Plotinus refers to *Timaeus* where the Father God addresses lesser divinities, saying: "Since you only possess derivative being, you are not immortals . . . but by my power you shall escape dissolution" (*Tim.*, 41A and B). The soul's immortality is often spoken of as being its disengagement from the body. In *Enneads*, I, viii. 8, Plotinus says: "Matter corrupts . . . the cause of evil is matter." And in I, viii. 10: "Evil in the soul is simple absence of good. If it is the denial of something which ought to be present or a denial of good by the soul, then the soul produces wickedness in itself by the act of its own nature and is empty of good, and although it is soul is without life. The soul if it has no life is soulless and the soul is not soul. But nay, the soul

3. The third argument is that the soul moves by an essential movement, and that thing which is moved *per se* (by its essence) cannot be corruptible, therefore the soul also is incorruptible.[1]

In substantiating the first proof we give the account of Proclus according to promise without abbreviation. It is a rule that when two things are mutually contrary and one of them proceeds from a certain power, then the other thing must also be contrary to that power. For instance, coldness is the contrary of heat and heat is produced by fire and so coldness is the contrary of fire also. According to this rule it follows that the rational soul (intellectual soul) is immortal and not susceptible to death because death is the contrary of life and life is essential to it.[2]

CAP. VII. AN ACCOUNT OF THE QUIDDITY OF THE SOUL, AND ITS LIFE, THAT LIFE WHICH IS THE PRESERVER OF THE SOUL AND BY REASON OF WHICH THE SOUL PERPETUALLY SURVIVES AND IS ETERNAL

When the famous philosophers saw that the soul bestows life on the body and confers all perfections on it, they came to hold that the soul was itself Life. But by this they did not mean that the soul was the form of life, because this was manifestly untrue and we have shown it to be untrue. But the meaning was that the soul brings life to the body. And because it is the purveyor of life to the body, it is itself primarily far more entitled to life and immortality. Therefore when the philosophers looked at the very essence of the rational soul in relation to the body, they came to hold that the soul itself bestows

has life by its own essence and therefore contains this denial of the good by itself. If the soul gives itself up to evil . . . it has adopted another nature namely, Evil, and as far as it is possible for the soul to die it is dead." Thus soul while it is soul is good and living. It is only by entertaining its contrary, which according to Miskawaih is impossible, that it can forfeit its immortality.

[1] The three lines of the Platonist argument are as follows: There are no absolutely new beginnings but simply alternations from one state to the opposite and this is the case with the cycles of the soul's apparent life and death, which latter cannot be in that case utter non-existence or annihilation. There seems an echo of this in the third argument which Miskawaih gives. Plato's second line of argument is the one familiarized for us in the *Confessions* of St. Augustine, namely, the memory of some previous existence's acquirement of truth. The last line of argument is similar to the first one given by Miskawaih. There is, however, not much emphasis on the soul's essential cognition or apprehension of the ideas which ranges it alongside those eternal verities. For the soul as the principle of life see *Phædrus*, 246B and the end of the *Phædo*. Proclus in his *Elements of Theology* says that every soul is self-animated (Prop. 189, cf. also Prop. 188). For the soul as self-moved see Proclus *op. cit.*, Prop. 20: " When there is soul present the body is in some sense self-moved . . . the body is naturally moved from without, whereas self-movement is of the essence of the soul." Also *Phædrus*, 246A and *Laws*, 895C–896C. Other clear statements on the subject are that the soul is indestructible and incorruptible, impossible to be dissevered from its substratum and indiscerptible (Proclus: *El. Theol.*, Prop. 187). Other references: *Republic*, 608–11, *Enneads*, IV, vii. (specially 9–12) and VI, iv. 16 (which deals with the point as to whether it is only the rational soul which is immortal).

[2] Not identified.

movement on its essence.[1] And Plato also said that the soul is itself motion: for in his book *The Laws* he wrote that the essence and substance of that thing which moves its essence is itself movement.[2]

It seems fitting here that we should cast a glance at the movement of the soul. We have already said that the soul is a substance but is not a body and not one of the six kinds of movement which we have previously described as fitting for this subtle substance. Now the motion which is fitting for the soul is circular motion,[3] i.e., we never find in any circumstances that the soul is without this motion. The soul continues always in this motion and because it is not bodily motion therefore it is not movement in place and it is also not outside the essence of the soul. For this reason Plato said that the substance of the soul, i.e., its essence, is motion. And this motion is the life of the soul. And because motion is an essential thing for it, therefore life also is essential for it. Therefore that person who has fully understood these three points namely, that motion is an essential thing for the soul, that that motion does not come under any time,[4] and that the soul is the mover of its own essence, has fully understood the substance of the soul.

By the expression " motion being under time " we mean that all the kinds of natural movement come under time [5] and that thing which is in time, its existence is found in past time, and it is obvious that if the existence of future and past time is anything, it is in the form of mutability and becoming (*taghayyur wa takawwun*), and so the natural movements are " becoming " (generation), which is not proper to the soul. On the basis of this Plato in his book the *Timaeus* [6] writes in the form of a question, " What sort of becoming thing is that which has no existence ? And what is that existing thing for which there is no becoming or change ? " That mutability which has no existence is movement in place and time, because its duration (quantity or dimension) of existence is found in some moment. And the relation between moment and time is as of point and line. So when the existence of time is found either in past or future, it is found in some moment. Therefore it is in no wise entitled to the name of being, but it ought to be said that time is always in flux and becoming. Those existences in which there is no variableness are things above and beyond time, for those things which transcend time must also be beyond natural

[1] *De Anima*, i. 3, 405b, 31 ff.

[2] *Laws*, 895C–896C. Cf. Proc.: *El. Theol.*, Prop. 20.

[3] This is the movement of procession and reversion. Cf. Proc.: *El. Theol.*, Propp. 33, 199, 200. Arist.: *Physics*, viii. 8, 9; *Timæus*, 36B ff. Porphyry: *Aphorisms*, xxx, Sect. 1: " *Cum enim perfectum sit, ad animam intellectu prœditam subrectum est; ideoque movetur in orbem: Anima autem ejus ad mentem; mens vero ad primum principiium subrigitur.*" Cf. also Pseudo-Arist.: *Theol.*, Cap. I, 172.

[4] Cf. *Enneads*, III, vii. 11 and IV, iv. 1.

[5] This is the view of Plotinus, cf. Inge: *Philosophy of Plotinus*, i. 171.

[6] The reference is to *Timæus*, 27D–28A.

movement. And it is clear that such are not under past or future, but their being is nearest to immortality and perpetuity and like eternity.[1]

Now we return to what we were saying before, that the motion of the soul which we have described is of two sorts—one towards the intellect and one towards matter. When the soul moves towards the intellect it acquires light and splendour, and itself becomes bright and illuminated. And when it moves towards matter it confers light and illumination on matter.[2]

For motion is an essential thing for the soul and therefore we have explained that it moves itself towards matter because matter does not move, nor is it fitting for it to move. Both of these movements of the soul which we have described are one in respect to movement itself, though in respect to that towards which movement is made they become two, from the one side the soul dispensing light and from the other receiving light.

Aristotle calls this motion, the dignity of the Creator (*Barz ul Bārī*),[3] and Plato " ideas " (*mu<u>th</u>ul*).[4] It has been proved that this movement of the soul is its essence and its life. And on this account the philosophers have said, " All life is soul ". It has also been learned that the soul is in one respect active (*fā'il*) and in another respect passive. And although the soul is of itself movement, that movement is not transient and not local. It is clear also that that thing which is not transient is fixed (constant) and constancy and rest are one and the same. Therefore a thing which is not transient is at rest. Thus it is proved that this motion is in the form of rest.[5]

Although this subject is very difficult and abstruse, nevertheless from our previous explanation much will have become clear. The whole of this question is difficult in the extreme for those persons who are not acquainted with the art of logic. For logic is the instrument of philosophy and the person who desires to gain insight into philosophy has no course open to him except to acquire logic. For instance, when a man wishes to be a scribe and to acquire the ability to read and write various kinds of script, he has no other course open to him but to seek out and gather together the writing of all scribes and to read them. Then if he practises perhaps he will learn to be a scribe. This is the case with logic and philosophy.

[1] These terms correspond to *τὸ ὄν, ἀθάνατος, ἀΐδιος, αἰώνος* which are differentiated in the Greek philosophers; cf. Proclus: *El. Theol.*, Propp. 87 and 105. See *Timæus*, 37D–38A for the discussion of time.

[2] This corresponds to the conception of the two acts of the All-Soul: in reverting to its Source and in its Providence, cf. *Enneads*, V, i. 3; IV, iii. 9, and IV, iii. 17, and also Pseudo-Arist.: *Theology*, Cap. II.

[3] The reference must be to the primary eternal and single movement spoken of in Arist.: *Metaph.* λ, 8, 1073a, 25. This is the *primum mobile*. But see also " Glory of the Lord," p. 71, *supra*.

[4] For the Aristotelian view in contrast to the Platonist see Caird: *Evolution of Theology in the Greek Philosophers*, Lect. 10, specially p. 280.

[5] Cf. Aristotle: *Physics*, ii. 3.

Now one more question has to be dealt with. When this rare and wonderful movement, which has connection with the soul and is unlike any of the motions which have been explained, is bestowed on natural bodies they move in a way fitting to them, i.e., with local movement. The simplest and most honourable local movement is the movement of the heaven, for the heaven is the first body which has accepted that motion and therefore it moves with a circular movement. This circular movement is the most honourable of all the bodily movements because in circular movement the parts of the body keep changing place, but the whole remains constant in its place. Similarly the parts of the heaven change place but the body of the heaven remains located in its own place ; and so it is as though in one respect the heaven is moved and in another respect at rest. Thus in reference to rest and constancy the heaven has the most perfect and complete likeness to the soul, and for this reason the life of the heaven is more complete and honourable than the life of all created things, because the universe of becoming and corruption is the lowest stage from the heaven and the movement of generated things is obtained from the soul by the medium of the heaven. And it is an agreed rule that the further the effect is from the cause, and the more intermediaries there are between, the lower will be the status of the effect and the less its likeness to its cause.[1]

After this preliminary statement, we revert to the former subject that our motion, i.e., the motion of the universe of " becoming " is gained from the movement of the heaven, and the movement of the heaven is taken from the movement of the soul. The soul always continues circular movement in order that its essence may gain completion and perfection from the Primal Intelligence. Because the Intellect is the First Creation of God, it is by essence able to dispense with perfecting and is always graced by illumination from the Creator. But although the Intellect is imperfect of existence, it does not move,[2] because movement is always towards completion and perfection, but here there remains no perfection towards which it could move, because it is impossible for the Intellect to become like its Cause (the Creator). But the Intellect is the most perfect and honourable of all created things, and if it were to move this would be futile and nothing futile can occur by the Primal Intelligence. So it is proved that the Intellect does not move, but the soul does in order that it may image the perfect Intellect. This movement is essential to it and its life, and keeps it

[1] See previous notes. Arist.: *Metaph.*, λ, 7, 8 and 9. For proximate and remote likeness see Arist.: *Phys.*, ii. 3, 12. Cf. Plot.: *Enneads*, V, viii. 1. Everything that reaches outwards is the less for it, strength less strong, heat less hot, every power less potent and so beauty less beautiful. See also Proc.: *El. Theol.*, Prop. 64. " All procession proceeds through similar things till it reaches what is utterly dissimilar."

[2] *De Anima*, iii. 11, 434a, 15 f. But the Neoplatonist idiom is obvious. Cf. *Enneads*, V, i. 6. " The first is immovable ; any second must issue from it without any assent in it, without its will and without any movement in it."

perpetually existing. The ancient philosophers have called this the Logos (*kalima*) and Idea (*mithāl*) and Demiurge and other names. This subject is very abstruse and deep, and if we proceed any further there will be still greater difficulties to encounter. Therefore we content ourselves with this much.

CAP. VIII. THAT THERE ARE TWO CONDITIONS OF THE SOUL. THE PERFECTION OF THE SOUL IS CALLED HAPPINESS, AND THE IMPERFECTION MISERY [1]

The one who has carefully read our former expositions and has made himself fully conversant with the contents of the previous chapters, will have learned that the movement of the soul is in two directions.[2] One moves the soul towards its essence, i.e., that motion which the soul makes towards the intellect, which is God's First Creation, and which is never in any circumstances or for any reason cut off from the bounty of its Principle and Cause. By the second direction the motion of the soul is towards the natural bodily instruments, so that by means of this motion it may perfect material bodies.

It is clear that one of these brings the soul to happiness and causes it to gain that immortality and perpetuity which is fitting to it. And the movement by the other direction is for the soul a cause of decline (*inḥiṭāṭ*) and exodus or projection from its essence. The names given to these two directions by the ancient philosophers are "high" and "low". But it is clear that by high and low they do not mean bodily movement which is downwards or upwards.[3] But the fact is that they had to use these terms for the two directions of the soul's movement for want of more suitable ones. It remains to say that the Law of Islam calls these two directions by the names "Right" and "Left".

In short, the soul when it turns towards the upward direction be-

[1] In general it may be said that the following chapters speak in terms made familiar in the *Nichomachean Ethics*. The ethical is explained as based on the eudaimonistic motive. But running through the whole is a thread of Neoplatonist thought.

[2] References have been given for the double motion of the soul. Dean Inge speaks of the diastole and systole of the soul's movement. Other references for the ascent and descent of the soul are *Enneads*, III, viii. 8, which speaks of the spiritual vision which is the soul's upward movement; *Enneads*, IV, vii. 13, where the Soul is represented as pregnant with spirit and must bring her offspring to birth, and this is why she creates in the world of sense. The desire for the Good, here represented by "upward movement" is spoken of by Arist.: *De Anima*, ii. 4, 415, and *Metaph.*, K. See also *Enneads*, V, ii. 1; III, vi. 5, and I, vi. 9. The soul's happiness is in detachment from the body and in elevation to the Spiritual World. The same idea is found in reference to abstention from carnal desires as the bliss of the soul. See *Enneads*, I, ii. 5, and Porphyry's *Aphorisms*, xxxiv. The theme of the Charioteer and his steed from *Phædrus* caught the imagination and is often found in the mystics (specially Jalāl ud Dīn Rūmī). There is, however, a subtle difference. The descent of the soul in Plotinus is fulfilment of its own being and its imitation of the Divine Providence. The soul's outgoing or descent to matter is therefore not in itself misery, but it is only when the soul is sunk in matter. Cf. *Enneads*, II, ix. 2.

[3] *Enneads*, VI, iv. 16. This is no coming down into place. The soul's descent consists in its being conjoined to body.

comes completely lost in its own essence and joining the essence of the Creator becomes unified with the essence, and so unified that from It oneness is introduced into every existence and immortality into the whole universe.

And when it turns towards the other direction, then dispersion and variability are produced in it, by which it becomes separate from its essence and reaps a sort of misery which this direction entails. On account of this theory Plato says that philosophy is habituation to death. For to Plato, death and life are of two kinds, because the life which the soul has by its motion upwards is other than that which is produced by its movement downwards. For this reason there are also two sorts of death, for there is an opposition in both kinds of life and death. The life which the soul has by moving toward the intellect, Plato calls "natural life" and he calls movement towards matter "voluntary life",[1] and on this basis he holds as opposed to these natural death and voluntary death. Having this classification in mind Plato said: "Die to will and thou shalt live to nature", i.e., Gain voluntary death and forsake material relations and thou shalt obtain natural life,[2] i.e., your soul will be graced by the illumination of the reason and the oneness of the Creator.

We have explained this abstruse and subtle doctrine in few words, but the more we think the more the idea of points of inquiry grows. It is the duty of that person to whom God vouchsafes grace whose eye of understanding God opens, to employ all his energy and endeavour

[1] Is the soul willing to descend? It would be better to translate this "appetitive" rather than "voluntary", but this would be to amend. Cf. *Timæus*, 44A. Natural motion is spoken of in *Timæus*, 44B. In all probability the reference is not to Plato but to Plotinus. In which case, *Enneads*, V, iii. 9 should be noted for the voluntary movement of the *souls*. "They began to revel in free-will. They indulged their movement. They went by the wrong way." This movement is said in *Enneads*, III, i. 9 to be "not of its higher nature". It is only when the soul acts by reason which is native to it that it can be described as an act of freewill. Thus freewill is the natural act and self-will is the contrary of it. The way Miskawaih expresses this, obscures the subtle distinction. The upward movement is disengagement from body; see *Enneads*, I, ii. 5.

Cf. also John of Damascus: *Dialectica*, Cap. III: "*Philosophia est meditatio mortis, sive naturalis, sive liberæ voluntatis sit.*" The Damascene quotes Ammonius: *Prolegomena to the Isagoge of Porphyry* (see Migne: *P.G.*, 94, col. 533–4).

[2] *Enneads*, I, viii. 10, where the death of the soul is spoken of as twofold: "While drowned in body to lie down in matter and saturate itself in it" and secondly, "when it has forsaken the body to lie in the other world until it bethinks itself and raises its eyes from the mire."

Phædo., 81C: "It behoves us to think of the body as ponderous, heavy, earthly and visible. Hence the soul, being of such a nature as we have seen, possessing such a body, is not burdened and dragged down again into the visible world."

Porphyry: *Aphorisms*, ix.: "Death is twofold, one known by all when body is loosed from soul, and the other that of the Philosophers where the soul is loosed from body."

Cf. *Enneads*, VI, ix. 9. The exact quotation I have not found, but the reference may be to *Phædo* where Plato says that the great concern of philosophers is the release and departure of the soul from the body. Cicero attributes to Plato in *Tusc. Quæst.*, I, Cap. XXX: "*Tota philosophorum vita commentatio mortis est.*"

See also *Nichomachean Ethics*, x. 7, end of 1177b.

in gaining everlasting life and eternal happiness, by which there will fall to his happy lot to be near to the Glorious and Supreme Truth; and by employing his God-given reason to abstain from the world and its evils and guard the rational soul from the contamination of carnal desires. For diligent application to the pleasures of the world [1] results in distance and alienation from the Creator and in the destruction of the rational soul and man becomes bound in all sorts of afflictions and receives most grievous punishment.

By this admonition and exhortation it is not our meaning that the world should be quite forsaken and that all connection with it should be completely severed. For this is what those people say who do not realize that man has been made of a sociable nature and cannot live his life without the help of his fellow men and without himself helping his fellows as they do him.[2] Then haply the purpose of man's life and sociability is possible of achievement.

The following is a detailed explanation of man's sociable nature. Man's creaturely nature is not of such a character that he can live alone and keep alive without mutual assistance as is the case with some birds and beasts, the creation of which is brought about in such a way that they do not depend on any one else for their survival. But if the matter is well considered it will be learned that all the needs of these animals are provided for in two ways, either in respect to their creation, or by way of divine inspiration (*ilhām*—probably instinct is meant), or in respect to the manner in which they are born, in the following manner: To each animal is given the kind of organs and provision which its circumstances and necessities demand. For instance, on the body of one is wool, of another hair, and of another feathers. If it is a grain-eating animal then a beak is provided, and for grazers lips and teeth suitable for snapping off and biting grass. And if they are wild beasts or carnivorous animals, they have been granted claws and talons to catch and rend their prey, and along with these necessary instruments there is granted to them sufficient natural courage. And by inspiration all the needs of animals are provided for in the following way: To every animal, whether beast or bird, such reason and power is given that by their aid it seeks and devours those foods which are agreeable to its disposition and liking, and abstains from harmful things. In the hot weather it lodges in one place and in the cold weather changes its place and provides its needs suitable to the time and season.

In short, by reason of that inspired power which is bestowed on it at its birth, it accomplishes all its work and does not depend for its life and survival on any teaching or instruction, but is sufficient and plentifully provided in itself.

[1] *Nichomachean Ethics*, VII, xiv. 1154a.
[2] *Nich. Ethics*, VIII, ix. 1160a; I, vii, 1097b; and *Politics*, I, ii. 1253a, 3.

But this is not the case with man. When a man is born he is quite naked and absolutely ignorant, neither has he any provision to provide for his necessities nor any instrument to avoid his troubles. Man's needs cannot be fulfilled without his obtaining instruction [1] and without the assistance of others. And even then a few assistants will not suffice, but he has need of a whole company of assistants. But in place of all these requirements the Creator has granted him the boon of intellect, by which he has subdued everything in the world and provided himself with every kind of instrument and tool, and by the aid of which he gains every beneficial thing of the dry land or sea and obtains the bounties of this world and the hereafter.

But the survival and life of man cannot possibly be without the aid and assistance of his fellows. The agents of man are so many that they cannot be numbered. All things to eat, to drink, to wear and all the paraphernalia which protects him in heat and cold, e.g., houses, etc., and all those things which man employs by way of adornment, if all were mentioned then one would have to reckon in all the things in this world and the bounties of God.

But there is no need to prolong this account, and it is sufficient to declare that in the provision of all these necessities and in deriving benefit from them, man has need of helpers : and because his case is different from that of animals, man is said to be sociable by nature, i.e., man has need of different kinds of help which cannot be realized except by people building towns and forming communities. The name for this gathering into communities is *tamaddun*—political or social life. Whether according to their requirements people set up tents to dwell in or build houses of earth or live on the tops of mountains in communities, whatever may be the case, because the need of mutual assistance has brought them together, their community is called *tamaddun* and the place a town (*madīna*).

In such a case, therefore, it is our duty and the demand of justice also that we should afford the assistance to our fellow men which they afford to us.[2] For instance, there is an army of soldiers in a city or country whose business it is to fight against marauders for their peace and security. But when they cannot do any other work but this fighting, or the preparation for it, it is the duty of the people of the country, the rich and the merchants, to guarantee their living and their allowances, so that receiving monetary help they may serve the country with a quiet mind.

And this is the case with all sections (of the community). One does one sort of work for the community and another another sort ; and so they ought, in order that the community may be in good case and that the social order may continue evenly and equitably.

[1] Arist. : *Politics*, IV, Cap. XIV.

[2] For the principle of reciprocation see Arist. : *Nich. Ethics*, v. 5.

Here it is necessary to point out that the section of ascetics and monks who work at no trade are in reality unjust and err from the path of justice because they obtain the things necessary to eat and drink from other people and do not serve them in return. It is their duty to render some aid just as they receive it. Perhaps the doubt may be expressed that the needs of such people are few. This is not correct, because in the provision of this little, innumerable men take part and toil, although at first sight it does not seem so. Thus it is obligatory upon every one to assist with equity and justice. If he receives much help from another, he should himself render much help, and if he takes but a little service, he should render a little, but in any case he should certainly serve and help.

By this "little" and "much" we do not mean quantity of service but quality. Thus, for instance, the mathematician may in one glance solve a problem which many men have not solved after years of toil.[1] And so if by this knowledge of his he does some work for his people then in reality it is much in respect to quality even if in respect to quantity it is nothing, i.e., even if he did it in a short time and with little labour. Or, for instance, the general of an army by his direct opinion devises a useful plan in comparison with which even if hundreds of men had wasted their lives they would not have achieved such a good result. Therefore this service is abundant in quality and he is entitled to a greater recompense.

It is fitting that every person should gain the world according to his dignity and rank. That of which he is worthy that he should receive. There should be no deficiency in what he gets and that which he does not receive he should not covet. He should continue to walk the straight path of the true Law and perform his religious duties, possess good morals and pleasing qualities. In short, this is the straight path of understanding. Acting on it is the way to salvation, and the way to happiness. And in this way the bliss and well-being of both worlds is possible. The subject required great detail but conciseness does not permit it.

CAP. IX. ACCOUNT OF THE INCITEMENT OF DESIRE TO OBTAIN HAPPINESS AND AN EXPLANATION OF THE METHOD BY WHICH IT IS TO BE OBTAINED

From the beginning, we have in each chapter dealt with those subjects which would form an introduction to the following subject. In the last chapter it was made plain what the perfection of the soul is whereby it gains happiness, and by that explanation the imperfection and misery of the soul will have been understood, for the knowledge of contraries and opposites is immediate. In this chapter it is intended to explain the way in which happiness may be obtained, so that it

[1] Cf. *Akhlāq un Nāsirī*, ii. 7.

may be easy for the seeker, after understanding it, to gain happiness. Happiness is gained by wisdom [1] and wisdom is of two sorts, one speculative, by the bounty of which man can form good and correct opinion,[2] and the other practical, by means of which man gains such a lofty position that praiseworthy acts and well-pleasing sincerity come to be practised by him. For the instruction and teaching of both these (the speculative and the practical) the prophets were sent, so that they might cure people's diseases of ignorance and bad morals, and produce in them good morals, beautiful manners, and worthy deeds. The prophets invite people to the aforementioned amendment and bring deniers to accept them by the argument of miracles. That fortunate person who follows them and believes in them has found the straight path, and he who denies is worthy of the fires of hell.

The one who wants to examine the invitation of the prophets—May God's blessing be on all of them !—with sound reason and correct speculation, takes the help of the rules of the sages and philosophers. And this important task can be achieved by the aid of wisdom, the definition of which is : what the philosophers of supreme insight have acquired of the two sorts of wisdom. The speculative is of such a sort as admits of many doubts, and in which the truth of the matter is hard to be learned. When a man thinks, he fancies that a certain matter is true, whereas in reality it is very far from the truth, or it may seem that some matter is near to the truth, whereas it is not so. The illustration of this is as when men make a black mark on a piece of paper and shoot arrows at it. The target aimed at is one, and all wish to hit it, but the arrows of most of the archers go wide,[3] and they are few whose arrows hit the mark. Or the centre of a circle is a single point, and every one tries to find this centre but few do so, and the majority err and go beating about hither and thither. Likewise truth is one, and those things which are nearest to it are all alike. All seek that truth but few reach it. The majority turn hither and thither and keep going astray. The reason for this is that those matters which are far from the truth are plain and clear to all, and those things which are near to the truth are extremely obscure, although people of acute penetration and meticulous in observation find the truth. Those people who know how to test copper coin can distinguish between copper coins and gold pieces. It does not follow, however, that they can assay gold pieces. Likewise it is easy to get to know gilt, but it is difficult to test pure gold correctly. So there are many testers, but that person is most perfect who can detect the least particle of difference or alloy between two pieces of gold. It is the same in the case of truth.

[1] *Nich. Ethics*, X, vii. 1177a.
[2] Plotinus : *Enneads*, III, vi. 2, where false opinions are considered to be the source of vice.
[3] Almost like an exposition of ἁμαρτία—missing the mark, the regular New Testament word for sin.

Those things which are far from the truth everybody knows, but in those which are near many people make mistakes. There are a few people of minute penetration and keen observation whose glance ignores semblances and goes straight to the root of truth, but for that great expertness and practice and mastery are needed, which are not gained without pains. When the necessity arose for escaping this sort of error in thought and speculation, an art was devised the name for which is "logic". Therefore the definition of the science of logic is that it is an instrument by means of which truth and falsehood can be discriminated and the difference learned between true statements and false. The science of logic was devised as a rule and standard for the examination of all those things about which thought and reflection are necessary. And the rule has been fixed that first of all there should be thought and reflection on such things as are nearest to the nature of man, i.e., natural matters.[1] For man has first of all the opportunity to study these things. After that by degrees he can turn his thoughts to the spheres (heavens), to abstractions (possibly separate substances), and to divinities, and at each stage by means of the art of logic he may save himself from error in thought, according to the particulars of such progression recounted by us in the preface to this book. Accordingly, keeping that arrangement in mind, it is proposed that the seeker should first of all add logic and afterwards natural philosophy and last of all divine philosophy. After traversing all these stages of speculative wisdom, books of practical wisdom are recommended, i.e., books of ethics by which the soul is cultivated, then afterwards household management should be taught, and after that politics. It is on this account that the philosophers have said: "The person who has got a grip on his enemy the soul and has corrected it, has become fit for domestic management, and he who has acquired ability in household management has become capable of political management, and he who has attained proficiency in political management has become fit for the rule of kingdoms." In short, that fortunate person who has attained proficiency in both speculative and practical wisdom, is entitled to the honourable appellation of "sage" or "philosopher", and has attained the desire of the soul in eternal happiness and everlasting salvation.

The Philosopher Aristotle in his *Ethics* has described those subjects which we have dealt with in the beginning of this part, that one perfect man is the possessor of insight and another has the ability to confirm him, etc. The Philosopher[2] said: "Man has need of an instru-

[1] Cf. Aristotle: *Nichomachean Ethics*, II, viii. 1108b (end).

[2] Aristotle's theory of "Right Reason". The ultimate source is *Nich. Ethics*, I, vii. 1177b, 27 ff. "But such a life will be higher than mere human nature because a man will live thus, not in so far as he is man, but in so far as there is in him a divine principle: and in proportion as this principle excels his composite nature, so far does the working of it excel that in accordance with any other kind of excellence: and therefore if pure intellect, as compared with human nature, is divine, so too will the life in accordance with it be divine compared with man's ordinary life."

ment to acquire acquaintance with virtues and good qualities, by means of which he can differentiate between the true and the false, and that instrument is divinely-given Right Reason. And he who is not favoured with this Right Reason, must naturally so form his thought after mental discipline, that it may accept the true things and reject the false. And the one in whom are neither of these qualities, i.e., he is neither excellent (*fāḍil*) so that he may understand of himself, nor pious (*ṣāliḥ*) so that he may find the way by the instruction of someone else, is eternally miserable and everlastingly wretched. There is a verse of the poet Isodorus: "One is excellent and one is pious." [1]

Having explained thus far, which is quite sufficient for a person of intelligence, we wish to explain further several matters concerning the above-mentioned happiness, in order that the seeker may be inflamed with desire for it. That person who may wish to gain the knowledge of existing things on the conditions which we have stated, and to travel by the easy process which the most eminent philosophers have recommended, will first of all have to inquire into the mode, composition and nature, and other matters found in the things of the universe, and he will learn what innumerable powers there are managing and ruling the macrocosm. He will also discover that all the governing powers are united with one another and that some govern others.[2] But all these powers have some relation to another universe of which no likeness can be given, neither is there any way of reaching that universe. But that other universe is spiritual and simple, and the ordination and planning, the generation and arrangement of all the existences of the first universe are connected with it. That universe permeates spiritually this first universe as these powers permeate natural bodies. But that universe has no need of this universe, but this is dependent on that, just as natural bodies have no need of bodies, but bodies are dependent on them. But if man does not observe the first universe well, and does not consider what exists in it, then the revelation of the second universe cannot be given to him. Because that is simple and this universe in which man lives is composite; that is spiritual and this physical. Then when after progress in thought and study of the second universe, he becomes familiar with it and contemplates the wonders of the effects of wisdom and the marvels of the mysteries of the supreme, which before this he saw neither in the first universe nor in the second, and it is discovered to him that all these effects are connected with one another and govern

[1] I fancy that the *Ṣāliḥ* must be the man of practical wisdom who does things for advantage (*Nich. Eth.*, X, viii. 1178a). It is not possible to say where the quotation ends. The fact that there is included a quotation from Isodorus, if the Neoplatonist is meant, would mean that it is not direct from Aristotle. It may be that Miskawaih was using the Porphyrian commentary which Isḥāq b. Ḥunayn is said to have translated.

[2] Cf. Philo: *Cherubim*, 31 (i. 158).

one another, man has the contemplation of a third universe which has no likeness to the other two. That, too, is incorporeal and has no need of place. It governs the second universe and encompasses it as the second does the first, and it assists the second universe by governing powers as the second does the first. The only difference is that this third universe is simpler than the second universe.

Then when man becomes familiar with this third universe there is revealed to him a universe so wide and simple (attenuated) that it has that relation to the third universe which the third has to the second. This fourth universe is so simple that if man did not contemplate the universe which precedes it and become familiar with that, the revelation of this would be impossible. The reason is that when man contemplates these universes and observes the wonders of the effects of wisdom and sees that every one of them is composite and dependent on some composer, then involuntarily he searches for cause and reason, for the cause is more honourable and simpler than what is caused. And when he casts a piercing glance on these four universes he sees in each one of them composition, and finds the effect of some wisdom and salutary counsel. And so, seeking continually for the effective cause and the bestower of composition, he reaches that Cause of causes of which there is no cause, One in whom there is no sort of multitude, a Simple in whom there is no composition, self-subsisting and self-dependent, not dependent on anything else, who gives aid to all things and takes help from nothing, because there is nothing above him. All powers come to an end in Him. There can be nothing before Him because He is the fountain of mature wisdom and most simple oneness.[1]

When the magnanimous reader reaches this point then it will be well understood by him that that Holy Essence is the Primal Source and the Original Cause and there is nothing prior to Him. And it is revealed to him that all the qualities of all the universes are not suitable for Him because they are all qualities of His effects.[2] At the same time

[1] The five worlds are not explicitly described and so it can only be conjectured what they really stand for. They might correspond to the Earth, the Spheres, the Soul, the Intellectual-Principle, the All-Soul, All the Souls, and Matter. According to Philo, we might have: The Material Universe (*Somn.*, i. 32), the Heavens (*Plant. Noe*, 1), Souls (*Somn.*, i. 22), Logoi-powers (*Post Cain*, 6), God. According to Proclus (an exposition in his *Platonic Theology* of *Laws* 895A6–B.2) we might, by the addition of the One, have the further four stages of the Unmoved, which is the Divine Intellect, the Self-moved, i.e., the Souls, that which is moved and moving, namely, material forms, and the moved, i.e., bodies. In his *Elements of Theology*, Proclus declares that there are four grades, namely, Bodies, the Soul's Essence, the Intellectual-Principle and the One.

[2] Damascene: *De Fide Orthod.*, Bk. I, Cap. II (*P.G.*, 94, 792). "Many of the things relating to God therefore, that are dimly apprehended cannot be put into fitting terms, but on things above us we cannot do other than express ourselves according to our limited capacity; as for instance, when we speak of God we use the terms sleep, and wrath, and regardlessness, hands also and feet and similar expressions."

Bk. I, Cap. XI (*P.G.*, 94, 842). "It is impossible for us men . . . to understand or speak of the divine and lofty and immaterial energies of the Godhead except by the use of images and types and symbols derived from our own life."

the doctrine is clearly understood that the names and attributes of created things which are used for the laudable and glorious Creator are all used metaphorically. For instance, cause and reason and wise and beneficent and other terms are used for the Essence of the Creator which are within the power of man, but none of them are fitting for that Highest Supreme, because He is the Author of all these excellencies and is other than them all and more honourable. This is that transcendent degree to which human reason cannot attain.

Finally it is worthy of explanation that when any fortunate and munificent person, contemplating all the universes, gradually reaches this supreme height, then in these contemplations he obtains a delight and pleasure which have no sort of resemblance to any physical pleasure, because this is the spiritual pleasure which falls to the happy lot of the soul, from the abstractions which are agreeable to and resemble it. These perpetual delights and pleasures never leave the fortunate people to whose lot they fall. No one can snatch them away, there is no stint in them being given to any one but the bounty and the pleasure increase from day to day. The one who reaches this supreme height learns that there are many degrees of it which are called stations [1] (*maqāmāt*). But the quantity and quality of these degrees can be estimated by those people who have traversed them and are acquainted with their sweetness and delight.

By this explanation will be confirmed the statement which we first made, that the person who sees existing things and thinks deeply on them and by correct progress advances from the lowest to the highest obtains knowledge of his Lord in such a way that he has no doubt or questioning. And it is possible that he may also see God in the way that it is possible for the creature to see God.

After this when a man turns his gaze from what is above to what is below, then he discovers that God Most High who is First and One and Simple, encompasses and embraces everything else and ordains and plans all beside, just as the intellect encompasses the soul, and the soul the nature and the nature bodies, although it has no need of the subordination or encompassing of any one of them, but all these are dependent on that Holy, Glorious and Mighty Essence.

CAP. X. IN EXPLANATION OF THE QUALITY AND CONDITION OF THE SOUL WHEN IT IS SEPARATED FROM THE BODY AFTER MAN DIES [2]

We have proved with powerful argument that after the death of

[1] The "stations" were afterwards amplified and elaborated in the Sufi system of ascension to union. The utmost and ultimate term of mystic contemplation is in the vision of the One when the All is seen in the One and the One in the All. Cf. ***Enneads***, V, iii. 6: "We had intellection and saw all things in the One." And VI, ix. 3: The soul, "shall take to itself all that the Intellectual-Principle sees and in this way shall see the One".

[2] There is a departure here to Islamic eschatology, but it is very slight and treated not at all in the manner of the orthodox theologians.

man his intellectual soul survives and is not destroyed. And in the state of immortality it must either be in a state of happiness or its contrary misery. We have explained happiness in detail, but the truth is that we cannot in any way know perfectly the nature of that happiness, only being able to indicate it remotely and understand or explain by symbols. For the conditions of that world are infinitely different from the conditions and customary usages of this. God Himself in His holy word has said about those conditions and delights, "No soul knows what is reserved for them of cheerfulness for the eyes" (Sura xxxii. 17), and the Messenger of Allah said, "There will be blessing which neither the eyes have seen nor the ears heard, neither has the thought entered into the heart of man."[1] Lo, in spite of our knowing that we cannot see those conditions nor fully understand them till we have put off the robe of humanity and severed our connections with all natural relations, nevertheless it cannot be that we should not try to understand and conceive them so far as our mortal power will allow, especially when we have from the beginning of this book explained many introductory matters to make the subject plain. Therefore in regard to this we wish to make it still plainer.

All existences are of two kinds, corporeal and spiritual. Corporeal existences are spherical creations, because the shape of the sphere is the most excellent of all shapes and preserves them from harm. The spherical shape is superior to all. All spheres are joined with one another and it is not possible that there should be anything dividing the spheres one from another.[2] For if anything dividing were assumed then it would have to be that there was some other body between the spheres or else a vacuum. The existence of a vacuum is impossible, i.e., it is not possible that without matter there should be found body composed of three dimensions. In the second alternative of some body being found between the spheres, it is impossible that such a body should not be spherical. And so it must be that one sphere encompasses another sphere.

Now the form of these spheres is this: Above the sphere of earth is the sphere of water and encompassing it, but from towards the north the water has receded from a small part of the earth. There is a great purpose in this, inasmuch as for the earth the centre of the sun is thus made towards the south of the earth. Therefore all moistures are drawn thither and so in the south heat is produced and from the north

[1] 1 Cor. ii. 9.

[2] For the spherical shape see *Timæus*, 33B, where its superiority is mentioned. Origen in *De Oratione*, Cap. 31, 29, considers that the resurrection body would be spherical. For the sphere see Arist.: *Metaph.*, λ, 8, but especially *De Coelo*, ii. 3, 286a, 12–22, where the special sense in which the centre of the earth is spoken of is explained. For the encompassing of one sphere by another, see Arist.: *Physics*, iv. 5, 212b. The scheme is as follows: the terrestrial globe is encompassed by the sphere of water, which is encompassed by the sphere of air, and this last is encompassed by the sphere of fire and so on. See Arist.: *Meteor.*, i. 2.

the water has receded. In this there is this great advantage that the earth may be inhabited and animals have the chance to live. Above the sphere of water the sphere of air encompasses, and the sphere of fire encompasses the sphere of air, and above the sphere of fire is the first heaven which is the sphere of the moon. The second heaven surrounds the first heaven, and on the same analogy all the heavens of the planets surround each other until the ninth which is super-planetary and is called the heaven of heavens and surrounds all the other heavens. This heaven of heavens is the *primum mobile,* and by reason of its own movement moves all the heavens. But the movement of these heavens is in the contrary direction to its own, the circuit of which is completed in a day and a night. Each one of these spheres is heavier and grosser than the one above it, as for instance, the earth is denser than water and is like its sediment. Likewise water is denser (more turbid) than air and air than fire, and the sphere of fire is denser than the heaven of the moon. On this analogy we conjecture that the second heaven will be clearer and so on by analogy, the heaven of heavens being the most translucent and most luminous of all the heavens. This is a brief account of the state of corporeal existences.

The second kind of existences is spiritualities. Although these have no bodies, nevertheless some of them encompass others, but this encompassing is spiritual, appropriate to spiritualities because they have no need of place.[1] To understand this spiritual encompassing we must believe that it is one of comprehension and regulation (*ishtimāl wa tadbīr*), i.e., one encompasses another in such a way that the encompassing constitutes the encompassed, and the regulation and fashioning of the encompassed is associated with it. The illustration for this is that we say of nature (*ṭabī'a*) that it encompasses all spherical bodies, but we do not mean by this an encompassing such as one body has in relation to another, but that nature confers movement on all spherical bodies,[2] and that their proportion and measurement are connected with it, and that the regulation and fashioning of all bodies is its charge. For nature is a divine power and permeates all bodies ; it constitutes or holds together all bodies. It regulates the outside and inside of every body to such a degree that no condition of the body is beyond its comprehension in any way.

On the same analogy, it should be understood that the soul encompasses the nature and the intellect the soul. The person of good understanding and high thinking who grasps these spiritual and

[1] *De Anima,* I, iii. 406a, 16 ff.

[2] The question of whether Aristotle taught that the sphere was moved by its nature was often debated. See *Physics,* ii. 3, in which it is declared that nature is the first principle of motion, and also *Metaph.,* 1072b, 5–10. Al Ghazzālī discusses the matter of the heavens' motion and whether it is living in *Tahāfut ul Falāsifa,* Quest. xiv (Bouyges, p. 239 ff.). Cf. also *Physics,* ii. 1.

transcendent modes of encompassing, can well understand how the Divine Designer and most Glorious and Mighty Bountiful encompasses all existing things and how His regulation and ordination, beneficence and goodness surround all created things.[1]

Now it demands some thoughtful consideration that when the relation of one of the above-mentioned spiritual degrees with the other is imagined, it appears that in regard to what is beneath it, every one is more honourable, and in reference to what is above inferior and gross. It is in this way that spiritualities [2] should be conceived. Howbeit there is the difficulty that we cannot use the term "turbidity" for spiritualities. We are perplexed what term to use for them. Therefore in such a case when spiritualities are conceived as incorporeal, nobility or low degree should be thought of, according to whatever is fitting to them.

The state of both sorts of existence has been suitably explained with details. Now we wish to explain what those spiritual existences are, because they are not bodies and are therefore in no need of place. When they meet one another there is no augmentation or diminution, but the condition of bodies is that when they are joined together they become greater in measurement. The reason for this is that the joining of bodies can either be by the intermingling and proximity of the parts of body or by the edges of the bodies meeting and the surface of one touching another. In both cases, the resultant composite body must be greater in measurement and must be greater in the three dimensions or in one of them. But because spiritualities are devoid of length and breadth, when they are joined together there is no increase or decrease.

We make clear this abstruse idea by an example from sensibles so that it may be easily understood. The rays of the planets, i.e., the rays of the stars in the sky, are manifold and numerous, and being emitted by them mingle with the air. It is obvious also that all these rays are different from one another because they issue from different heavenly bodies. But no observer can conjecture that those lights mingle together in the air and lose themselves in one another. No matter how many exist, they may become a hundredfold or a thousandfold more, nevertheless they cannot increase in measure by reason of their multitude. Probably this illustration will suffice for the understanding of the case that when spiritual powers are joined together they are not greater in measurement and do not disappear by being joined, and neither does any constriction or mixture result. This theory should

[1] This theory of order due to nature, etc., is in marked contrast to the later Ash'arian system. Cf. Cicero: *De Natura Deorum*, ii. 57, 142. These "spiritualities" are reminiscent of the "Physicals" in Proclus: *El. Theol.*, Prop. 111. A common division is into Corporeal, Psychical and Intellective, σωματικός, ψυχικός, νοερός.

[2] For nine corresponding spiritual orders see Pseudo-Dionysius: *Celestial Hierarchy*, iii. 2.

be understood by another example. We have already explained how the intellect encompasses and comprehends the soul, and however manifold the degrees of spirituality may be, nevertheless no person considers that by reason of multiplicity they have become mixed or become one. For though none of them belongs to corporealities or spatial things, nor are they things perceiving, nor things perceived nor self-distinguishing (self-conscious ?), nevertheless, the intellect discerns them all as separate, and perceives that the state of one is other than the state of another. Consider that in every one of the parts of the body these powers are assembled together : the nutritive, the digestive, the retentive, and the eliminative, but no person thinks that all these powers are one or joined, and neither does he think that one is mixed with another or that one does not leave room for another. Nevertheless, everyone perceives that one is distinct from another. The proof of this is that some are sometimes weak and some similarly remain powerful, and the physician tries to make the weak power strong and bring it into its normal state.

So when you can understand these matters, you ought in the same way to understand that when the soul separates from the body, it also has various states, and these are not one (i.e., do not form a unity) nor are they intermingled nor pressed together. Probably these two examples are sufficient for the understanding of this abstruse question. But we will nevertheless explain the matter further for greater clearness.

It has been learned that there is only one spiritual power [1] which governs and moves the world of bodies, and that in every respect comprehends and encompasses all corporealities. The name for this is " nature ". So assume that the universe be so big and that the existences in it become a hundredfold more, and that the created things of the universe be also multiplied and become innumerable. Nevertheless there will occur no difference in the encompassing and governing exercised by nature, and similarly there will be sufficient for its arrangement and movement, without there being any augmentation of the essence of nature. Or assume that the universe should become much smaller than it is at present, and that the individuals should become far fewer, nevertheless there will be no lessening of the movement and government of the nature or any decrease in its essence. In the same way it should be understood and believed that when the soul becomes separate from the body its condition is the same.

Here the reader may have the doubt that the souls are various, one is bad and another good, one is miserable and one happy, and the

[1] Much here and elsewhere is owed to Galen. See Aristotle's definition of nature in *Physics*, ii. 1, 193b, 4–6 : " Nature is a principle of motion and rest." " The form or species of such things as have within themselves a principle of motion, such form or characteristic not being separable from the things themselves except by reason."

degrees of the souls also various and differentiated, so what is the state of these souls after separation from the body and in reference to whatever happiness and misery were acquired while living in the body in this world, what is the end of the soul? In reference to this problem we wish to explain several matters for the purpose of making the point clear, and after this we will address ourselves to reply to it. When we spoke of nature, soul and intellect, and told how these three encompassed each other, we referred to their stations and various degrees also. Now it should be heeded that the mode of stations and the various orders of every one of these is that each one has a special relation to the orders above and below it. The lower does not encompass what is above it, i.e., it has no knowledge of the order above it, and knows nothing about its condition except that it also has some existence, but the higher order has information of the nature of the orders under it.[1]

The example of this is that the nature has no knowledge of the rational soul although, because the soul causes benefit (*fayḍ*) to reach it (i.e., overflows upon it) and because the nature is in a condition of dependence upon it, therefore it only knows that the soul exists. But the soul comprehends the nature with its knowledge and causes aid and benefit to be outpoured upon it.

Such also is the state of the Soul in respect to the Intellect and the state of the Intellect in respect to the Creator. Therefore in regard to the Creator, except for His being, no one has any knowledge,[2] and His

[1] Cf. Plotinus: *Enneads*, IV, v. 9. Throughout the scheme of things the lower things are included under what is one degree less low and the higher things under those still higher, one thing under another until the first is reached. This first having nothing prior to it cannot be surpassed by anything and must therefore surpass all.

But when Miskawaih proceeds to say that the higher has only knowledge of the lower, there is a certain ambiguity and in some senses this is not consonant with Neoplatonist thought. In Neoplatonism it is taught that the Intellectual-Principle eternally knows and has its intellection by virtue of the self-contemplation of the One, and it is denied in Proclus (*El. Theol.*, Prop. 167) that an intelligence knows that which is consequent upon it. Further, in Prop. 124 of the same we find that Proclus declares that the divine does not get knowledge extraneously from its inferiors. Still further Plotinus (*Enneads*, V, vi. 2) says that the One will be intelligible to the Intellectual-Principle, although the Intellectual-Principle is lower than the One. To show how ambiguity might arise we might further note that Prop. 123 of the *Elements of Theology* informs us that the One is unknowable. Miskawaih would therefore seem to postulate degrees of unknowableness. The lower only knows the existence of the higher by effects, but the higher in knowing itself knows its effects.

A partial solution is the assumption that there is an ambiguous use of the term "knowledge" (see further note on the unknowability of God).

[2] Plotinus referring to Plato's *Parmenides*, 142 in *Enneads*, V, i. 10, shows that what was said about the *unknowability of God* was regarded by the Neoplatonists as based on the utter transcendence of God. He who transcends even existence must transcend knowledge. Plotinus has many references to the same subject and in various terms. In *Enneads*, VI, viii. 11, he asks how we can make a statement about the One "since everything else we say of It is said negatively". In VI, ix. 3, he even goes so far as to say that when we call the One a Cause, we are not saying anything about It but about ourselves. "We are speaking of what we derive from It while It remains wrapped up in Itself." Yet it is admitted that God is spiritually apprehended by

being is known because we are dependent on that Majesty and the Intellect perpetually draws grace from Him. The state of the knowledge of the soul which we have explained is in the form that the soul keeps on moving and desires to gain information. During its movement it gains the information sought, as though one should ask and someone should give more than was sought. Thus the soul takes knowledge without knowing the form of the Giver and how He gives.

The movement of the soul is sometimes not straight, i.e., sometimes the soul is held in the grip of matter [1] and so, when it seeks, it moves distractedly, much as the movement of the palsied who wishes to walk straight but staggers. If the soul did not make this sort of crooked movement, its perceptions would always be correct, but because of this there is often error in its perceptions, otherwise from the side of the benefiting intellect no imperfection or error occurs.

Now we turn our attention to the removal of that doubt mentioned and desire to state what is the end of the bad and of the good soul. Whatever degrees and stations there are of the nature, of the soul, and of the intellect, their state is this: every station has no acquaintance with the one above it, but comprehends and is informed of the degrees under it, and according to the extent of their desert [2] and capacity, bounty reaches each. E.g., every one of the degrees of the happy soul is comparable and conformable to another. Thus every station and degree remains always in delight and joy because, by reason of the conjunction of the degrees, the delight and happiness which is in achieving perfection of form and the overflowing bounty of the divine plenitude, is everlasting.

Likewise with the opposite of the happy soul, the wicked and miserable. The wicked soul is perfected by its bad form, for the form of everything is its perfection. And because the overflowing bounty of the divine is cut off from it, due to its being unreceptive to the overflow, and having no capacity for the spiritual, the wicked soul is continually in affliction and trouble essential to it, and this affliction and punishment are never separated from it.

Now the happiness which we have formerly mentioned, we shall

mystical union even though He is not known in the ordinary sense. But one might say that that which may be described by negatives must be known in some sense. Thus Miskawaih says that the higher order has knowledge of the *nature* of the orders below it, and has knowledge of the order above it so far as to know that it exists, and specifically with regard to the soul, it knows what is given and therefore must know that there *is* a Giver, but cannot go any further.

[1] *Enneads*, IV, iii. 15. Such souls are heavily burdened and deadened into forgetfulness, carrying a great weight which bears them down.

[2] Cf. *Enneads*, I, viii. 10. By ascending from virtue we come to the Beautiful and Good and by descending from Vice we come to essential Evil. Taking Vice as the starting point we attain to the vision of Evil, so far as that is possible, and we become evil ourselves, in so far as we participate in it. In *Enneads*, I, iv. 5, Plotinus commends cutting away the body or the sensual life of the body to secure the integral unity essential to our highest happiness. For "imaging" see *Enneads*, I, iv. 10.

explain more clearly. It will have become clear from the former exposition that lower degrees are not happiness for higher degrees, but the happiness of the lower is from the higher. And the happiness in the higher degree is complete and pure, while in the lower degree it is imperfect and impure, as though a mere shadow of the higher.

Wherefore, from all this exposition it has been learned that we ought to understand and believe that those things which we think constitute happiness while our connection with body continues,[1] and those things in which we gain our delight by means of the senses, are in reality like the shadow and image of the higher degrees ; the highest joys are really perfect and complete happiness, although we cannot properly picture them. And just as we recognise the revolution of the heaven and know the extent of its happiness, but also know that its happiness is not comparable with ours, so also we know that our happiness, in comparison with the happiness of the heavens, is quite mean and base and even non-existent.

The illustration for this is that when we were in our mother's womb, and when we were in infancy and suckling, the very mention of the things we thought happiness then and separation from which was a vexation to us, now fills us with loathing. Similarly, when our souls part from the body those things we now think sheer happiness and unadulterated enjoyment we will come to consider low and mean.

In this way, because the soul will become pure and clear of contamination with nature and corporeality, it will gain an existence which is superior and more excellent than the human existence and mortal order, and then its happiness will be in accordance with those conditions. The likeness of the soul to a young bird is manifest. It is first in the egg, and when it achieves the perfection of its form, it casts off the eggshell and throws it aside, taking a form which is more honourable and higher than before. Likewise the soul gains a form after separation from the body, by which to obtain delight to the limit of its capacity, i.e., on account of imaging the things of the world it becomes miserable or happy. We have already explained that there is a special and essential act of the soul (movement towards the higher) which perfects it and brings it to happiness ; and we have also explained the quiddity and condition of that special act. So when some hindrance is made to the special act of the soul, it prevents it from reaching happiness, and this hindrance is the cause of its descent (*tanazzul*) from its degree and order ; and the more the soul descends the greater misery it receives. Sometimes this descent (*inḥiṭāṭ*) is but little and

[1] For the pleasures of the body and how these are contrasted with the pleasures of the soul, see *Nich. Ethics*, III, x. 1117b–1119b and X, v. 1175a, 21, 28, etc. "In the fool, grasping after what is pleasing is insatiable and undiscriminating. Every practice of desire foments the corresponding habit and if the desires are great and violent, they expel reason utterly." *Enneads*, I, iv. 12 declares that the adept's pleasure cannot be licentiousness.

does not expel it from the bounds of happiness, and sometimes it is much, and this expels it from happiness and brings it within the bounds of misery. And it has been made clear that that which hinders the soul from its happiness is its obliteration by the perceptions and delights of the senses. For the things outside the soul are joined with the soul by means of sense and the sense turns the soul towards the concupiscible or irascible and provokes it.

Both these souls, the concupiscible and the irascible, corrupt with the corruption of the body, because both are made of matter and corporeal form. But when desire prevails over the sense and the sensibles, then it moves the soul to occupy itself with the delights of the body as, for instance, the pleasures of food, clothes and copulation, etc. When wrath spreads it moves the soul to vengeance and stirs it up to occupy itself with the pursuit of honour, dominion and the love of pre-eminence and rule. But all these desires plunge the soul into error and hinder it in its proper motion. They are like superficial adornment and gilt and have no reality in themselves. Wherefore we have already recorded the testimony of the philosopher Plato to the effect that he did not consider they were worthy of even the name of existence. If then they cannot be even called existing then what must their condition be?

These desires make the soul impotent to do its work and hinder it from happiness. They make a veil for the soul just as when tarnish adheres to a mirror preventing it from its perfection.[1] In such a case if those desires be used to fulfil the demands of the intellect, and if it is chosen to follow the commandments of the Law, the soul descends but a little way and is not excluded from happiness. For in such a case the intellect is the ruler of the soul. Every task is according to its command. It is also dominant over desire and wrath. Then the intellect is like a king,[2] and these concupiscible and irascible souls are like slaves and servants which act according to the command of the king. If the soul is diligently occupied with desires, then they dominate the intellect and at such a time the aid of the intellect is taken in planning how to satisfy them. This is a most perilous condition. In it the coveting of wickedness and obscenity and all manner of iniquity increases exceedingly. In it, contrary to the Divine Will, a man becomes expelled from obedience to the intellect and becomes trammelled in perpetual evil and everlasting wrath. The reason for this

[1] *Enneads*, I, iv. 10: "When the intellect is ordered to the higher that which contained the Soul's life is, as it were, cast down and becomes like the reflection on the smooth and bright face of a mirror. . . . When the mirror is in place the image appears, but if the mirror be not there or have become tarnished, nevertheless what would have produced the reflection is still there. It is thus with the soul. When there is peace the images of the rational appear in that which is within us capable of reflecting them," etc. The *Nichomachean Ethics*, IV, 7 declares pure happiness to be contemplative.

[2] Al Ghazzālī in the *Iḥyā* uses a similar figure of speech.

is that the first prophet that God sent to His creatures is the intellect, and the result of disobedience to it is to be bereft for ever of the good-will of God and bound fast in perpetual misery.

In philosophical discussions it has been proved that the name for the enjoyment which the soul experiences agreeable to it is "bodily pleasure", and it is clear that this enjoyment cannot be real enjoyment. An illustration of this is that when one has loosened a rope by which a man is hanging by the neck, he experiences pleasure, but this is not real pleasure, for his neck is still tied, and it is only that the knot has been loosed. There is a fuller exposition of this in its proper place in the philosophy. In this book it would violate the brevity which is our aim. Such deep and abstruse subjects really belong to the final topics of philosophy and to understand them is beyond the understanding of many people. Ordinary people only know the external sensibles and phantasy which accompanies sense and perceives particulars. So that thing which is not received by the senses or phantasy is untrue to the ordinary man. He does not regard it with any favour at all, because he has not the eye to perceive such things. Secondly, the thick veil of the senses intervenes between such people and fundamental truths, and for this reason they consider realities to be fabulous and false. Through this lack of understanding, people of insight and masters of intellect have compassion on their state, just as the blind are objects of pity to those who can see. Since ordinary people cannot understand reality, it is necessary to explain to them a thing of this sort by giving them similes from sensible things. And this use of illustrations is convenient in order that they may be satisfied. Otherwise they will consider that reality worthless and untrue, and turn their attention away from it.

On this account some philosophers have said: "The ordinary people consider the truth to be nothing and what is nothing to be something." This is nearly the same in meaning as the saying we have previously recorded from Plato, because you will often have seen and heard that when you explain some mode of intelligibles abstracted from matter, they immediately say that this describes some non-existent thing or, "This thing is non-existent and is nothing". But I say with absolute conviction that this idea of theirs is an error. The fact is that they seek for that intelligible and abstract matter in the senses, although it is not there but has genuine existence in itself. These people have not the eye of insight that they may have the capacity to perceive it! What hope have they other than this, that being reckoned blind from birth they should be held excused, and that we should guide them and have compassion on them and direct them as far as they have the capacity and ability to be guided. This is the work of the reverend prophets (on whom be peace) who bear the greatest pains and afflictions in order to instruct men in the Unity and lead them to believe on God and consider Him One. But those people on account of their stupidity and the weakness of their mind, think that the God who is the Creator of the whole universe must be extremely big-bodied and corpulent, and must be seated on a great throne with thousands and millions of His servants standing before Him, etc.

And even the best of them also attribute the qualities and names of created things to the Divine Essence. If to the common ignorant people the abstract realities and ideas above referred to are explained, they begin to say (we take refuge with Allah): "The Essence of the Creator does not exist and all this is deception." For this reason the learned and the philosophers have declared: "Leave such ignorant people as they are and whatever they think God is then let them keep to it. Otherwise if abstruse ideas are taught them they will even become deniers of the Essence."

O God, Thou knowest the weakness and the strength of creatures and art acquainted with the extent of everyone's knowledge. Grant forgiveness and mercy to all. Amen.

PART III. PROPHETHOOD[1]

CAP. I. OF THE ORDERS OF CREATED THINGS OF THE UNIVERSE AND THAT SOME ARE JOINED TO OTHERS

Because it is our object to explain the doctrine of prophethood, it is fitting that we should first of all explain the orders of created things and that the divine wisdom should be revealed in the production and creation of these various orders of being, so that it may be learned that God Most High favours every existing thing with its being and perfection according to its worth and capacity. And to whomsoever the Truly Just gave whatever He gave, He gave according to worth and capacity. It is also necessary for us to describe all the orders of existing things from the beginning to the end, and forasmuch as it is our aim at present to explain prophethood, it is essential that we should recount in detail all the orders superior and inferior to it, in order that the original purpose may be quite clear and well-fixed in the mind. These propositions have already been proved in the appropriate place and learned men have explained with powerful arguments that some of the bodies of existing things are joined to others and that the whole is one, i.e., all existing things from the centre of the earth to the topmost surface of the ninth heaven are one. And the living is one, although it has various parts.[2]

[1] The tracing of a line of ascent in the manner undertaken in the following pages emphasizes that this is more than a theology, it is a cosmology.

[2] Not a pantheistic statement, though at a time so near to that of Bāyazīd Bistāmī and Junayd, and the infiltration of Indian ideas into Islam, such a statement might not have been surprising. Here the unity is expressed up to the ninth sphere and not

There are two kinds of this whole. One is the world of becoming and corruption in which we live. The other is that universe in which generation and corruption, i.e., mutability and change, life and death, are not. That is the universe of the heavens and the planets, the mode of the composition and form of which is that between the heavens there is no gap or breach, and neither is susceptible to alteration. This theory has been proved in the science of astronomy by conclusive arguments which leave no room for uncertainty. The conjunction of those bodies which are found in this universe is proved by observation. One party holds that there is a vacuum, i.e., that a dimension is found in which there is no body supporting the dimension. But this has been proved false in physics by conclusive argument. The mature divine wisdom has made the existing things of the universe linked one with another in the following manner : Every species is linked to another in a continuous and ordered way. It is as though the Tirewoman of Nature's blessed hands had made this universe into a garland of a surpassingly wonderful kind, the particulars of which are as follows. By the joining of elements the first effect manifested in this universe from elements was that the rational (*sic*) soul was manifested in the form of plants. And plants were distinct from inanimate substances in the respect that plants move and obtain nutriment. In reference to this effect there are so many kinds of plants that they cannot be numbered. But we agree that there are three orders of plants, the higher, the middle and the lower. This division of orders is so that our meaning may be properly understood, and that all the orders may be fixed in the mind. Otherwise the orders of plants are innumerable and bound up with each one of them are endless accidents; but between all three orders also there are numerous other orders.

The first order of plants is that which grows of itself from the earth and has no need of shedding seeds, and neither is there any need to preserve seed for the survival of its species. Such, for instance, is the common grass of the jungle. This order is like the inanimate things. There is only a difference between it and them to the extent of that feeble movement which the form of the plant undertakes in receiving the effect of the soul.[1]

This noble effect (of soul) continually increases and becomes more powerful in other plants until some grow bigger and branches sprout in them and they preserve their species by means of seed. In these plants the effect of the divine wisdom is manifested far more than in the first mentioned. All these plants are in the first order.

beyond. The whole is integral and continuous, a contrast in some respects to the later atomism. One species merges into another and distinctions are declared to be only for the purposes of thought. This is the point in the repudiation of the doctrine of the vacuum, because the vacuum is denied in the interests of a theory of universal *continuum*.

[1] Plants have a portion of soul, *De Anima*, ii, 12, 424a, 33.

In other plants the effect of soul becomes so strong that among them are found trees in which there are trunk, leaves and fruit, and by the fruit is the preservation of their species. For such trees a gardener is necessary to set and tend and preserve them that then haply they may bear fruit and be verdant. Among plants this is the middle order. And in the middle order also there are various degrees and species, e.g., some approximating more to the first order as, for instance, trees found in mountains and wild places, in islands and forests. In these, though there is seed and the other qualities by which their species are differentiated, they have no need to be planted, cared for and tended.

Nobler and superior to this sort are trees in which the noble effect of soul is found to a greater extent than in other kinds, e.g., the olive, pomegranate, fig, quince and apple for the production and preservation of which seed is necessary, and for their cultivation, good soil, sweet water and pure air, if the balanced disposition of such noble plants is to be maintained.

Now this effect increases gradually till it comes to manifestation in the most noble palm in which plants come to their highest order, so that if they were to advance in the slightest degree from this they would pass the limits of plant life and take animal form. The effect of the soul in the date palm is so strong and great that abundant resemblances to the animal are produced in it. There is, for one thing, sex in it like animals, and secondly, for fertilization it is necessary for the male to be brought into conjunction with the female. This joining is called *talqīḥ* and is similar to sexual connection in animals. Thirdly, in the date palm there is, in addition to root and stem, a thing like the brain of animals called in the Arabic *jummār*, i.e., the pith of the date palm. This is so necessary to it that if any harm happens to it the palm will die. This is in contrast to other trees of which there is only one stock namely, the root, which is fixed in the earth and so long as it remains the tree will not die. But for the date palm there are two sources: one the root, and the other the pith which issues from the trunk. The fourth similarity (of the palm with the animal) is that the seed (i.e., its pollen) smells like human seed, and it is by means of this that fertilization takes place. In addition there are many more resemblances to be found between the palm and animals, but considerations of brevity forbid their mention here. Having these points in mind the Prophet said in a delightful manner: "Honour your sister the date palm; for behold, it was created from the remains of the clay of Adam."

It has been shown that the final stage of plants is this, where we arrive at the highest of plants and reach the lowest of animals. And although the last order of plants is the most noble of them it is only the lowest and meanest stage of animal. When the body advances from the stage of plants and even from the last stage of plant life, its case is that it becomes separated from the earth, and such a body has no need like the plants for roots to keep fixed in the earth in order to survive, for it obtains voluntary movement.[1] This is the initial stage of animals, but it is superior to the highest order of plants. But this stage is weak because in it there is only manifested the weakly effect of one sense, i.e., only the sense of touch which is called the common sense, is found in this stage.[2]

An example of this stage of the animals is the shell-dweller found in streams and on the seashore. These animals are known to possess the sense of touch in the following way: When any one lifts them up gently and quickly, they become separate from their place and are easily raised. But if you wish to pick them up slowly, they grip the place and fasten on. It thus appears that they become aware by their sense of touch that someone is holding them and trying to separate them from their place, and so they grip the place, and because they become fast it is difficult to pick them up and part them from it. The reason for this is that their likeness to plants is so strong and they are nearest to the plant kingdom. So when in changing place they become separate from the earth they become weak and very little life remains in them. Then when they progress from this stage they attain that in which there is change of place and movement also, and in which the power of sense is strengthened as, e.g., in insects, moths and a multitude of creeping things.

Advancing from this stage, when the effect of the soul increases, an animal is produced having four senses, such as the mole which has, excepting sight, the four other senses, or other animals in which there is one sense but not another. Animals thus progressing, reach another stage in which there is the sense of sight but only weak, as, for instance, the ant and the bee and other animals which have beadlike eyes and no eyelids wherewith to cover their eyes.[3]

After this when the effect of the soul becomes still more powerful the perfect animal is formed which has all five senses. But the animals which have five senses differ in their degrees. Some are stupid in whom the senses do not act well; and the senses of some are fine and keen so that they learn what they are taught, and accept commands and prohibitions, and have the capacity to discern and understand, like the horse among beasts and the hawk among birds.

Progressing from this order, the supreme order of the animals is

[1] Note that the greater part of this is Hippocrates and Galen. The Christian Syrian translators Ḥunayn b. Isḥāq, Qusṭā b. Lūqā, ‘Isā b. Yaḥyā translated Hippocrates into Arabic (see *Encyc. of Islam*, art. *Buḳrāṭ*), Galen's *Ars Medica, De Elementis Secundum Hippocratem, De Temperamentis, De Sanitate Tuenda, De Alimentorum Facultatibus, Therapeutics*, etc., and several commentaries of Galen on Hippocrates. The Commentary on *Timæus* was translated by Ḥunayn.

[2] All have at least one sense. *De Anima*, ii. 3, 414b, 2.

[3] *De Anima*, ii. 10, 421b, 29 ff., and *De Sensu*, v. 444b, 25 ff.

reached which is closest to the degree of humanity. And although this order is the most honourable and excellent of all the common orders of beasts, it is inferior and lower than the order of humanity, as, for instance, the monkey and other such animals which in form quite resemble men and between whom and men there is but little difference. If from that order the slightest advance is made we come to the order of humanity. Here among the animals the effect of the soul is strongest ; understanding and discernment have come, and the slightest things come to be understood. The stature is upright. It comes to accept direction in good things and to acquire what is taught with understanding, and is fit to constitute a separate species. Although this degree is superior to all the orders of beasts, it is in humanity the lowest of the low. If compared with perfect men then these are of the lowest order. Such men inhabit the remote north and south and its adjacent parts, such as the blacks who live in the furthest part of the land of the blacks, and like them other brutish men which are found in certain islands. Between these savages and the last-mentioned order of beasts there is a great difference, for these people also cannot fully discern what is beneficial for them, neither is there in them the ability to receive knowledge and wisdom. Therefore they cannot acquire excellence from the neighbouring peoples who are civilized and educated. And because they are not civilized and educated they continue to be in a low state. Therefore the educated and powerful nations exact service from them like the servitude of beasts and, in fact, except for servitude and slavery they have no capacity or aptness to any other kind of progress.

After this stage of humanity, the rational soul goes on progressing until, when you look at the men of the third, fourth and fifth climes, how perfect in reason and of quick intelligent nature they are ! They have ability of the highest degree in every sort of art and craft, and acquire deep penetration and wide proficiency in abstruse sciences and fine arts.

Again the most noble and eminent effect goes further till we have most learned and perfect men who for their sound thought and right opinion are famed throughout the ages and incomparable. They are so quick in understanding and so powerful in penetrating intelligence that they gain knowledge of future states and events. Their bright genius has so increased that they see unseen things as though they were under a thin curtain.

When man reaches this noble degree he comes near to the plane of the angels. By angels we mean that existence which is above the existence of man. In this case certain stages remain between the degree of humanity and the sublime degree to which (intermediate stages) that progressive man quickly attains.

In the following chapter we will explain in detail the state of the powers of the microcosm (*'ālam ṣaghīr*) and their interrelation. We will also show how near by the senses and powers of man, progressing to something higher than themselves, reach the order of angels and derive benefit and help from angels.[1]

By the following explanation the reader will be able to estimate the term of the plane of humanity and its noble and supreme degree, and will also learn in what manner the relation of the Spirit (*rūḥ*) occurs, called in the Qur'ān " Holy Spirit ".

Further, from our forthcoming explanation the various orders of existences will be fixed in the understanding of the readers. And we will show that the Order of Mission (*risāla*) and prophethood is the most noble and excellent, if God will.

CAP. II. WHEREIN IT IS EXPLAINED THAT MAN IS THE MICROCOSM AND THAT HIS POWERS HAVE CONNECTION ONE WITH ANOTHER

It is now for us to prove that whatever things are to be found in the macrocosm, i.e., in this universe, e.g., the four elements and wildernesses and habitations, sea and dry-land, plain and hill, minerals, plants and animals, in short, all things, are also to be found in man,[2] as though man were a kind of smaller universe and were composed of all these things of the universe. Some things are found in him manifestly and others obscurely. Here in accordance with this claim we will give a brief explanation by which readers possessed of intelligence and conviction may understand the theory comprehensively. Otherwise, all these subjects are so abstruse and wide that a book would be found necessary for the subject of every chapter. Nevertheless, in this book there is no room for an elaborate explanation and so it is explained concisely.

Because man is composite, it is not possible for simple elements to be found in him in their simplicity because if that were so the simples would immediately dissolve man and cause him to be non-existent, e.g., if the fiery particle came into the human body in its simplicity, it would burn up the other parts which were in the body and all those parts would dissolve and find their centre. Similarly with the rest of the elements. These also being simple, if they were found in the composite body then the same would be the case. We have given the illustration of fire because its action is so manifest. Thus it seems that all the elements will be found in man in composition. Now if it be considered, it will be learned that in the human body there are things which in heat and dryness are instead of fire, and some which in

[1] Cf. John of Damascus : *De Fide Orthod.*, II, Cap. XII (*P.G.*, 94, 921). " God then made man without evil, upright, virtuous, free from pain and care, glorified with every virtue, adorned with all that is good, like a second microcosm within the macrocosm, another angel capable of worship," etc.

[2] *De Fide Orthodoxa*, Bk. II, Cap. XII (*P.G.*, 94, 925). " The bond of union between man and inanimate things is the body and its composition out of the four elements."

heat and moisture are in the place of air, and some which in coldness and moisture are in the place of water.[1] In the body, in the place of fire is the gall which hangs by the liver, because that is hot and dry and the humour of this temperament, namely, the bilious, is situated here. The effect of heat and dryness reaches the whole body from this. In the place of earth is the spleen, the disposition of which is cold and dry and the humour of this temperament is situated here, i.e., the melancholic, and from it the portion of this humour is distributed according to necessity. In the place of air there is blood which flows in the veins, for its temperament is hot and moist which is the temperament of air. In the place of water is phlegm, the temperament of which is cold and moist, for that portion of food is called *balgham* which, after cooking, remains raw and so, contrary to the other humours, has the capability of being cooked again. Thus when it is digested it becomes perfect nutriment and nothing is wasted. Therefore for its situation, unlike other humours, there is no special receptacle provided.

In another respect man may be likened to the macrocosm in that the heart is the source of heat and dryness, and so it is like fire ; and the blood is the source of heat and moisture, and so its disposition is like that of air ; and the brain is the source of coldness and moisture, and so its disposition is like that of water ; and bones of the body are the source of coldness and dryness and so are in the place of earth.

And it is as if these four members are the principles of the four elements and the elements their derivatives, and similarly in general the other things which are found in man, the microcosm, like the macrocosm. Some are these : those moistures which issue from the eyes and mouth are like the springs and streams of the earth. The vapours of the body are like clouds and the sweat is like rain. The big veins of the body are like those waterbeds in which water continually flows, and the small veins are like streams and small springs. The hairs of the body are like the plants, and those living things which are produced on the surface of the body, such as the flea, are like living creatures of the dry land. And those living things which are born

[1] The scheme is composed of the elements of Empedocles, the four cardinal humours according to Hippocrates and the four temperaments according to Galen.
The scheme may be set out in the following table :

Element	*Organ or Secretion*	*Quality*	*Temperament*
Fire	Gall or yellow bile	Hot-dry	Bilious or choleric
Earth	Spleen or black bile	Cold-dry	Melancholic
Air	Blood	Hot-moist	Sanguine
Water	Phlegm (no special organ)	Cold-moist	Phlegmatic

Note the similar references to the physiological scheme, e.g., Damascene, *op. cit.*, II, xvi. (*P.G.*, 94, 932). "Anger is ebullition of heart's blood produced by bilious exhalation or turbidity."

within the body are like the living creatures of the sea. The upper half of the body on which is the face and other organs, is like the inhabited portion of the earth in which are cities and towns inhabited, and the lower half is like deserts and wildernesses. The eyes in respect to their light and rays are like the stars and the layers of the eyes are the heavens in which the stars are set. The likeness of the accidents of the body is exactly as the happenings in the universe when in the earth the winds blow, earthquakes come, and storms arise; similarly sneezing, cold and fever are diseases of the body like these events.

Thus as in the universe there are various conditions of various things, likewise in the body some limbs move by their essence and nature and are susceptible to rest, some by their own essence are at rest, and some move accidentally or by someone who moves them. Some members of the human body have a relation or peculiarity similar to the twelve constellations and the seven planets, and the nature of those members is made according to the constellations and the planets. The exposition of this theory is given fully in the science of astrology; there would be a danger of exceeding in length if the matter were to be discussed here.

Now we have to explain the important point that the macrocosm is round and that this round shape is the most excellent and noble of all shapes. Therefore the likeness of the microcosm to the macrocosm is not complete until this microcosm be round also.[1]

From consideration it seems that this microcosm was created round, for what is intended by the whole human body is its nobler and higher member, i.e., the head. In this all the senses reside and by the means of it all the effects of humanity, i.e., discernment and understanding, memory and thought, etc., are manifested. Further, the connection of all the powers of the soul is with the head and to it is given roundness which is the most excellent of shapes. This head is what is essentially intended by the whole human body, but if it had been created separate and without connection with the other members then it could not continue to survive for any length of time and it would not be able to complete its allotted span. For man needs to change his place, to exert effort, to seek what he wants and to repel hurtful things, and all this work is by movement and it is obvious that the movement of a round thing is rolling. Therefore when man moved for his needs and was round in shape like the head, then he would always be in danger of numerous calamities and in a short time would perish. Therefore he is made with other members.

As well as this convenience the head has need of such heat as would preserve the special proportion (mean) of its disposition and be extremely mild. For this heat it was also necessary that it should have its place in the middle of the head in order that like the centre of the

[1] *Timæus*, 33B and 44D–45B.

sphere its effect might be uniform in all directions and preserve the whole body of the sphere. But the substance of the brain is cold-moist,[1] and so if the abode of this heat were fixed in the middle of the brain, then the cold and moisture of the brain would immediately quench it and man would perish.[2] Secondly, if that heat were to meet the moisture of the brain, then many vapours would be produced, and because they did not find their way to the air would again turn to the heat and destroy it.

For the above-mentioned conveniences and other advantages, the details of which would be tedious, it was necessary that this heat should remain at a distance from the brain. Therefore the heart was devised as its place. But because the heart is far from the brain, it was therefore necessary that between the substance of the brain and the place of heat there should be a road made by which heat might reach the brain. For this purpose the arteries were made which are between the heart and the brain and by which spirit reaches the brain. And because from the storehouse of the heart the distance to the brain is far, there was therefore the necessity that the heat should be created great, so that in traversing the road it might decrease gradually, and reach the brain to the degree necessary and preserve its temperature. For this reason was heat created greater in the heart.

Now because in the heart there is great and intense heat, smoky vapours continually issue from it.[3] In such a case, to let out these vapours and to draw the outside air which is agreeable to its disposition, there was the necessity for a bellows which would always be at work and lessen the vapours and not allow excessive heat to be generated. For this advantage the Wise and Powerful One made the lungs, the work of which is to expel from within the hot air and vapours and to filter from outside that air which it draws in, and to send it in a condition proportionate and agreeable towards the heart and so be the cause of its survival and continuance.[4] Now because the brain continues to do its work, and since by heat its strength is diminished and it becomes dissolved, it was necessary that some nutriment should be given to it which would compensate for the dissolved particles. For this purpose all the instruments of nutriment, the stomach, liver etc., were created in the human body ; and last of all hands and feet were created for the need that man had for such organs and instruments for the quest of his desire and to repel hurtful and unpleasant things.

In addition to these conveniences which we have explained there are hundreds of others and these are fully explained in books which

[1] *De Sensu*, ii. 438b, 29.
[2] *De Part. Anim.*, ii. 7.
[3] *De Somno et Vigilia*, iii. 458a, 1.
[4] *Timæus*, 70C and D ; Arist. : *De Respiratione*, 475b, 19, and 480a, 20.

have been written on this subject. At any rate, from all these external and internal advantages, and these hidden and manifest benefits, are learned the nature, power and perfect wisdom of the Creator—may His name be honoured!—And blessed be Allah the most beautiful of Creators!

By this explanation it has been proved fully that man is the microcosm, and together with this it has been made clear that his powers have mutual relation such as there is in the macrocosm, and further, that just as in the macrocosm there is progress from the lowest degree to the highest, likewise the powers of man continually progress from the lowest to the highest.

It was our original intention to explain the powers of man, but without writing of the above subjects these intentions could not be fulfilled. Under this compulsion these matters have been first related, and in the following chapter they will be explained, if God will.

CAP. III. IN THIS CHAPTER IT IS EXPLAINED THAT THE FIVE SENSES RISE TO A COMMON POWER (SOMETIMES CALLED COMMON SENSE AND SENSORIUM) AND BY THE GRACE OF GOD RISE EVEN HIGHER THAN THAT

It was formerly stated that there is a power, the common sense,[1] which gathers what the five senses perceive and know and arranges these things. If there had been no such power then when sensibles disappeared from before us there would be no preservation and accumulation of what the sense learns. We now explain how the rational soul is connected with the body, so that body and soul may become capable of receiving the effect of one another.

Because the body in comparison with the soul is in the final degree of grossness and turbidity,[2] the soul, when it moves lower and desires to become joined to the body, is under compulsion by the mutual relation. For until the composite body is refined, as far as possible, by means of several (interposing) mediums, the soul by reason of its perfect rarity and fineness cannot join to it. Similarly, the soul moves towards the lower and as far as possible turns its powers towards the body and then it can attain connection with the body. In short, both soul

[1] Common sense has the power of discriminating between the sensations of the special senses, and is the perception of the common sensibles such as movement, rest, shape, dimension, number, and is the conscious faculty of memory. See *De Anima*, III, i. 425a, 15 to III, ii. 427a, 9.

[2] Cf. Arist.: *De Partibus Animalium*, iv. 10, 686a, 25 ff. and 687a, 7 ff. There is progressive refinement, the soul of plants is nutritive, of animals nutritive plus sensitive, appetitive and motive, of man the foregoing and the intellective in addition. In sensation, the form of the sensible is abstracted from matter and reaches sense through a medium, as sound through air. Correspondingly there is a modification brought about in the sense. Passive reason receives sense impressions and active reason meets these impressions with interpretative forms of thought. The whole idea is organic and seems an attempt to resolve the dualism of body-soul. Nevertheless, the dualism remains in spite of the " intermediate stages ".

and body incline towards each other and the soul decreases in purity and the body puts aside its impurity and so there may be mutual conjunction.

This abstruse doctrine should be understood by an example. When the food reaches the stomach, that organ first refines it by means of digestion and then sends it to the liver, whereafter, making it finer still, the liver turns it into blood and sends it to the heart. The heart makes that thick blood still rarer by its heat [1] and by means of the fine veins, the name for which is " arteries " and which are empty inside, sends this (refined blood) to the brain. That refined and thinned blood flows in the veins like water in streams. That is, in these veins there is some space which remains empty, lest being filled with blood they become choked.[2]

This blood is like the heat of the heart, and so in that space left in the veins to the brain, rare vapours are produced by the blood and mount to the brain.[3] The more these vapours rise the more refined they become, until, arriving in the brain, they spread to all parts of it by means of veins as fine as a hair, and the heat of those vapours meets the coldness of the brain [4] and obtains equable proportion (i.e., a mean) and this properly proportioned thing is called " natural spirit ".[5]

By the suitability and appropriateness of the fineness and subtilty of this spirit, the powers of the soul are poured out on the instrument of the spirit, i.e., so far as clear spirit is produced in the brain, to that extent there is in it the capacity to receive the effects of the soul, i.e., sense, understanding, etc.[6]

Now from the brain, nerves spread throughout the whole body, and by means of these there is sense and voluntary movement.[7] This sense and voluntary movement is the special characteristic of the animal, distinguishing it from the plants.

Of these nerves, one hollow nerve comes to the eye, called the pupil, and into this the spirit comes exceedingly pure [8] and fine, and by means of it sight is obtained. Similarly one nerve goes to the ear, by which the work of hearing is done, and on the same analogy for the remainder of the senses.

[1] *De Somno et Vigilia*, iii. 458a, 11 ff.
[2] *Ibid.*, 458a, 6.
[3] *De Somno et Vigil*, 458a, 1.
[4] *De Partibus Anim.*, ii. 7, 652a, and *De Somno et Vigil*, 457b, 30.
[5] *De Somno et Vigil*, 456a, 11, *τὸ σύμφυτον πνεῦμα*.
[6] It should be noted that thus spirit is subordinate to soul. This was entirely altered when *Rūḥ* took the higher place and body became associated with soul. Here spirit has more of the character of vital breath. Much of the above is from Galen.
[7] The brain thus becomes the centre and this is not Aristotelian. It is, however, to be attributed to Galen (*De Usu Partium*, Bk. VIII).
[8] John of Damascus has a phrase which constantly occurs : " The organ is . . . the anterior (or mid or posterior) ventricle of the brain and *the vital spirit* which it contains." See *De Fide Orthod.*, Bk. II, xix and xx (*P.G.*, 94, 937 f.).

When the effect of sensibles is obtained in any sense, it proceeds to the common sense. This perceives and senses the sensation of all the senses; the common sense is a power of the soul which is the final stage of this subtle substance of the body, i.e., the spirit, and accepts all these effects. And as each sense perceives the sensibles of its proper species, and accepting their effect distinguishes between the individuals of that species, so the assembling or common sense alone accepts all the effects of all the senses and distinguishes them; but the method of perception in these two differs, for the five senses receive the effects and forms of the sensibles gradually, one after another,[1] but the common sense receives and perceives the forms of the senses all at once,[2] and it is not affected by their forms because the common sense is itself form, and one form cannot accept another form by way of effect, but only by some other way which is superior and nobler than this method of effect (*ta'aththur*) and in this way it receives all the sensibles without regard to time, analysis or division.

And no intermixing of many forms takes place in the common sense in the same way as when several pictures can be drawn on some body in one place, one must be on top of another and become mixed up and cramped, but each form remains quite distinct to it.

Above this power is yet another power the name of which is "the power of presentation" (imagination).[3] Its place is the forepart of the brain. But some people think that the common sense and the power of presentation are one and the same. After this there is the power of memory which is like a storehouse in which all the forms of sensibles are kept safe.[4] And although a long time may have elapsed since the perception, nevertheless when the occasion arises, the power of memory takes from its storehouse the perceived form and presents it to us. The place of its abode is the hinderpart of the brain. Superior and more excellent than all of these is another power of the soul, the name for which is "thought". This is the power whereby there is movement towards the abstract reason. This reflective power is peculiar to man and is not found in any other animal.[5] This power has its place in the middle portion of the brain.[6] The power of imagination and memory are in animals also, and the portions in which these

[1] Senses receive sensibles successively. *De Anima*, III, i. 425a, 23 ff. Common sense receives them simultaneously. *De Sensu*, vii. 449a, 14 ff.

[2] Cf. *De Anima*, III, ii. 427a, 5 ff.

[3] This is *phantasma* and not imagination as we understand it. Presentation seems to be the best equivalent. Galen, *op. cit.* John of Damascus: *De Fide Orthod.*, II, Cap. XVII (*P.G.*, 94, 933).

[4] *De Fide Orthod.*, II, Cap. xx (*P.G.*, 94, 940). "The organ of memory is the posterior ventricle of the brain which the Greeks call the παρεγκεφαλίς and the vital spirit which it contains."

[5] *De Fide Orthod.*, II, xii (*P.G.*, 94, 928). "Man's reason unites him to incorporeal and intelligent natures."

[6] *De Fide Orthod.*, II, xix (*P.G.*, 94, 937). "The organ of thought therefore is the mid-ventricle of the brain and the vital spirit which it contains."

powers are situated are in their brains also. But the middle lobe is not in their brains and so animals are devoid of thought.

The name of this power (of thought) is humanity. The more this power grows and the more sound it is, the more is man distinct from the beasts. And the man in whom this power moves most and accepts the bounteous effect of reason, the more the quality of humanity is increased in him. So the man who uniformly uses this power in his sense perceptions, and continues always to consider the causes and primary principles of everything sensed and perceived, and keeps moving towards the intellect in search of causes, upon him, reason bestows the realities of things perceived. And in man the form of humanity is capable of being perfected and his soul comes to conceive the reality of things. And because these realities are of eternal existence, the mortal hand of generation and corruption and time cannot reach them, because they are simple. Thus the possessor of thought and consideration becomes occupied in the perception and investigation of those realities, and the realities of things become the centre of all his endeavours and purposes. In addition, because these things have no connection with time, there is no past and future in them but the condition and existence of every reality is the same at every time. In this noble degree man progresses until he arrives at a stage, which if he should surpass he would pass from the bounds of humanity and attain to the degree of the angel, which is more abstract [1] and luminous than humanity. Here it is fitting that this degree should be explained in detail as other degrees have been explained. And here it is proper to explain the condition of revelation (*waḥī*) and its relation to man.

CAP. IV. IN EXPLANATION OF WAḤI [2]

The person who has read thoughtfully the former explanations and understood them, will have learned that the degree and station which we explained last of all is the noble goal of mankind and the end of the perfection of the children of men.

When men reach this stage either one of two states befalls them. A man either makes continual natural progress, i.e., as long as he lives he deeply studies existing things in order that he may become

[1] Cf. the " separate substances " of later Scholastic.

[2] Plotinus does not provide revelation but ecstasy. Proclus speaks of Plato in his commentary on *Timœus*, iii. 63, 24 in terms which make us feel that we have an expression of belief in an inspired man who enjoys special illumination, which almost corresponds to the philosophical illumination of " prophethood " in these early Muslim writers. Cf. also the *Commentary* of Proclus on the *Republic*, lix. 19. " In accordance with the good counsel of the higher powers who revealed their mysterious reason to souls inhabiting this lower world." For the Philonic view : *De Migrat. Abrah.*, 7. The prophet is passive. He is insensible to externals and comes to image and form ideas while in a state of trance. See also his *Quis Rerum Div. Heres.*, 53.

Yet a combination of certain elements from the ecstatic view of attaining to the unknown who is otherwise unknowable, is to be found in Philo, as it is to be found in those Muslim writers who seek to explain the mode of prophethood.

acquainted with their realities, to the utmost of his mortal power, and by that perpetual thought his speculation becomes so acute and powerful that divine matters and spiritual mysteries become revealed to his soul as self-evident matters. This clearness (manifestation) is such that the highly intelligent person has no need for syllogistic reasoning, because in the latter there has to be progress by degrees from lower to higher, whereas here in his illuminated reason there is such light and clearness that everything becomes manifest to him.

(That is one alternative) otherwise his state may be as follows: Divine things may come to be received by him without any progress towards them at all, but in the manner that the abstract matters in themselves descend upon the lofty enlightened mind by reason of mutual affinity.

This second condition should therefore be understood in detail. Man's progress is always in the following way: He progresses from the power of sense to the power of imagination, and from the power of imagination he advances to the power of thought, and from the power of thought he turns his attention to the power of reason. Then he has the perception of the realities of those things which are in his intellect. This gradual progress is because all the powers are joined by spiritual links, as we have explained in the previous chapter in detail. But this form of progress becomes reversed in some dispositions, i.e., because the powers by reason of their conjunction become most powerful in receiving impressions and in effectiveness, the powers of some men come to overflow in the downward direction. In this case the reason begins to affect the power of thought, and the power of thought the power of presentation, and the power of presentation the sense. Then the man begins to see the realities of intelligibles, causes and origins in such a way as if their entity were in this world outside the mind (i.e., as if he were actually seeing these things outside the mind in the phenomenal world) and as though he saw them with his own eyes and heard them with his own ears, just as the sleeper sees in sleep resemblances to sensibles in his imagination and thinks that he is seeing them externally. Similarly this man of highest rank observes intelligibles. And frequently the things which he perceives are correct, in some of them being good news for the future and in some fear and danger. And sometimes he regards intelligibles in their identical state, and in this case there is no need for interpretation; and sometimes he perceives them enigmatically (or obscurely), and then there is need for interpretation.[1]

There are various reasons for the difference of conditions, but there is no room for explanation of them in this book of ours. When the

[1] This scheme was afterwards used by Ibn K͟haldūn in the *Muqaddima* to his famous *Universal History*. Is Ibn Miskawaih the source for Ibn K͟haldūn or had they a common source?

power of the intellect prevails on the man of powerful understanding and lively mind, then sensibles become, as it were, absent and separate from him, and in the power of presentation he so contemplates as if he descended to sensibles. In such a case, respecting anything the possessor of *waḥī* sees and hears he has no doubt or dubiety whatever, and the things perceived are exactly correct and worthy of credence. And because the past and future of those intelligibles are one, the reverse of sensibles, therefore they are present and manifest together at the same time, i.e., as they contemplate past events so do they the future, and when they give information to the people of the world concerning the past and the future, it is proved correct. And when they compare what they perceive with those learned ones who discern reality, the revelations of both agree [1]; for when the principles and causes are one, then the results must also be one. That is, although there is a difference in the mode of revelation and perception, nevertheless the causes of the perception are one and so why should the consequences and results be not also one? So when they relate their perceived realities and inspired doctrines to those sages and philosophers who have obtained the realities by their own gradual advances and power of perception, the opinions of both agree, and so both prophets and philosophers confirm one another; but rather the sages and philosophers are the first of all creatures to confirm the prophets, for both agree in the perception of those matters of reality. For the difference between them is only that the philosopher comes to his contemplation by advancing from the lower to the higher and the prophet has descended from the higher to the lower to apprehend reality. Just as the distance from the higher plane to the lower is one but in reference to that person who is below is called ascent and in relation to that person who stands above is called descent, such is the case with these realities and contemplations, namely, that the philosopher ascends and the prophets descend and perceive; but the realities are one.

Nevertheless there is this difference: that by reason of the perception of the power of presentation, those realities and quiddities are coloured with a corporeal and material colour; because as material things ascend towards the reason they leave their original forms, so also when intellectual things descend to the power of imagination they adopt material forms appropriate to them. So when the true prophets observe and contemplate those intelligibles, their pure soul recognizes them and is convinced of their truth without doubt, because these are the realities which man perceives by gradual movement and

[1] With this conception of the unity of revelation and philosophy should be compared Ibn Rushd's discussion of the relations of philosophy and theology in *Kitāb Faṣl ul Maqāl fī mā baina'sh Sharī'ati wa'l hikmati mina'l ittiṣāl*. Later days were to experience a revulsion from the ideas expressed by Miskawaih; and Al Ghazzālī, Ibn Taimīya and Ibn Hazm all wrote books in refutation of philosophy—though they used philosophic method!

thought, and so he has no doubt at all of their truth. Similarly when thought descends and contemplates them there is no room for doubt.

This degree is very extensive and the degrees of prophecy and the prophets' orders in it are very diverse. Sometimes existing realities appear to these honoured persons quite clearly and there is nothing obscure in them, but sometimes some obscurity remains in them as if a veil or curtain were hung between. And in the same way there is diversity in the perception of future things. Sometimes events which occur centuries afterwards, e.g., wars and seditions, are manifested and sometimes they contemplate conditions which are to happen even after thousands of years.

The honoured prophets, on whom be peace, had to adopt a style of explanation which was near to the understanding and could benefit all classes of men in common, in order to proclaim their message and teach men. So they used riddles and proverbial sayings which, beside being commonly understood, satisfied the elect also. Each man was informed by the prophet's word according to the extent of his intelligence and power, and received admonition and wisdom. And when these honoured persons see that the intelligence of some follower and believer is great, they instruct him the more according to the breadth of his understanding. Thus we know without doubt that the Prophet did not instruct Abū Huraira in the way that he instructed Lord 'Ali. Likewise what he taught to intelligent Arabs he did not teach to Bedouins and wild Arabs. For knowledge for the soul is as food for the body and the perfection of food is that it should preserve the body, perfect its form and make it increase in power. If too much and too strong food is given to a weak body then it will not be able to digest it, and it will be a danger to its life ; and so, contrary to the intention, the body will become sick. It is the same in the case of knowledge. If a load beyond its power is put upon the soul then instead of its being benefited, it is injured. In teaching knowledge it is fitting to adopt that expedient which is resorted to in the case of food for a child of tender years. It is first given milk to drink and the gradually soft and light foods are given for a long time till it becomes able to eat heavy foods like meat and corn.[1] If heavy food is given at once then the child will get sick and sometimes die. We think that what we have said will be sufficient for the understanding of this abstruse subject.

CAP. V. THAT THE INTELLECT IS A KING WHO RULES AND DOMINATES ALL CREATED THINGS NATURALLY [2]

The rank which the Creator conferred on the Intellect surpasses all other ranks, because all generated and created things are less than the

[1] Cf. Alexandrian idea of two classes of men.

[2] For the kingship of reason see *De Anima*, I, v. 410b, 10 ff. and John of Damascus : *De Fide Orthod.*, II, xii (*P.G.*, 94, 928). "The reasoning part naturally bears sway over that which is devoid of reason."

intellect and depend on it. Furthermore, the intellect, by reason of excellencies and perfections, confers benefits upon all, and is the cause of assistance reaching them.

Although some contingent things, by reason of their remoteness from the intellect and their contamination with bodily defilement, withdraw from obedience to it, nevertheless, when they catch but a glimpse of its bright countenance, they immediately bow the head in reverence before it. Thus Reason is like a King who remains secluded from his servants and slaves, but while they are unable to see him, keeps observing them. For this reason they oppose and disobey him, thinking him not to be present. And they think he does not see them, but when he lifts the veil and his servants come to know that he is looking at them, as soon as they see him, they make their obeisance to him and cease their opposition.

It is the characteristic of beasts that they naturally fear man and serve him, although some animals are so strong that several men could not restrain them, and if they were to seize several men would defy their united efforts to get free. Thus in power and might all those animals are stronger than man, but one man can rule many strong beasts and make them serve him. This superiority is due to intellect. It is also the case that among men, ordinary people when they come across any person who possesses a greater portion of intellect, obey and fear him, e.g., the chief of a village, and such will themselves be subject to those who are superior to them in intellect, e.g., a ruler, a judge, a governor or a viceroy.

The reason for this is that the intellect is naturally served and obeyed. Wherever it is found, it makes other things subject to itself. It is found more in ordinary people than in animals, and so they are obeyed by animals ; more in chiefs than in common people, and therefore ordinary people obey them. Proceed in this way and you will discover that the one in whom is the greatest intellect, will be obeyed and served by all the universe. It does sometimes happen that a man is thought to have more intellect than he really has, and he is obeyed on that account. Sometimes it happens that people who love to dominate and rule, wish to become leaders by their wickedness and cunning. They give proof of quick intelligence and cunning, and make people obedient to them by ostentation and display and they often succeed in their object.

By this it will have become clear to our readers how noble and excellent is the rank of the intellect and that it is naturally served and obeyed. All contingent things are inferior to it, and they are its servants and subjects, deriving help and assistance from it. For the nobility and plenitude of the intellect is intrinsic (essential), and there is no intrusion of display in it. There are some cases in which by ostentation, or by chance, or by good luck, some persons attain to rule and become the objects of service, but there is no occasion to describe such here. Should it be fitting this will be related later.

We have dealt with this subject in a separate chapter so that it may be learned that people, in the time of the prophets, see with their own eyes those effects of the pure intellect of the prophets, which we learn only by report and hearsay (*khabr wa sam'*). For this reason the people naturally obeyed them and dedicated their life and property to them, even coming to regard as enemies their own friends and kindred and the people of their own households for the sake of the prophets. Furthermore, they feared them in a way that they would not fear even a tyrannising king, unparalleled in awe, wielding armies, victorious and conquering; and this notwithstanding that a king gives honour and wealth to his warriors and fulfils their legitimate and illegitimate desires, in contrast to the prophets, who forbid and prohibit people's illegitimate lusts and pleasures.

The real cause of this fear and subservience which we have described is that men and animals are subordinate to him whom they find to be greater in intellect, and the effects of whose intellect they observe.

Here it may be objected that some people, even in the time of the prophets, declared them to be false, and instead of rendering homage and submission, were at enmity with them, and instead of regarding them with reverence, held themselves to be the more honourable. This doubt is the result of limited observation and lack of thought, for in the natural properties of all things it always happens accidentally that a person, for some special reason or some particular object, goes contrary to his natural virtue. Likewise, opponents and infidels were all at pains to decline to confirm the truth of the prophet and to render obedience to him. Often the reasons for opposition are exceedingly strong. For instance, they do not obey the commandments for fear of the loss of their leadership, or for fear of losing their desires and pleasure, on account of covetousness, or else because the love of following the ancient customs of their forefathers prevents them from submission, etc.

But what we have said is simply an account of the natural property of the intellect, that wherever it is it is obeyed and that the majority of people will submit to him in whom it is strong. And it is the rule for natural things that no trouble or difficulty faces a man when he sets himself to act according to them. On the other hand, there are accidents which are adventitious to every natural thing. E.g., it often happens that a man's nature demands some particular thing, but for some other reason he leaves what is natural to him and chooses what is contrary to it, so doing something in violation of his soul and conscience. E.g., he is cowardly but makes a show of bravery, stingy but makes a parade of generosity, unjust by nature, but for some advantage or under compulsion does justice. Such examples are numerous, and it is a strange calamity for man. Such a man is called *mu'jib.*

CAP. VI. SHOWING THAT TRUE VISION IS A PART OF PROPHETHOOD

We have already spoken of the conditions of the reality of the soul and its natural movement. Taken in conjunction with this and by the description of prophethood and the reason for sleep this doctrine will become well fixed in the mind.

The reality of sleep is as follows. When the soul becomes tired of using the instruments of sense, it becomes detached from them to take rest and so leaves the instruments of sense unemployed. The condition which supervenes is called sleep. This taking of rest is essential because the senses are bodily instruments and like all bodies they tire with labour and weariness falls upon them. At such a time it is necessary for them to rest and for the nature during rest to make up the deficiency which has resulted by working.[1] The example of this is that the eyes fulfil their task of seeing in the following manner. In the arteries within the brain pure spirit comes into the hollow nerve which reaches the pupil of the eye. That spirit is so subtle that, passing through the layers of the eye, it becomes dissipated and being turned into a ray issues from the pupil of the eye. This ray complements the light from without and the ray which results in the crystalline lens of the inside of the eye becomes saturated with the light which proceeds from the things seen. This condition is called sight.

So when man perceives things in this way and the refined and pure spirit becomes quite dissipated, turbid and impure spirit takes its place. In such circumstances trouble and pain in the eyes is experienced and the man appears to be seeing but dimly, or as if there were sand in his eyes. The eye resembles a reservoir filled with clear water. If there is a hole in it, then first the clear water will issue forth and afterwards turbid and muddy water. So if its vent be closed and it be again filled with water, the reservoir will remain in its original condition. Otherwise all its water will be exhausted. Likewise, if from within the eye the pure spirit is exhausted, it is necessary for its vent to be closed and the eyelids to be closed so that the pure spirit, which is the means to sight, should gather again. And this condition has to be prolonged in order that the action of the eyes should move according to its natural fitness (*mujrā*). The name for this rest is "sleep" which, according to the explanation given, is necessary for the eyes and all the senses. Therefore in this case the senses become idle and the soul does not get any opportunity to move. But it is impossible for the soul to remain idle. Thus when it does not find any external particulars to perceive, it turns towards those particulars which it has previously perceived by sense, and which have been stored

[1] *De Somn. et Vigil.*, i. 454a, 25 ff.

up in the power of memory. It now begins to occupy itself with these by forming compositions of some particulars with others. By this composing and occupation of itself, the perception which it obtains is sometimes strange and rare, as if it were seeing unseen things. E.g., it sees a man flying, and a camel riding on some bird, or a cow with a body smaller than a man's, and such kinds of false composition. All these are called confused dreams (*aḍghāth ul aḥlām*) which cannot be interpreted.

But when the soul turns its attention in sleep towards the intellect, and is not occupied in the perception of sensibles, it observes those things which are to occur in the future. Now if in this observation it has complete enjoyment and perfect insight then whatever it sees is true and correct and has no need for interpretation, for the soul sees it in its real identity. But if the attention is less, then what it sees is enigmatic and symbolical and needs interpretation. This is called true vision.[1] This is awareness (*khabr*) and prophethood, because this is always the state of the prophet and this condition overwhelms him whether asleep or awake. Other people only have this condition in sleep, and then only now and again, and this quality cannot be gained by instruction and learning or by volition. Therefore, if once in a lifetime a person has a dream of this sort, he should ponder deeply on the state of the soul and its happiness, and understand that the happiness of the soul is an everlasting boon. So he should try to gain it and gain also the true happiness of the two worlds, the present and the hereafter.

CAP. VII. THE DIFFERENCE BETWEEN PROPHETHOOD AND SOOTHSAYING [2]

It seems proper here to discuss the nature of soothsaying and then show the difference between soothsaying and prophethood. This sort of power of the soul is often manifested at a time when the mission of some prophet is near. The reason for this is that when a "shape" comes to be produced in the heavens by which some important matter or great change in the universe is to take place, from the beginning of the manifestation of that form till it is completely and perfectly manifested, several existences appear in the world of manifestation which approximate to the perfect things intended, but are imperfect because their cause, i.e., the heavenly shape is still incomplete. But when that shape appears in the heavens complete and perfect, there is produced in the universe a perfect existence necessitated by the shape.

[1] A departure from true Aristotelianism, cf. *De Somniis* and *De Divin. per Somnum*, *passim*.

[2] It should be noted that there is a similar juxtaposition in the discussion of prophethood and the difference between prophethood and soothsaying, in the *Muqaddima* of Ibn Khaldūn.

But such an existence appears in the place of manifestation for only a short time, because the heavens are at all times making diverse movements and rapidly changing shape. So the perfect power necessitating that particular shape appears only in one person or in two or three. Such person or persons accept the effect of the shape perfectly and completely grasping it perfect the power. Thus the man who is born at about the same time, before the perfect completion of the shape, will be deficient in power and the greater distance he is from the perfect shape, the more deficient in power will he be.

The effect of this perfect shape is manifested in this universe in prophethood. And the effects of the defective shapes come to manifestation in the form of soothsaying. For this reason, a single person obtains prophethood only after a long period or in certain periods perhaps two or three persons are honoured with the blessed prerogative of *waḥī*.

Now as the power of guidance of the common people is exercised in various countries and cities, to fulfil this requirement the Lord Creator, glorious and sublime, sometimes sends prophets into several cities and countries, and sometimes gathers more than one in a single city. So when prophethood becomes manifested—the complete effect of that perfect shape—the imperfection and weakness of the powers produced before and after it are most apparent in comparison with the perfect power of prophecy. Therefore at the time of the appearance of every prophet there is more frequent occurrence of things to be displayed in their perfection and completeness only by means of the prophet of high degree. Wherefore the learned among the *mutakallimūn* have said : " In that nation which lays claim to perfect ability and consummate excellence in some particular quality, Allah sends a prophet perfect in that very quality, in order to amaze and render impotent such people by the miracle of the manifestation of his perfection, and they are not able to perform anything comparable with it in any way. The advantage of this is that if another sort of miracle were given to that sublime prophet, the people would say that he had exhibited something of which they had no knowledge, and that if they had possessed such knowledge, they could have displayed something better than it."

This true statement of the learned exponents of dialectic is in accordance with our exposition, and they have explained the matter most fittingly.

Now the condition of the soothsayer should be considered carefully. When he feels this power (of soothsaying) in his soul he uses conscious art [1] to perfect the power, but because in itself the power is imperfect, it is manifested in sensible things, and the soothsayer shows such signs

[1] The difference urged is the artificiality of the soothsayer's methods compared with the spontaneity of the prophet. Cf. Cicero : *De Divin.*, i. 18.

as people see in omens, or in divination by the flight of birds (*zajr*), or like some people who make a clatter with gravel so that the attention may be drawn in a certain direction and other similar devices, the soothsayer makes similar motions in order to reply to people's questions. Sometimes he speaks in rhyme and verse in which he is at pains to use metre and rhyme. By this it is his purpose to draw the attention away from the senses and occupy it with his speech. Thus by such contrivances his soul becomes detached and the effect of soothsaying becomes powerful. And what he says with his tongue has its effect on his heart.

By these forms and devices what he foretells is sometimes in accordance with fact and sometimes not. This is because he desires to perfect his deficiency, but because he is trying to perfect himself and is in himself imperfect, he is sometimes true and sometimes untrue, and in consequence of his irresolute and unstable condition he does not credit his own predictions. So with the idea that if he predicts something quite clearly and it should turn out false he will have a "bad market" and lose his reputation among the common people, he frequently uses ambiguous and general statements which are capable of being interpreted in two ways. Sometimes he deceives and gives messages which are in themselves nonsensical. Often in regard to some matter which is placed before him there is no movement of his soul and so he says something by conjecture. Sometimes some soothsayers are near to the final limit of humanity and some are far off, and so in soothsaying there are various degrees and ranks.

Nevertheless the honoured prophets, on whom be peace, have this distinction and difference from all soothsayers that in the prediction of soothsaying there is bound to be falsehood, and secondly the soothsayer often makes claim to impossibilities. For some things are revealed to them which are apparently impossible, but because of the imperfection of their power they cannot interpret them correctly. Therefore they relate them as they are, without interpretation or attention. And because they cannot possibly happen they are proved to be signs of imperfection.

If by chance some soothsayer is true and of sound opinion, then he does not go beyond his real degree and original station, and fully understands his own ability and condition. When such a truth-loving and intelligent soothsayer learns about the message and mission of some true prophet chosen by the Absolute Creator, he immediately believes on him, and is the first to confirm his prophethood and to accept and perform the submission as, e.g., Sawād b. Qārib and Ṭulayḥa, etc., of whom it is reported that these were most enlightened soothsayers and that they believed on the Prophet with a true heart, were reckoned among the perfectly believing companions, and died happily in Islam.

CAP. VIII. OF THE PROPHET WITH A COMMISSION AND THE PROPHET WITHOUT A COMMISSION (MURSAL WA GHAYR MURSAL)

The Prophet with a message is distinguished from all mankind in many characteristics and qualities, among which one special characteristic is that the excellent qualities and perfect excellencies gathered together in the prophet without a message are found in no other man, and in respect to this concourse of virtues he is the most noble and excellent of all mankind. But the case of the prophet without a message is that many realities of things are revealed to him and by the outpouring from the presence of the Lord Creator, glorious and sublime, he is benefited and illuminated according to his dignity and spirituality. And he has such spirituality and God-given enlightenment that he has no need to progress from lower to higher by instruction and gradual progress, but the realities manifested to him he is under no command to bring and preach to others.

For this reason it is not necessary for such to pass beyond or descend from the power of thought to the power of imagination in what is revealed to them. Nevertheless this honour is vouchsafed to them that they can hear with the ear the commands and declarations of the True Giver which are addressed to them, and this lofty quality is called inward converse (communion—*munājāt*).

Any man honoured with the rank of prophet with a commission is the most noble and distinguished of men and he is set apart by the peculiar grace of the Creator and commanded to preach and guide. Thus if the prophets without a commission give counsel and admonition, and guide people to goodness and holiness, then this is only on account of their kindness and goodwill. Otherwise it is no official duty of theirs, and it is not obligatory on them from Allah that they should guide people.

In the prophet sent with a message there are numerous qualities, but in one not sent with a message there are only eleven qualities necessary. Of these, ten are found also in *imāms* and *khalīfas* who are substitutes for the prophets. But there is one quality which is peculiar to the prophet without a message which is not found in *imāms*, i.e., that the prophet without a message has a special power by reason of which he comprehends the favours and illuminations of the divine, and there is no necessity that he should gradually progress and seek wisdom and morality by the method of philosophy.

CAP. IX. OF THE KINDS OF REVELATION (WAḤĪ)

The kinds of *waḥī* must be as many as the different sorts of powers of the soul, because the graces and favours which flow from the Divine Presence upon the rational soul in the form of *waḥī* are received by the soul either by all its powers or by some of them. Therefore the kinds of *waḥī* are to be held distinct in reference to each respective power. As to the first classification, there are two kinds of powers in the soul; one is sense and the other intellect; of each of these there are many kinds, and those kinds may be still further divided until the particulars of the kinds of soul are found to be infinite and innumerable. It is because there are numerous instruments and perceptions of the soul that there are these numbers of classes and there is a separate and distinct name and class for each one.

The powers of the soul found in the senses are also of various kinds. Certain kinds of senses are such as may be included in the plant order, and others in the order of brute beasts. Some senses can be reckoned as belonging to the plane of humanity. Sense of this degree is the highest and most noble in rank of all the senses, i.e., sense of hearing and sense of sight.

We have already set forth in detail that the effect of the soul which the animal accepts in the first place, is the sense of touch found in the kind of animal called the shell-dweller. Sense superior to this is taste and smell which is found in many creeping things and moths, etc. Then in the final stage, when the animal receives the forms of the powers of hearing and sight, the most noble animal is produced as we have previously sufficiently indicated and have explained by examples and clarification.

By this account it is intended to explain that the senses of hearing and sight are nobler than all the other senses for the reason that they are both simpler than the other and have less contamination from the material,[1] for both of these senses receive the forms of things without coming into contact with them, in contrast to the other senses, which cannot receive the effect of a sensed thing without contact or intermingling with bodies and without material change, i.e., without being brought into contact with the sensed body, they can have no sensation of it.

Now because the forms of the realities which light upon the soul from above have no admixture and commerce with matter, therefore they cannot go further than the senses of hearing and sight, because it is beyond the capacity and power of the other senses, to receive such realities in any way on account of their materiality. And besides, when the noble realities and simple natures reach the hearing and sight and so terminate, it is certain that a faint effect of matter will be produced in them as though the shadow of matter had fallen upon them; and they will be clothed to some extent in material garb. However, those realities cannot accept materiality or turbidity to any greater extent for if they did those simple natures (*ma'ānī*) would

[1] Cf. *De Sensu*, v. 445a, 5 ff., where there is a division of the senses into tactual and those which use a medium.

be deprived of their simplicity and abstractness and this is quite impossible.[1]

It has thus been shown and proved that the kinds of revelation must be as numerous as there are kinds of powers of the soul. Nevertheless three kinds of powers of animals are excluded, namely, those which are to be found in brute beasts and those which are close to plants. These are the sense of touch, taste and smell upon which revelation cannot alight. A powerful degree of *waḥī* is when with the exception of these three the soul receives it by means of all the remaining powers. Still more powerful and better than this is when the soul receives and perceives revelation by means of a few powers, and the highest and best degree of *waḥī* is when the soul receives it by a single power.

CAP. X. THE DIFFERENCE BETWEEN THE PROPHET AND THE FALSE PROPHET

Although the difference between the prophet and the false prophet is plain to the intelligent thinker and well-informed philosopher, it is hidden from those people who are vulgar or who would consider themselves elect but in reality resemble the vulgar in thought and discernment. Therefore it seems fitting that we should describe in brief this difference also, so that the subject of this book may be completed and that there may not be excessive length.

We have, with great detail and by the method of argument proved that all prophets and messengers (God's blessing be on them !) are by virtue of that special degree, the most excellent, noble and distinguished of mankind. And as the vulgar and the elect,[2] the needy people of mankind are dependent on gaining worldly pleasures and always remain absorbed in them, the exalted prophets have no need at all of these desires and pleasures. And by reason of their absorption in the realities and spiritual apprehensions with which they have become familiar, their attention is always cut off absolutely from these pleasures.

These reverend persons perceive such simple natures and noble realities in two ways. One is that they see such realities with their own eyes in ordinary waking life, and hear them with their own ears, as we have explained in one chapter hearing and sight and its pos-

[1] This reads very like a description of clairvoyance and clairaudience. There is, however, a slight inconsistency in the whole and it is, that when prophethood is first explained, the link with the divine is assumed to be the Intellect, which is directly moved and by which divine movement a process is set going from the higher to the lower. In this chapter, however, we fall from this high estate to the idea of the soul's reception of *waḥī* by means of sense. The author is not clear. It cannot much matter if the initial movement is from the intellect and descends to the sense whether the descent is to one activity of the soul or not. It may be that the author's meaning is that inferior forms of *waḥī* may affect the lower powers of the soul with certain exceptions, and that the highest form of *waḥī* is when only the intellectual power of the soul is moved.

[2] Cf. division of men into two classes in the Alexandrian school.

sibility in detail. Such knowledge and perception is one of the states of revelation, the exposition of which is that the preliminary effect of this true reality, when it is poured out from above is in the distinguishing power of the prophet, i.e., in his intellect. After that, by reason of the power of the effect, it goes on affecting the other powers inferior to the intellect and reaches the final powers in the downward direction, i.e., those powers which are on the animal plane, namely, sense of hearing and sight. The second method of the perception of realities is that they hear but they do not see, as though they hear from behind a curtain. God refers to these two forms of *waḥī* in His word when He says: "It is not for any mortal for God to speak to him except by *waḥī*, or from behind a veil or by sending a messenger and inspiring, by His permission, what He pleases" (Sura xlii. 50).

When the prophets hear revelation of the second mode fear and awe fall on them, after which they are put at ease and the degree of conviction and assurance is attained. In any case in both forms of revelation such reverend persons are commanded by the Divine Majesty to bring to their fellows the realities and spiritual apprehensions (*ma'ārif*) received by them, and to guide them by beautiful ways into the straight path, in order that thus they may rectify the morals and manners of the people, and extricating the souls of the common people from the mire of ignorance and misguidance, illuminate and purify them; as though the prophets are the curers of the distresses of the soul, as physicians cure the diseases of the body.

It is the duty of the prophet to cause people to walk by the Holy Law which is like a ford through water. For a path in the water is called *sharī'a*, and so the Arabs used the name *sharī'a* for religion because religion is the way of guidance.

Because the prophets are commanded to preach the commandments of God they have to undergo many persecutions and difficulties in this task and have to bear such troubles and hardships that death is nothing in comparison. For this reason, in the performance of this duty these reverend people do not fear even death.[1] Any man with the above qualities, i.e., who is honoured with the robe of prophethood, has a special property and wonderful power to win hearts and to give satisfaction by the bounty-scattering word. And such confirmation of the divine is obtained that he draws all men to his commands and opinion, and subjects them. And to make clear his lofty purpose and make it commonly understood, he can bring parables suitable to the occasion and the subject, and by means of them guide the common people. Again, in the prophet there is a special power to manifest

[1] In general speaking smooth things with a desire for popularity would seem to be a mark which the Jews recognized for the false prophet. See 1 Kings xii. But there is always the criterion not mentioned by Miskawaih, namely, the radical difference in the conception of God held by the false and the true prophets.

those obscure realities and subtle meanings in various ways. In all there are in the prophet upwards of forty distinguishing characteristics which are found in no other men.

But the false prophet (*mutanabbī*) is the opposite of the prophet because he desires to obtain worldly pleasures and desires, and true prophets desire to forsake these. So if the false prophet is covetous of property together with honour and marriage, good food and clothes, etc., no matter how he tries to hide his purpose and prevent it becoming known to the public, at last the veil is pierced and in a short time he becomes demeaned and dishonoured in the eyes of men. For he keeps hankering after pleasures and lusts and is continually in anxiety to obtain them, and so, in spite of concealment, in some way or other, his glaring quest of the world comes to men's notice in his motions and his rests. It often happens that in the beginning, by the cunning practices and devices of the false prophet, people of ordinary intelligence come to be deceived by him, especially when he adopts silence and continence, abstinence and devotion and, to gain the attention of people, spends little on himself and is generous to others. Moreover, sometimes he displays such jugglery and trickery that the less intelligent public conceives these to be miracles and comes to consider him as a prophet sent by God. At such a time, when they inquire from him the realities of things and matters of origin and of the hereafter (source and return), about which it is customary to inquire from prophets and which the vulgar and the elect alike are avid to learn, there is no help for him except that he should give a reply by one of the methods previously mentioned. Firstly, he refers to something about the things in question related in the heavenly books sent down on the prophets or in the traditions about them, and replies to those who believe in him almost in the same words. But the false prophet cannot expound or comment on the traditions of the prophets or verses of the heavenly books, because in them are parables according to fact, but the obscure words and symbols of such verses and traditions are ambiguous, and the understanding of them is not the work of every man. Secondly, when questioned, the false prophet gratuitously invents some oracle of his own and thus gives his reply in such a manner (i.e., his speech is not God's Word). And because he is most assuredly unacquainted with the subtle meanings and deep doctrines (about which he is asked) and replies without the divine corroboration, his speech is confused; one thing he says contradicts another, and numerous discrepancies are found in his replies. By such contradiction and discrepancy, observant and thoughtful people find out that he is not genuine and not sent by God.

We have now satisfactorily set out the three doctrines of the Being of God, the Conditions of the Soul, the Prophethood. More detailed and amplified treatment would have been contrary to the brevity laid down as a condition for this book, and so an explanation thus far is deemed sufficient.

We will give an account of those subjects which require greater detail and exposition in our book *Al Fawz al Akbar* which is about to be written, if God pleases ; and it is He who vouchsafes assistance.

INDEX OF SUBJECTS

A

Ablutions, 36
abrogation, 80 f.
abstraction, 181 f.
accidents (*accidens*), 64, 114 f., 118, 120
accommodation in teaching, 55, 173
activity or actuality, 64, 102, 126, 137
adoptianism, 44, 58 f.
Alexandria, 3 f.; theological school, 46 ff.; eclecticism of, 46; Jewish teachers of, 52 f.; Christian teachers of, 53; orthodoxasts, 53
allegorism (*vide ta'wīl*), 50, 54 f., 66 f., 101
almsgiving, 36
Alogi, 60
alteration (kind of motion), 102
Angels: in Qur'ān, 22 ff.; Holy Spirit an angel, 23; and jinn, 23 f.; Christ an angel ? 28 f.; called *'abd* in Qur'ān, 30; called *rasūl* in Q., 30
animal, 141, 160 ff.
animal power, 95
Annunciation, 13, 26, 29
anthropomorphism, 78 f., 112 f.
Antioch, 3, 45, 49 f., 54, 61, 63
Aphthartodocetists, 3
apollinarianism, 61
Apologists, 64, 66 ff.
Apostles' Creed, 56
Arabic, 4
arianism, 28 f., 59 f.
aristotelianism and Aristotle (see also under "Authors and Books"), 3 ff., 47, 48–53 *passim*, 61, 62, 64 f., 84 ff., 90 f., 107, 113, 116, 122, 123, 130, 131, 133, 137, 145
asceticism, 16, 34 f., 40, 70 f., 73, 83, 99 ff., 155 ff.
Ash'arites, 63, 151
Asia (Christians in), 2
atomism, 97, 159
augmentation (kind of motion), 102

B

begetting (crude ideas of), 72
Bidpai, Fables of, 4
Black Stone (Ka'aba), 65, 68
blessedness of soul, 139 ff.; urge to, 143 ff.; degrees of, 154 f.
blood, 132
body, 102 f., 109 ff., 113 f., 115, 116 f., 118 ff., 128 f., 130 ff., 134, 135 f., 148–152 *passim*, 155, 163–168
Book (Heavenly), 25; mother of the, 25; of Fate, 26; of Law, 25 f.; God's knowledge in a, 26
brain, 132, 166 f., 168, 169
Buddhism, 4
burning bush, 11
Byzantium, 2, 59

C

Cappadocia (school of theology), 48 f.
cause, 84, 106 ff., 109 f., 113 f.; motor, 104 f.; effective, 105 f., 109; composite, 107; accidental, 108; instrumental, 108; *ex necessitate naturæ*, 109; simple, 107 f.
change (kind of motion), 102, 116 f., 126; of form requires outside agency, 117
China, Christians in, 2
Christ: only a man ? 28; humanity of, 49, 82; Ebionites on, 58; Monarchians on, 60; Second Adam, 29, 32; called *'abd* in the Qur'ān, 30; prophets called Him "servant," 74; Why did He pray ? 74; called *rasūl* in Q., 30; denial of divinity in Q., 31; divinity questioned, 74; in Ikhwan uṣ Ṣafa, 37 f.; events of His life, etc., 70; death of, 79 f.; crucifixion of in Q., 30; crucifixion of, 39, 67, 79 f.; sinless, 74; ascetic, 40 f.; virgin birth of, 59, 67; an angel ? 28, 32; a spirit in the Qur'ān, 29; Messiah in Q., 32; works miracles, 12 f., 33, 36; the Paraclete, 33; in Muslim tradition, 36 ff.; a sign of the Last Day, 34; "Word" in the Qur'ān, 29; two natures in, 73 f.; "Why callest thou Me good ?" 74; divinity of, 68, 73; controversy of the Person of Christ in the Church, 44 ff., 72 ff.; docetism, 30 f.
Christianity: Muhammad's acquaintance with, 2, 32 f., 57 f., 65; relations of Arabs with, 2; in Asia, 2; controversies in, 4, 28, 44 f.; influence on Islam, 6, 42 ff.; in Muslim tradition, 36 ff.; provided theological background for Islam, 42 ff.; Was it properly presented to Islam ? 43, 57 f.; fashionable by law, 45; a new philosophy, 71
Christology: of the Qur'ān, 27 ff.; general, 50, 57, 58–61 *passim*, 65,

66 ff., 71, 72 ff. (see also Logos, God the Son, Incarnation, etc.).
Church : Eastern, 45, 62 ; Syrian, 45
clairvoyance and clairaudience, 182
colour, 126 f.
composition, 106 f., 115, 133
concupiscible power, 107, 131 f., 156
contemplation, 148
corporeal form, 115, 116
corporeal universe, 149 f.
corruption of Scripture, 58
corruption (kind of motion), 102, 134
creation, 53, 67, 75, 77, 87, 113 ff.; continuous, 114 f. ; *ex nihilo*, 116 ff.
Creator (see God).
crucifixion, 67 f., 79 ff.

D

death, 132 ff., 140
definition, 64
deification, 71
deism, 53
Demiurge, 139
demonstration, 112
desire, 155
detachment, 97
dialectic (see also *'Ilm ul Kalām*), 51, 53, 64 f.
differentia, 64
dimensions, 121
spiritualities not dimensional, 150 f.
diminution (kind of motion), 102
disciples of Christ (in Muslim story), 39
disposition, 118, 120
divorce, 36
doceticism, 30 f., 58, 79
doctrine : absence of rigidity in early statement of, 56 ; Quranic, 17 ff.
dreams, 176 f.
dualism, 84, 86, 87

E

Ebionites, 32, 58
Eden (heavenly), 29
effects : diverse from same cause, 107 ; impossible without cause, 108
Egypt, plagues of, 11
elements, 49, 94 f., 103 f., 121 f., 163
emanation, 47, 59 f., 84 f., 106 f., 108, 113, 116 f.
eschatology : of Qur'ān, 33 f. ; of the Cappadocia School, 49
esoteric teaching and discipline, 49, 54 f. (see also mysticism and Sufism).
eternity, 105, 110 f.
ether, 110
Eucharist, 12 f., 49
evil, creation of, 67, 134
exegesis : Origen, 48 ; Paulus Persa, 86
exemplars (Platonist), 109
existence : accidental, 104 ; essential, 104 f. ; grades of, 158 f. ; plant world, 159 f. ; animal, 161 f. ; human, 162 f.

F

falsity, 144 f.
Fate, Book of, 26
fear in religion, 15, 33
Firdaus (see Paradise), 34
Flood, the, 10
flux, 96 f., 114, 115, 116, 136
food, ritual restrictions, 36
form, 49, 64 ; sensible, impressed on mind, 95 f., 102, 126 f. ; general, 115, 116 ff., 120 f. ; sequence in existence and non-existence, 117, 118 f.
freewill, 61 ff., 67 f., 80
future life, 148 f., 152 f.

G

generation (kind of motion), 102
genus, 64
" Glory of God," 71, 137 (see also *Barz ul Bārī*).
gnosis, 54, 57, 147 f.
gnosticism, 4, 44, 57, 58 f., 85
God : the Abiding, 20 ; above all likeness, 112 f. ; arguments for His existence, 93 f. ; argument from motion, 101 ff. ; the Afflictor, 20 ; All-knowing, 18 ; All-seeing, 18 ; Ample, 19 ; His anger, 20 ; attributes of, 17 ff., 78 f., 112 ; the Avenger, 19 ; His Being, 17, 78 f. ; common consent of philosophers concerning His existence, 98 ff. ; Creator, 18, 19, 21, 113 f. ; Equitable, 21 ; His Essence not known, 111 ; eternal, 105, 110 f. ; existence of, 93 ; existence essential to, 105, 110 f. ; Exalted, 19 ; the Favourer, 20 ; Faithful, 18 ; the First and the Last, 20 ; Forgiving, 18, 20 ; the Former, 19 ; is not in a genus, 112 ; the Gatherer, 19 ; the Giver, 19 ; the Grace of, 22, 62 ; grace, righteousness and truth in O.T., 22 ; the Great, 19 ; the Guardian, 18 ; the Guide, 18 ; the Hearer, 19 ; the Hinderer, 20 ; the Holy, 18 ; incorporeal, 75 f., 78, 109 f., 112 ; mode of attribution *in sensu eminentiori*, 111, 113 ; judges, 18, 22 ; justice of, 21 ; *knowledge of God* : not by reason, 78, 93 ; by reason, 93 ; analogical, 99 f. ; self-evident, 99 ; the Living, 19 ; the Lord, 21 ; love of, 62 ; the Merciful, 18, 21, 22 ; the

Mighty, 19; names of, 18 ff., 110 f.; necessary existence, 105, 110 ff.; the Opener, 19; the Patient, 20; the Preceder, 20; Propitious, 20; the Provider, 21; the Pure, 19; positive qualities of, 113; the Reckoner, 19, the Relenter, 19; the Self-subsisting, 21; Sovereign, 18, 21; simplicity of, 105, 108, 109, 110, 115; the transcendence of, 18, 111, 114, 153; unity of, 18, 21, 70, 75, 76, 100, 105, 106 ff., 112; unknowability of, 153; the *via negativa*, 111 ff.; the Watchful, 20; the will of, 18, 61 f., 67 f.; the Wise, 18; the Preserver, 18, 21, 114 f.
God the Father, 71 f.
God the Son, 71 f., 73, 75
golden calf, 11
Gospel (see also *Injīl*), 11 f., 81
Gospel: spread of, an argument for Christianity? 70
Grace, 57, 62, 72
Greek learning: Græco-Syrian medicine, 3; philosophy, 3, 5, 50 ff.; in the development of Christian Theology, 52; Jewish teachers of, 52 f.; influence of, 54, 113 ff.; translation of Greek works into Pahlawi, 86; the Academy, 86; mathematics, etc., 86 (*vide* Ibn Miskawaih, Aristotle, Plato, Proclus, Plotinus, etc., etc.).

H

habit, 64
Ḥadīth (with a capital used as a collective for Muslim Tradition), 6, 23, 35, 36 ff.
Hagarites, 65
Ḥanafites, 42
happiness, 154 ff.; true—contemplative, 156
Hell: guardians of, 24, 34; names of, 34; fear of, 33
heresy, in Christianity, 45, 56 f., 57 ff.
historical relation of Islam and Christianity, 1 ff.
holiness of God in O.T., 18
Holy Spirit: an angel? 23; Gabriel, 23; Paraclete, 32 f.; female? 32, 71, 75 (see also Virgin Mary).

I

iconoclasts, 4, 63
ideas, 137 f.
illuminism, 84, 171
illusion, 97
image worship, 63, 65, 68, 69
imagination, 126, 169 (see also phantasy and presentation).
immortality (of soul), 130–136
inanimate things, 103 f.
Incarnation, 31 f., 48, 57, 61, 68, 72 ff.
individua, 64
infinite series, 91, 104, 106, 115
inheritance (laws of), 36
Intellect: Primal, intellectual-principle, 60, 84, 106, 113; and sense, 125 ff.; conceives its own essence, 129; does not decay with the body, 129, 132 f.; First, 134, 138; immortal, 135; soul's motion towards, 137; does not move, 138; the first prophet, 157; first creation, 139; compasses the soul, 150 ff., 154; its Lordship, 173 ff.; active intellect, 113
intelligences, 106
intelligibles (intelligible species), 96 f., 120 f., 123 f., 125 f., 127 ff., 157
intercession (of Muhammad), 69
intermediaries, 107 ff.
irascible power, 107, 131 f., 156
Ishmaelites, 65
Islām, 7; early development of, 42 f.; development against Christianity, 43

J

Jacobites, 2, 28, 79
Jesus, 8; miracles of, 13 f., 33; annunciation of His birth, 13 f.; nativity, 13 f.; unwritten sayings of, 16, 37
Jews: in Arabia, 1; used to refute Christianity? 2; Jewish elements in Christianity, 53
Judgment (of God), 33
Julianists, 31

K

knowledge (human): through sense, 95; self-evident, 99; speculative and necessary by contemplation and observation, 99; degrees of, 146 ff.
knowledge of lower being by higher, 154

L

Lateran Council (A.D. 649), 60
law and legalism, 53, 62, 80
Laws (religious), 35 f., 70
life, 130 f., 132 f., 135 ff., 140
Light of Muhammad, 60
light-myth, 84

literalism, 54, 66 f.
literature, early Christian, in Asiatic languages, 4 f.
liver (psychological), 132
logic, 111, 145
Logos, 29, 48, 50, 53, 60 f., 71, 139, 147

M

Malkites (Byzantine Church), 2, 79
Man, 49 ; a social being, 141 f. ; a microcosm, 163–167 ; originally righteous, 163 ; crown of animal world, 163 f.
manichæism, 3, 5, 73
Marcionites, 44, 58, 59
marriage, 36
matter, 84, 87 ; hinders reason, 95 f. ; diversity of material, 108 ; eternal and immutable, 116 ; general, 115, 127, 134, 137, 139, 154
Mazdakians, 73
memory, 169
memra, 29
Messiah, 32
Messianic prophecy, 74
metaphysics, 4, 51 f., 56 f., 76 f.
microcosm, 49, 163–167
midrash, 7
Mi'rāj of Muhammad, 40
miracles : of Muhammad, 36 f., 69 f., 80, 82 ; apocryphal, of our Lord in Qur'ān, 13 ; doctrine of, 51 ; why Christ's followers no longer work miracles, 70 ; confirming Scripture, 80 ; to procure faith, 82 f.
misery of soul, 139 ff.
monarchianism, 59 f.
Monophysites, 2, 28
monotheism, 21, 63 (see also God, unity of).
Moses, 11 ; called son of God, 74
Mother of the Book, 25 (see also *umm ul kitāb*).
motion, argument from, 101 ff.
movement, 101 ff. ; essential, 103 ; of inanimate things, 103 f. ; of animals, 104 ; natural and voluntary, 105, 109 f. ; of soul and spheres, 113 f. ; of soul, 132, 135 ff. ; circular, 138 f. ; celestial, 150 ; crooked (of soul), 154 ; voluntary, 161
Muhammad, 1 ; Did he know Christianity ? 2 ; miracles of M. in tradition, 36 f., 69 f., 80, 82 ; supernatural journey of, 40 ; genius of M. in Islam, 42 ; Light of M., 60 ; *al Ḥaqīqat ul Muḥammadīya*, 60 ; praised by Christian apologist, 69 ; character of, 69 ; defence of M. by Tabarī, 70 ; prophecy of in the Bible ? 33, 71, 74, 81 ; sinless, 74 ; general, 82
multiplicity, origin of, 106 f., 110 (see also One and Many).
Mu'tazilites, 63
mystery (see esoteric).
mystics and mysticism, 47, 48, 49, 54, 57, 58, 60, 86, 92, 98, 148

N

Nativity of Jesus Christ, 13 f.
nature, 64, 102, 105 f., 115, 150, 152 ff.
Neoplatonists, 3, 45, 47, 50, 56, 84, 85, 91 ff., 106 f., 113, 127, 138, 151, 153 f. and *passim* throughout notes on Section Two.
nerves, 168
Nestorians, 2 f., 28, 32, 45 f., 50, 61, 62, 63, 77, 79, 85, 86
New Testament, 8 ; apocryphal, 1 ; in Qur'ān, 13 f. ; criticism by Ṭabarī, 70
Nicæa (council), 44, 45, 59 f.
night vigils, 14 f.
notions, universal, 120 ff.

O

objective, 121
Old Testament : narrative in Qur'ān, 8 ff. ; attributes of God in, 18 ff. ; criticism by Ṭabarī, 70
One and Many, 106 ff., 109
original sin, 62
Orthodoxasts, 53
ousia, 48, 64 (see also list of Greek words).
outpouring or overflowing, 113

P

Pahlawi translations of Greek works, 86
palm tree, 160
Paraclete, 33, 71, 82
Paradise, 34 ; sensual, 34 ; dwellers in, 42 (see also Heaven and *Firdaus*).
passivity or potentiality, 64, 102, 125 f.
Paulicians, 59, 63
pelagianism, 46, 61 ff.
People of the Book, 26
perception, 95 f., 101 ; a function of the soul, 120 f. ; by organs, 121 f. ; general, 122 ff. ; 125–129, 152
peripatetics (see aristotelianism).
Persia, Christians in, 2, 86
Persons (Trinity), 53, 64, 71, 76 ff.
phantasy, 95, 100, 120 f., 169
philosophers, physicians of the soul, 100

philosophy: intro. into Islam, 84 ff.; harmony of Christianity with, 89; toilsome quest, 93 f., 97 f.; begins with exact sciences, 98; p. and revelation, 172
physics first concern of philosophy, 95
place, 64
plants, 159 f.
platonism, 5; reconciliation with Moses, 46; general, 46 f., 49, 53, 95, 106, 109, 134, 137, 140 (see also under Authors and Books—Plato).
pleasure, 154–157
political conditions: at Muhammad's advent, 1; in early Islam, 5 f.
politics (community), 141 f.
position, 64
prayer, 14 f., 42
Prayer of Joseph, 25
predestination, 62, 67
predicamenta, 64, 128
predication, 64
pre-existence, 92, 135 (see also soul).
presentation, 169
preservation, 114
Preserver (see God).
priest, can a sinful one officiate? 42
Primum Movens and *Primum Mobile* (see list of Latin words).
property (logic), 64
prophet and prophethood, 24, 27, 51, 58, 69 ff., 79, 84 f., 100, 157–183; difference between false and true, 182 ff.; difference between commissioned and uncommissioned, 180; difference from soothsaying, 177 ff.; how explain rejection of prophets? 175; confirmed by reason, 172; Ebionites, 58; Sethians on, 58; the highest degree of humanity, 162 f.
pseudepigrapha of Philosophers, 85
pythagoreanism, 53, 84

Q

quality (see also God: qualities), 64
quantity, 64
Qur'ān: shews knowledge of Judaism and Christianity, 1; first book in Arabic, 5; Biblical and apocryphal influences on, 6 ff.; foreign words in, 6 ff.; rhapsodical style of, 17; piecemeal delivery of heavenly book, 25 f.; known to Damascene, 65; a miracle, 69 f.; alleged corruption by Ḥajjāj, 69; mysterious letters at head of chapters of, 76; appealing to, against the, 79; whether from God, 80

R

reason: in religion, 56; impotent to know God, 78; function of, 93 f., 95 f.; stimulation from above, 171; and revelation, 171 f., 174 (see also *'aql*).
Reason (Primal) (see Intellect); dethronement of in sensual pleasure, 156 f.; right reason, 145 f., 156
redemption, 57
relation, 64
reserve, 54
resurrection: age of body at, 41 f.; general, 51, 53, 56
retaliation (law of), 36
retribution, 51, 154
revelation: Qur'ān's teaching, 24 ff.; Holy Spirit agent in, 25; doctrine in Islam, 51; and reason, 53, 55 f., 171 ff., 182 f.; stimulation of reason in, 171; kinds of, 180 ff. (see also *waḥī*).
reward, 51, 154 f.
ritual worship, 14 f.

S

Sabellius and sabellianism, 60
Sabians, 85
Satan, 9 f., 24
scholasticism, 64 f., 84
sciences, 98
Scripture, 48, 50, 59, 70, 80 ff.
Sepher Jazira (Abraham's), 10
self-evident knowledge, 99, 129
Semitic elements in Islam, 7, 10
sense, 95 f., 101 f., 120 ff., 122–124, 125 ff., 127, 128 f., 131 f., 161, 167 ff., 181, 182 f.; common-sense, 169; sensibles, 96 f., 123 f., 127 ff., 151
Sethians, 58
shape (circular), 165
shellfish, 161
shooting stars, 24
Shu'ūbīya, 5
simplicity (the non-composite), 105, 110
sleep, 130, 176
soothsaying, 177 ff.
Sophia (see also Wisdom), 25
soteriology, 57, 80
soul, 84, 92, 104, 114, 118–158; rational, 119; not in place, 120 ff.; rational soul corrects sense, 123; unity of, 124; perceives particulars and universals, 125 ff.; potential, 126; separate, immortal, 127, 128, 130 f.; faculties of, 131 f.; not composite, 133; immortality of, 133 ff.; life and death of, 139 ff.; bliss and misery

of, 139 ff.; urge to bliss, 143 ff.; condition of when body dies, 148–157; bad and good, 154; descent of, 154 f.; effects of: plants, 159 f.; animals, 160 f.; humanity, 162; bound by bodily condition, 167 f.; powers of, 180 f. (see also World-Soul, *nafs* and *rūh*).
species, 64; are interlinked, 159
speculative knowledge, 99
spheres, 114, 149 f.
spherical shape, 149
spirit: kind of fluid, 168, 176; spiritual universe, 150; spiritual things incorporeal, 96
Spirit: Christ, 29, 66, 68 f.; meaning to Muhammad, 29 f., 32; Aphraates, *passim*, 32; general, 75 f.
stars, influence of, 177 f.
stoicism, 47, 53
substance, 64, 114 f.
success as proof of truth, 83
suckling, 36
sufism, 47, 49, 99, 109, 148
suppositum, 116, 130 (see also list of Latin words).
Syriac translation from Greek, 50, 86 ff.
Syrians: contribution to early Muslim state, 5 f.; lectionary, 14 (see also Syriac).

T

tablets (heavenly), 25 f.
temperaments, the four, 164 f.
temporal, 110
Theology: Christian theological background to early Islam, 42 ff.; the great schools, 46 ff.; pre-Islamic philosophical theology, 50 ff.
Theotokos, 28, 32, 45
thing, material and immaterial, 120 f.
thought (power of reflection), 169 f.
time, 64, 110, 136
Timothy's *Apology*, 71 ff.
tradition: Muslim, Christianity in, 36 ff.; reflects early Muslim controversy, 36; miracles of Muhammad in, 36 f.; Christ in, 37; Christian, 49
traditionalism, Christian, 54
transmigration, 92 (see also metempsychosis and *tanāsukh*).
transposition (kind of motion), 102
trinitarianism: in Alexandrian philosophy, 47, 107
Trinity, the Holy, 32, 49, 53, 57, 65, 67, 68, 69, 70, 71, 72, 75 ff.
tritheism, 31 ff., 61; accusation of, 75
truth, unity of, 54, 144 f., 157
"two lives," 54, 97 f.
two-nature theory, 39
typology (Origen), 50

U

understanding, 119, 120 f., 123
union of soul with God, 141
Unity of God (see God).
Universe: material, 147; four, 146 f.; is one, 158; of corruption and incorruption, 159; of Heaven and planets, 159 (see also *'ālam*).

V

vacuum, 96, 129, 149, 159
vanity of present world, 34
via negativa, 157 ff.
Virgin Mary, 13, 28, 32, 45, 73, 74 f.
virtue, 145 f.
vision: part of prophethood, 176 f.; of God, 51, 148

W

wicked man—can he lead worship? 42
Will of God (see God).
Wisdom of God (see God).
Wisdom (personified), 25, 71
wisdom, the soul's bliss, 144
Word, the, 29, 68 f., 71, 77 ff. (see also *Logos*, Scripture and *Nāmūs*).
world, 34, 84 (see earth).
World-Soul (All-Soul), 103, 113, 114, 137 (see also *nafs*).
worship, 14 f.; motive to, 15

Z

Zandaqa, 73
zoroastrianism, 86, 93

INDEX OF PROPER NAMES

(Certain names will be found in the subjects index since their inclusion there seems more appropriate, e.g., Muhammad, Paradise, etc., and also the names of sects, e.g., Ash'arites. Other names not in the following list may be found in the Index of Authors and Books.)

A

Aaron, 8, 11, 58
Abba Joseph, 16
'Abbāsid Caliphate, 86
'Abdullāh b. Mas'ūd, 40
'Abdullāh b. 'Umar (Ibn 'Umar), 71
Abgar IX, 3
Abraham, 9, 10, 58
Abū Aḥmad b. Kirmast, 94
Abū 'Alī 'Īsā b. Isḥāq b. Zur'a (d. A.D. 1007), 66, 89
Abū Bakr (d. A.D. 634), 71
Abū Huraira, 37
Abū Ibrāhīm b. uṣ Ṣalt, 94
Abū Qārib (pre-Islamic king), 2
Abū Sa'īd, 42
Abyssinians, 2, 12
Adam, 9, 29, 32, 49, 58
Aden, 3
Agathadæmon, 84 f., 93
Al Akhtal, 5
Alexandria (see Subject Index).
'Alī, 71
Anaxagoras, 127
Anushirwān Khusrū I (A.D. 530), 3, 85 f.
Apollonius of Tyana, 84, 91
Arabia, 1 ff., 28
Arbil, 2
Arius, 50
Asia (see Subject Index).
Aswad b. 'Abd Yaghūth, 70
Ayyūb (see Job).

B

Bactria, 2
Bardesan, 3
Barthold, 1, 4
Basilides, 46, 58
Basra, 2, 3
Bathsheba, 12
Bāyazīd Bistāmī, 158
Beryl (Bp. of Bostra third cent.), 60
Bulīnus (see Apollonius).
Buqrāṭ (Buḳrāṭ, Hippocrates), 161
Byzantium, 2, 59

C

Cain and Abel (Qābil and Ḥābil), 10
Cappadocia (see Subject Index).
Celsus, 47, 55
Ceylon, 3
China (see Subject Index).
Coelestius, 62
Constantine the Great, 44 f.
Constantine Sylvanus (seventh cent. A.D.), 59
Constantinople, 45, 60
Constantius (Emperor of Byzantium fourth cent.), 60
Cosmas Indicopleustes, 3
Cyriacus (Jacobite Patriarch of Antioch A.D. 793–817), 66
Cyril of Alexandria (d. A.D. 444), 46

D

David, 12
Dhū Nuwās, 1 f.
Diocletian, 44
Dionysius (Greek philosopher), 85
Dionysius of Alexandria (c. A.D. 200–265), 44, 57
Dioscorus of Alexandria, 46

E

Eden (see Subject Index).
Edessa, 2, 3, 85
Egypt, 3, 4
Elijah, 8
Elisha, 8
Eliyya of Nisibis (A.D. 1008–49), 66
Enoch, 10, 85
Ephesus (Council A.D. 431), 45
(Council A.D. 449), 46
Ephraim the Syrian, 34
Eutyches, 46
Eutychius, 31
Ezra (see Uzayr).

F

Al Fārābī, 47, 51, 52, 86, 92, 106, 107, 113, 115
Flavian, 46

G

Gabriel, 8, 23, 29
Gīlān, 2
Gog and Magog (see Yājūj and Mājūj).
Goliath, 11

H

Hadramaut, 3
Ḥajjāj b. Yūsuf (A.D. 661–714), 69
Ḥarrān, 66, 84 f., 93
al Hāshimī (Mḥd. b. 'Abdullāh), 68 f.
Heraclius (Byz. Emp.), 65
Herat, 3
Hermes Trismegistus, 84 f., 91, 93
Hermias, 53
Himyarites, 1 f.
Hippocrates, 91, 161
Huns, 3
Hur, 11

I

Iamblichus, 91
Ibn Abī Usaybī'a (b. A.D. 1203), 90
Ibn 'Arabī, 47
Ibn Mas'ūd (see 'Abdullāh b. M.).
Ibn 'Umar (see 'Abdullāh b. 'U).
Idrīs, 10
'Īsā (see Jesus, Subject Index).
'Īsā b. Yahyā, 161
Isaac (Isḥāq), 10, 58
Ishmael, 10
Isodorus, 146
Israelites, 11

J

Jacob (Patriarch), 10 f., 25, 58
Jacob (Jacobite Bishop), 2
Jacob Baradaeus, 3
Jāhiz (d. c. A.D. 864), 73
Jālūt, 11
Jibrīl (see Gabriel)
Job (Patriarch), 8
Job of Edessa, 3
John the Tritheist (Philoponus, see Authors and Books).
Jonah, 8
Joseph, 10 f.
Joshua, 58
Julian of Halicarnasus, 31
Junayd (d. A.D. 910), 158
Jundishābur, 3, 50
Justinian, 31, 79, 85

K

Karkūk, 2
Khaibar (battle), 36
Khusrū I (see Anushirwān).
Korah (see Qārūn).

L

Lahab, 70
Leo the Isaurian (eighth cent. A.D.), 4, 63
Lot, 8, 9
Lucian the Martyr (c. A.D. 311), 50

M

al Mahdī (Caliph A.D. 775–85), 31, 36, 69, 72 f., 75, 77, 79 ff., 85
Malabar, 3
Mālik, guardian of Hell, 34
Ma'mūn (Caliph A.D. 813–33), 68
Mani, 58
Mansūr (Caliph A.D. 750–75), 86
Ma'rib, 3
Marius Mercator, 62
Maryam (Moses' sister), 11
Maximus (A.D. 580–662), 91
Merv, 2
Mesopotamia, 2 f., 5
Michael, 8, 23
Migetius, 59
Mīkāl (see Michael).
Milan, 60
Moderatus, 47
Moloch, 34
Moses (see Subject Index).
Muḥammad b. 'Abdullāh al Hāshimī (see al Hāshimī).
Mu'tasim (Caliph A.D. 833–42), 87
Mutawakkil (Caliph A.D. 847–61), 88

N

Naḍir (tribe), 1
Najrān, 3
Nichomachus, 47
Nishapur, 2
Nisibis, 2, 3, 50
Noah (Nūḥ), 8, 10, 58
Numenius, 47

O

Orpheus, 84

P

Paul of Samosata (third cent. A.D.), 44, 49, 58, 59
Persia, 3, 85
Pharaoh, 8, 11
Pythagoras, 85, 91

Q

Qābil and Ḥābil (Cain and Abel).
Qārūn, 8, 11
Quraiza (tribe), 1

R

Rasain, 85
Rayy, 2
Rome, 60
Rufinus, 48, 63

S

Salmā, 36
Samaritans, 14
Samarqand, 3
Sassanids, 3 f.
Saul, 11
Sawād b. Qārib, 179
Scythia, 3
Seleucia, 2, 3
Serenus of Marseilles, 63
Seth, 58, 85
Shammai (Rabbi), 15
Sinai, 11
Smith, Margt., 57
Socotra, 3
Socrates, 85, 91
Solomon, 8, 12
Synesius, 53, 56

T

Tālūt (see Saul).
Tamīm ud Dārī, 37
Thales, 93
Theodosius (Emp. of Byz.), 45
Theodotus, 58
Theophilus (Syrian missionary), 1
Thomas of Marga, 15
Timothy (Nestorian Catholicus; see also Subject Index), 31, 36, 66, 68
Transoxania, 2, 4
Ṭulayḥa, 179
Turks, 3

U

'Umar b. 'Abd ul Azīz, 41, 71
'Umar b. ul Khattāb, 41, 71
Umayyads, 5, 41
Urfa (see Edessa).
Uzayr (Ezra), 8, 74

V

Valentinian (Emp. of Byz.), 60
Valentinus the Gnostic (A.D. 120–60), 46, 58

W

Walīd b. Mughīra, 70
Wāthiq bi'llāh (Caliph A.D. 842–47), 88

Y

Yājūj and Mājūj, 34
Yathrīb (tribe), 1
Yazīd II (ibn Walīd, Caliph A.D. 744), 63

Z

Ẓafār, 3, 66
Zamzam, 7
Zeno (Greek philosopher), 53
Zeno (Emp. of Byz.), 3
Zoroaster, 58
Zulaikha, 10

INDEX OF AUTHORS AND BOOKS

(Included are the names of some Syrian translators. General references appear opposite the names of authors or books. Particular references are given in certain cases. P.G., P.L., P.O. and P.S. stand for *Patrologia Graeca, Latina, Orientalis* and *Syriaca* respectively. *E.R.E.* refers to Hastings: *Encyclopædia of Religion and Ethics* and *E.I.* to the *Encyclopædia of Islam.*)

A

'Abdu'l Masīḥ b. 'Abdullāh Nā'ima al Ḥimṣī (translator of the Pseudo-Aristotelian *Theology*) . . . 89, 91
'Abdu'l Masīḥ b. Isḥāq al Kindī (Christian Apologist ninth or tenth century) 36, 66, 69, 82
Abū Bishr Mattā b. Yūnus al Qannai (d. A.D. 940 Syrian translator) . . 88 f., 94
Abu'l Faraj (d. A.D. 967) *Kitāb ul Aghānī* . . . 1, 5
Abu'l Faraj Qudāma b. Ja'far (d. A.D. 922), Commentator on the *Physics* of Aristotle . . . 94
Abu'l Khayr ul Ḥasan b. al Khammār (b. A.D. 942) . . . 89, 93
  Commentary on Aristotle's *De Anima* . . . 130
Abū Rashīd Sa'īd an Nīsapūrī (A.D. 937–1608)
  Kitāb ul Masā'il . . . 97
Abū Rūḥ Ṣafā'ī
  Translation of *Physics* . . . 85, 89
  Commentary on *Physics* . . . 94
Abū Yūsuf Ya'qūb b. Isḥāq al Kindī (mid ninth century A.D.), philosopher and editor of Pseudo-Aristotelian *Theology* . . . 69, 91, 92
Abū Zakarīyā' Yaḥyā b. 'Adī, the logician (*al Manṭiqī*), d. A.D. 974, Syrian translator . . . 66, 87, 88, 89, 93, 94
  Acts of John, Peter and Philip (see *Apocrypha N.T.*).
Alexander Aphrodisias . . . 90, 91, 94
  Physics . . . 94
  Commentary on Aristotle's *Topics, Hermeneutics,* and *Generation and Corruption* . . . 88, 89
'Alī Ṭabarī (see Mingana).
Ammonius Saccas (Neoplatonist) . . . 88, 91
  Prolegomena to Porphyry's *Isagoge* . . . 140
Aphraates of Edessa (fourth century A.D.) in *P.S.*, Vol. I . . 32, 66, 74, 83
Apocrypha: New Testament . . . 8
  Acts of John . . . 30
  Acts of Peter . . . 30
  Acts of Philip . . . 79
  Arabic Gospel of the Infancy . . . 13
  Gospel to the Hebrews . . . 32
  Gospel of Pseudo-Matthew . . . 14
  Gospel of Thomas . . . 13
  Protevangelium of James (see also James, M.R.) . . . 13
Apocrypha: Old Testament (including *Pseudepigrapha*)
  Apocalypse of Moses . . . 23
  Baruch . . . 23
  Fourth Ezra . . . 25
  Book of Jubilees . . . 23, 25, 27
  Secrets of Enoch . . . 23, 24, 26, 29
  Sclavonic Enoch . . . 34
  Testament of Abraham . . . 23
  Testament of Twelve Patriarchs . . . 25
  Vita Adæ et Evæ . . . 9, 23
  Sirach (see also R. H. Charles) . . . 25, 26

De Somno et Vigilia
I, 454a, 25 ff. 176
II, 456a, 11 168
III, 467b, 30 168
III, 458a, 1 . . . . 166, 168
III, 458a, 6 168
III, 458a, 11 ff. 168
De Coelo 86, 88, 89, 90
I, iii. 110
II, iii. 286a, 12–22 149
De Part. Animal. 89
II, vii. 166
II, vii. 652a 168
IV, 686a, 25 ff. and 687a, 7 ff. . . 167
Politics
I, ii. 1253a, 3 141
IV, 14 142
De Respiratione
457b, 19 166
480a, 20 166
Meteorology 89, 110
I, ii. 149
I, iii. 339b 110
De Somniis 177
III, 461b, 5 ff. 123
III, 461b, 25 ff. 123
Categories 86, 88, 89, 90, 93
XIV, 15a, 13 ff. 102
Post Analytics 88, 89, 90
II, vii. 92b 104
Rhetorica 88, 90
Hermeneutics 85, 88, 89, 90
Poetica 89, 90
Prior Analytics 88, 89, 90
Topica 88, 89, 90
De Divin. per Somn. 177
Generat. et Corrupt. 88, 89, 90
Sophistica 85, 89
Pseudo-Aristotelian *Theology* (Athalūjīya) 89, 91, 107, 113, 132, 133, 136, 137

Asin y Palacios, Miguel
Logia et Agrapha Domini Iesu 16, 37
Islām and the Divine Comedy 40

Assemani
Bibliotheca Orientalis (ii. 105) 63

Athanasius (A.D. 296–373), *P.G.* 25–28 45
De Decretis (c. v. 24) 59
De Sent. Dion. (4) 57

Augustine (A.D. 354–430), *P.L.* 32–47 58
Confessions 135
De Libero Arbitrio 62

Averroes (see Ibn Rushd).
Avicenna (see Ibn Sīnā).

B

Baghdādī (d. A.D. 1037)
Al Farq baina'l Firaq 58

Barnabas, Ep. of 58
Bartlet, V. (see *E.R.E.*).
Basil of Cæsarea (A.D. 330–379) 48
Basil (unknown), translator of Aristotle's *Physics* with Porphyry's *Commentary* . 89
Baumstark
Geschichte der Syr. Lit. 90

Bell, Rd.
Origin of Islam in its Christian Environment 1, 34, 35
Qur'ān, a New Translation 28, 30, 34

o 2

al Birūnī (A.D. 973–1048) 86, 87, 91, 92
Tārīkh ul Hind (ed. Sachau as *Alberūnī's India*) . . . . . . 90 f.
i. 35 . . . . . . 90 | i. 123 90
i. 36 . . . . . . 88 | i. 222, 231 91
i. 40, 42, 43 . . . . . 91 | i. 320 . . . . . 90, 92
i. 57 . . . . . . 91 | i. 385 90
i. 65 f. . . . . 90, 92 | ii. 166 90
i. 85 f. . . . . 91, 92 | ii. 168 91
i. 95 and 98 . . . . . 91 | ii. 171 90

Bonaventura (A.D. 1221–1274)
Commentaria Quatuor Libros Sent. Mag. Petri Lombardi 95
Itinerarium Mentis in Deum 98

Brockelmann, C.
Geschichte der Arabischen Litteratur 88, 89, 94

Browne, L. E.
Eclipse of Christianity in Asia 1, 43, 63, 66, 73, 82, 86

Budge
Thomas of Marga's Book of Governors . . . . 16 ff.
Coptic Texts (v. 726 f.) 33

Bukhārī
Ṣaḥīḥ 40

Burkitt
Early Eastern Christianity 32

C

Caird, Ed.
Evolution of Theology in the Greek Philosophers 137

Carra de Vaux (see *E.I.*).

Cassiodorus (sixth century A.D.)
De Institutione divinarum Literarum . . . . 86 f.

Charles, R. H.
Apocrypha and Pseudepigrapha of the O.T. 9, 26, 34

Cheikho
Al-Nasranijja 15
Vingt Traités théologiques d'auteurs arabes chrétiennes 66, 73, 82
Trois Traités anciens de polémique et de théologie chrétiennes 66

Chrysostom (A.D. 347–407)
P.G. 48, 813 ff. 66, 83

Cicero
De Natura Deorum (ii. 57, 142). 151
De Divin (i. 18) 178
Tusc. Quæst (I, xxx.) 140

Clement of Alexandria (A.D. 150–213) . . . . 44, 46 ff., 53 f., 55–56 *passim*, 71
Protrept. 79
Stromateis (vi. 15, 124 and vii. 16, 196) 56

Clementine Homilies (Pseudo-Clementines) 58

Cyprian (*P.G.* xlviii. 1075 ff.).
Liber Testimentiorum 71, 72, 74, 82

Cyril of Jerusalem 28

D

Damascius (Neoplatonist) 86
Com. on Aristotle 90

Dante 40
Paradiso (see also Asin y Palacios) 120

Dawson, C.
Mediæval Religion 72
De Boer (see *E.I.*).
De Slane (see Ibn Khallikān).
Dialogue of Papiscus and Philo (ed. McGiffert) 72
Diodorus of Tarsus (fourth century A.D.) 50, 61
Donaldson, Dwight M. (in *Macdonald Presentation Volume*) 37

E

Encyclopædia of Islam
i. 432 ff. *Aristūtālīs* by De Boer 94
784 f. *Bakrāṭ* by Carra de Vaux 161
ii. 524. 'Īsā by D. B. Macdonald 29
1129. *Kurbān* by Wensinck 17, 35
iv. 124 ff. *Samaritans* by Gaster 8, 14
Encyclopædia of Religion and Ethics
vi. 248. *God* (*Arabian, pre-Islamic*) by Margoliouth 21
viii. 779. *Monarchianism* by Pope 57
ix. 695 ff. *Paulicians* by Scott 59
xii. 770. *Worship* (*Christian*) by Vernon Bartlet 15
Epiphanius (A.D. 315–403) 75
Haer.
xix. 4 . . . . . 32 li. 60
xxxix. 1 58
Erdmann
History of Philosophy 85
Euclid, translation by Ḥunayn b. Isḥāq 88
Eusebius (A.D. 263–339) 44, 49

F

al Fashānī
Al Majālis as Sanīya fi'l Kalām 'ala'l Arba'īnwan Nawawīya (Com. on Forty Traditions of Nawawī) 37
Finlay
History of Byzantine Empire 94
Fisher
History of Christian Doctrine 32

G

Gairdner (see Ghazzālī : *Mishkāt ul Anwār*) 54
Galen 88, 90, 91, 92, 134, 152, 164
Ars Medica, Comm. on Hippocrates, De Alimentorum Facultatibus, De Elementis sec. Hippocratem, De Sanitate Tuenda, De Temperamentis, Therapeutica 161
De Usu Partium 168, 169
Gaster (see *E.I.*).
Geiger . . . . 10 ff., 23 f., 34
Was hat Mohammed aus dem Judethume aufgenommen ? . . . 7 ff., 34, 36
Al Ghazzālī . . . . 51–56 *passim* 172
Iḥyā 'Ulūm 'd Dīn 16, 40
Maqāsid ul Falāsifa
ii. 82 and 85–86 . . . . 115 iii. 239 116
iii. 236 102
Tahāfut ul Falāsifa (ed. Bouyges) 51, 150
Jawāhir ul Qur'ān 51

Mishkāt ul Anwār (Gairdner's trans.) . . . 54 f.
La Perle Precieuse (French trans. by Gautier of *ad Durra ul Fākhira*) . . 41
Maḍnūn uṣ Ṣaghīr wa'l Kabīr. . . . 51
Goldziher
Muhammadanische Studien . . . 37
Gospel to the Hebrews, Pseudo-Matthew, Thomas, etc. (see *Apocrypha N.T.*).
Gregentius (see *P.G.* 86, 621 ff.) . . . 66
Disputation with Herban the Jew . . . 73, 75, 80, 82 f.
Gregory I (*P.L.* 67, 1027) *ad Seren.* . . . 63
Gregory of Nazianzus (A.D. 330–390) (*P.G.* 35–38).
Orations (xl. 45) . . . 49
Eccles. Hist. (vii. 29) . . . 49
Gregory of Nyssa (335–394) . . . 48, 55, 73
Or. Cat. . . . 31
Translation of his *Nature of Man*, *Ṭabī'at ul Insān* . . . 89
Guillaume . . . 37, 66
Traditions of Islam . . . 37
Nihāyat ul Iqdām fī 'Ilmi'l-Kalām (see Shahrastānī).

H

Harnack
History of Dogma . . . 53
Homer
Iliad and *Odyssey* . . . 85, 91
Horovitz
Koranische Untersuchungen . . . 7, 9
Horten
Indische Strömungen in der Islamischen Mystic . . . 57
Ḥunayn b. Isḥāq (Syrian translator d. 873) . . . 66, 82, 87, 88, 89, 161

I

Ibās of Edessa (c. A.D. 457) Syrian translator . . . 50
Ibn Biṭrīq (Christian translator ninth century A.D.), see Yaḥyā b. B.
Ibn Ḥajar al Asqalānī (A.D. 1372–1449) . . . 37
Ibn Ḥanbal (A.D. 780–885) . . . 41
Ibn Ḥazm (b. A.D. 994) . . . 172
Ibn Hishām (d. A.D. 834) *Sīra* (Life of Muhammad) . . . 40
Ibn Khaldūn (A.D. 1332–1406)
Muqaddima . . . 171, 177
Ibn Khallikān
Biographical Dictionary (trans. De Slane) . . . 87, 88
Ibn Miskawaih (d. A.D. 1030) . . . 71, 86, 87
Al Fawz ul Aṣghar . . . 49, 55, 84, 92, 93
English Translation . . . 93–185
Tajārib ul Umam . . . 93
Ibn Qayyim ul Jawzīya (Shams ud Dīn thirteenth century A.D.)
Kitāb ul Qadr . . . 22
Ibn Rushd (Averroes A.D. 1126–1198) . . . 47
Kitāb Faṣl ul Maqāl fī mā baina'sh Sharī'ati wa'l Ḥikmati mina'l Itliṣāl . 172
Tahāfut ut Tahāfut (ed. Bouyges) . . . 51
Ibn Sīnā (Avicenna, also Bū 'Alī, A.D. 980–1037) . . 47, 51, 86, 90, 91, 92, 106
Ishārāt . . . 60
Najāt . . . 104, 116
Shifā . . . 52

Ibn Taimīya (A.D. 1263–1328) 172
Ar Raddu 'ala'l Manṭiq 51

Ignatius (d. c. A.D. 115)
Epp. ad Smyrn. et ad Trall. 58

Al Ījī ('Aḍud ud Dīn d. A.D. 1355)
Al Mawāqif fī 'Ilmi'l Kalām 64

Ikhwān uṣ Ṣafā (Brethren of Purity) *Risā'il* (Cairo 1928) 37

Inge
Philosophy of Plotinus 136

Irenæus (A.D. 130–200) 44, 45, 52
Haer. 52

Isḥāq b. Ḥunayn (d. A.D. 910), Syrian translator 88, 146

J

Jacob of Edessa
Enchiridion 85

Jalāl ud Dīn Rūmī (A.D. 1207–1273) 139
Mathnawī (ed. Nicholson) 30

James, M. R.
New Testament Apocrypha 30

Jeffery
Foreign Vocabulary of the Qur'ān 1, 6, 8, 14, 19, 21, 24, 25, 34, 35

Jerome (A.D. 345–420)
Com. on Mat. 34

Jilī
Al Insan ul Kāmil 49, 60

John of Damascus (Damascene d. c. A.D. 750) . . . . . 5, 16, 63 ff.
Disputatio Christiani et Saraceni (*P.G.* 94, 1585 ff.) . . . . . 64, 66 ff.
Disputatio Saraceni et Christiani 64
De Imaginibus (*P.G.* 94, 1376) 63
De Haeresibus (*P.G.* 94, 677 ff.) 64, 65, 68
Dialectica (*P.G.* 94, 525 ff.) 53, 64, 140
De Fide Orthodoxa 64

Bk. I, ii. (*P.G.* 94, 792) . 96, 110, 111, 147
(*P.G.* 94, 793) . . 111
iii. (*P.G.* 94, 793 f.) . 103
(*P.G.* 94, 796) . 95, 114
iv. (*P.G.* 94, 797) . 109, 110, 111, 112
(*P.G.* 94, 800) . . 113
viii. (*P.G.* 94, 816) . . 110
xi. (*P.G.* 94, 842) . . 147
xii. (*P.G.* 94, 845) . 99, 113

Bk. II, xii. (*P.G.* 94, 921) . . 163
(*P.G.* 94, 924) . . 119
(*P.G.* 94, 925) 95, 119, 163
(*P.G.* 94, 928) 132, 169, 173
xvi. (*P.G.* 94, 932) . . 164
xvii. (*P.G.* 94, 933) . 95, 169
xix. (*P.G.* 94, 937) . 168, 169
xx. (*P.G.* 94, 937 f.) . 168
(*P.G.* 94, 940) . . 169

Barlaam and Ioasaph (probably wrongly attributed to Damascene) . 16, 33, 35

John of Ephesus (*P.O.* xvii. 40) 15

John Philoponus (sixth century ? Yaḥyā Naḥwī, also John the Tritheist). 61, 87 f.
Com. on Nemistius on *Physics* of Arist. 94
Com. on *Physics* of Arist. 89

Jonathan b. Uzziel (see *Targum*).

Junilius Africanus (mid sixth century A.D.)
Institutio Regularia . . . . 86 f.

Justin Martyr (d. c. A.D. 165) 44, 53
Apol. (i. 46, 2) 71

Jubilees, Book of (see *Apocrypha O.T.*).

K

Kashf uẓ Ẓunūn (see Mustafa).
al Kindī (see 'Abdu'l Masīḥ b. Isḥāq).

L

Land
Anecdota Syriaca 87
Levonian
Studies in Relationship of Islam and Christianity 119
Liber de Causis 91, 106
Lombard, Peter (d. A.D. 1164)
Libr. IV Sententiarum (Vol. I, lib. i.) 95

M

Macdonald, D. B. (see also *E.I.*) 29, 33
Margoliouth (see also *E.R.E.*) 21
Schweich Lect. on Relations between Arabs and Israelites 1
Early Development of Mohammedanism 41
Massignon, L. 36, 57, 66
Mattā b. Yūnus (see Abū Bishr).
McGiffert
Dialogue of Papiscus and Philo. 72
Mas'ūdī
Les Prairies d'Or (ed. Barbier de Meynard, Paris, 1861–77) 87, 92
i. 19–20 . . . . . 92 iv. 8 91
i. 200 . . . . . . 58 iv. 61 . . . . . 88, 90
ii. 250 . . . . . . 90 iv. 64–66 84
iii. 68 . . . . . 90, 91 iv. 180 ff. 88
iii. 134 . . . . . 90, 91 vi. 385 f. 58
iii. 362 f. . . . . . 90 viii. 293 58
Midrash 9, 11
Mingana, A.
Syriac Influence on the Style of the Qur'ān 7, 8, 35
Timothy's Apology for Christianity . . 31, 36 ff., 68 ff., 72, 74–82 *passim*
Woodbrook Studies (ii. 37) 37
Synopsis of Christian Doctrine in the fourth century according to Theodore of Mopsuestia 42, 80
Kitāb ud Dīn wa Daula (by 'Ali Ṭabari) . . . . 66, 70 f.
Mishkāt ul Maṣābiḥ (compiler: Waliyu'd Dīn Abū 'Abdullāh Maḥmūd)
Riqāq 41
Fitan 37, 42
Mishna 26
Moslem World Quarterly (1925) 66
Muḥammad Bāqir
Rawḍat ul Jannāt 93
Muir, Sir Wm.
Apology of Al Kindy 66
Muslim
Ṣaḥīḥ (*Masājid* 236) 37
Mustafa b. 'Abdullāh Kātib Chelebī (see *Brock.* ii. 227 f.).
Kashf uẓ Ẓunūn 94

N

Nadīm (c. A.D. 980)
Fihrist 85, 87, 88, 89
331–370 87
342 91
343 88
344 . . . . 88, 89, 90
344 f. 90
352 . . . . 88, 90
353 90
354 91
355 . . . . 90, 91
356 . . . . 88, 94
357 . . . . 89, 90, 91
369 89
370 130
373 91
Nadhīr Aḥmad
Ḥuqūq wa Farā'iḍ i Islām 42
Naṣīr ud Dīn aṭ Ṭūsī (A.D. 1201–1272)
Akhlāq i Nāṣirī 143
Nemistius
Exposition of Aristotle's *Physics* 94
Nicholson, R. A. (see also Jalāl ud Dīn Rūmī) 57
Nicolaus
Com. on Aristotle 90
Nöldeke, Th. (see also Schwally-Nöldeke) 30
Sketches from Eastern History (art. *Qur'ān*) 12

O

Olympiodorus
Com. on Plato's *Sophist* 88, 90
Com. on Aristotle's *De Anima* 90
Onkelos (see *Targum*)
Origen (A.D. 185–254) 3, 44, 46, 47, 48, 50, 53, 55
De Principiis 48, 55
De Oratione 149
Com. in Joan 48
Com. in Mat. 48

P

Paulus Persa (Paul of Nisibis A.D. 530–380 ?) . . . . . 4, 86 f.
Logic 86
Philo (20 B.C. to A.D. 50) . . . . . 46 ff., 49, 53, 54, 71, 111, 114, 170
De Cherubim, 9 (i. 144) 53
31 (i. 158) 146
De Posteritate Caini, 6 (i. 229) 147
De Plantatione Noe, i. (i. 329) 147
De Migratione Abrahami, 7 (i. 441) 170
Quis Rerum Divinarum Heres., 53 (i. 511) 170
De Profugis (*De Fuga et Inventione*) 25
De Somniis, i. 22 (i. 641) and i. 32 (i. 649) 147
Vita Mosis, iii. 14 (ii. 155). 33
(The above references are to Tauchnitz, followed by Mangay in brackets, for uniformity, though in the text Cohn-Wendland has been referred to in some cases.)
Philostorgius (b. A.D. 368) 1
Pirke Aboth 11, 33
Plato 84, 91, 92, 95, 109, 133, 134, 137, 140, 157
Timæus 47, 92
translations, etc. 88, 89, 90
27D–28A 136
33B 149, 165
36B ff. 136
37D–38A 137
41A and B 134
44A and B 140
44D–45B. 165
70C and D 166
71 95

Plato—*continued.*

Laws, translations, etc. 88, 89, 90
895 A6–B2 . . . 104, 147 Bk. X 103
895 C-896C . . . 135, 136

Phædrus 139
translations, etc. 89, 90
245C . . 104 246A . . 135 246B . . 135

Phædo 92
translations, etc. 90, 140
81C . . . . . . 140 end 135

Parmenides 107
translations, etc. 90
142 . . . . . . 153 142B ff. 105

Sophist, translations, etc.. . . . . 88, 90
Republic, translations, etc. 88, 90

The following works are also mentioned :—
Alcibiades, *Apology of Socrates*, *Athleticus* (?), *Clitipho*, *Crito*, *Cratylus*, *Charmides*, *Euthydemus*, *Euthrypo*, *Gorgias*, *Hipparchus*, *Hippias*, *Ion*, *Laches*, *Minos*, *Menexenus*, *Meno*, *Politicus*, *Protagoras*, *Theages*, *Theætetus*, *Thaion* and a *Geometry*. 89–90

Plotinus (A.D. 205–270) . . . . . 5, 46 f., 91, 111, 113, 140, 170
Enneads 91
I, i. 3 f. 98
I, ii. 5 . . . . 139, 140
I, iii. 5. 97
I, iv. 5 154
I, iv. 10 . . . 154, 156
I, iv. 12 155
I, vi. 9 139
I, viii. 5 97
I, viii. 7 134
I, viii. 8 134
I, viii. 10 . . 134, 140, 154
II. ix. 2 139
III, i. 9 140
III, ii. 2 107
III, vi. 2 144
III, vi. 5 139
III, vii. 11 136
III, viii. 8 139
IV, iii. 9 137
IV, iii. 15 154
IV, iii. 17 137
IV, iv. 1 136
IV, v. 9 153
IV, vii. 9–12 135
IV, vii. 13 139
IV, viii. 5 124
IV, ix. 3 125
V, i. 3 137
V, i. 6 138
V, i. 10 153
V, ii. 1 . . . . . 124, 139
V, iii. 6 148
V, iii. 9 140
V, vi. 2 153
V, viii. 1 138
VI, iv. 16 . . . . 135, 139
VI, v. 9 106
VI, viii. 11 . . . . 112, 153
VI, ix. 3 . . . . . 148, 153
VI, ix. 9 140
(Creuzer and Moser's edition and translation by S. McKenna.)

Plutarch 85, 91

Porphyry . . . . 86, 91, 99, 100, 107, 108 f., 136, 146
Life of Plotinus 99
Aphorisms 136, 139, 140
Isagoge 90, 93, 140
Com. on Categories 88, 90
Com. on Ethics 88, 90
Com. on Prior Analytics 90
Com. on Physics 85, 89, 94

Proclus 5, 47, 88, 90, 134, 147, 170
Elements of Theology 90, 91, 106, 147
Prop. 5 107
9 105
14 104
17 124
20 . . . . . 135, 136
21 106
33 136
40 ff. 105
46 105
56 ff. 113
62 106
64 138
80 128
Prop. 81–83 124
87 and 105 137
111 151
123 153
124 153
167 153
186 . . . . . 119, 130
187 135
188 and 189 135
195 118
197 128
199–200 136
(Creuzer and Moser edition.)
Platonic Theology 147
Comm. on *Phædo* and *Gorgias* 90
Com. on *Timæus* 90, 170
Com. on *Republic* 90, 170
Shorter Elements of Theology 90
Protevangelium of James (see *Apocrypha N.T.*).
Pseudo-Dionysius 47, 91
Divine Names 107, 111
Mystical Theology 111
Celestial Hierarchy 151

Q

Qusṭa b. Luqā (fl. A.D. 835), Syrian translator 89, 94, 161

S

Sam'u'l Kiyān or *Sam'u'ṭ Ṭabī'ī*, Arabic name for Aristotle's *Physics* . . . 94
Sanūsī
Catechism 113
Sbath
Vingt Traités philosophiques et apologetiques d'auteurs arabes chrétiens . 66, 82
Schwally-Nöldeke
Geschichte des Qorans 1
Schwally
Idioticon 34
Shahrastānī 91
Nihāyat ul Iqdām fī 'Ilmi'l Kalām (ed. Guillaume) 66
Al Milal wa'n Nihal (Cureton) 85, 87
Shibli Na'mīnī
'Ilm ul Kalām 52, 56
Simplicius 86, 91
Comm. on *De Cœlo*, *De Anima*, *Categories*, etc. 86, 90
Com. on *Physics* 86, 90, 115
Steinschneider
Die Arabischen Übersetzungen aus den Griechischen 88
Stephen of Alexandria, Commentator on *Hermeneutics* and *Categories* . . . 89
Studia Sinaitica (vii and viii) 66, 72, 75, 78
As Suyāṭī (A.D. 1445–1505)
Mutawakkilī 7

T

Talmud . . . . 8 ff., 24, 23
Abodah Zarah 11
Berachoth 14
Chagiga 34
Erubin 34
Gebhamoth 36
Kethuboth 36
Sanhedrin . . 9, 10, 11, 23
Targum
of Jonathan b. Uzziel . . 10
of Onkelos 10
of *Canticles* 26
of *2nd Esther* 12
Taylor
Plato's Parmenides 107
Tertullian (latter half of second century) 53, 57
Adv. Prax. 60
Testament of Abraham (see *Apocrypha O.T.* and Charles, R. H.).
Testament of the Twelve Patriarchs (see *Apocrypha O.T.* and Charles, R. H.).
Thābit b. Qurra (translator) 85, 94
Themistius 90, 91
Com. on *De Anima* 125
Com. on *Physics* 94
Comm. on *De Coelo, Poetics and Topics* 88, 89
Theodore Abucara (Abū Qurra) 66, 68, 69, 73, 82
Theodore of Mopsuestia (d. A.D. 428) 29, 50, 61, 62
Synopsis (ed. Mingana) . . . . 41 f., 80
Theodore: translator of *Prior Analytics* of Aristotle into Arabic ? . . 88, 89
Theophilus of Edessa (d. A.D. 785), translator of Aristotle into Syriac . . 89
Theophilus of Edessa (d. A.D. 785), translator of Homer into Syriac . . 85
Timothy, Nestorian Catholicus (see Mingana).
At Tirmiḏhī (d. 892) 42
Tor Andræ
Der Ursprung des Islams und das Christentum 1, 33, 35
Muhammad: the Man and his Faith (Eng. trans.) 2, 15, 16, 34

V

Vita Adæ et Evæ (see *Apocrypha O.T.* and Charles, R. H.).

W

Wensinck
Muslim Creed (see also *E.I.*) 113
Wright
Comparative Grammar of Semitic Languages 24
Short History of Syriac Lit. 85

Y

Yaḥyā b. 'Adī (see Abū Zakarīya').
Yaḥyā b. Biṭriq (ninth century) 88, 89
Yaḥyā Naḥwī (see John Philoponus).
Ya'qūbī
Tā'rīkh 37
Yāqūt
Dictionary of Famous Men (ed. Margoliouth) 93

INDEX OF SCRIPTURAL PASSAGES

GENESIS . . 22
i. 1 . . . 19
26 . . . 76
ii. 7 . . . 19
iv. 3 ff. . . 8
vii. . . . 8
xxv. 22 . . 7
xxx. 22 . . 19
xxxi. 49 . . 20
EXODUS . . 11
vii. 1 . . . 74
xix. . . . 7
xxii. 23 and 27 . 19
xxiii. 14 . . 7
xxv. 9 and 40 . 26
LEVITICUS . . 35
ii. 4 . . . 35
vii. 18 . . 19
ix. 24 . . . 13
xvii. 4. . . 19
xix. 9 ff. . . 36
xxvi. 25 . . 19
xxvi. 44 . . 83
NUMBERS . . 35
xviii. 27 . . 19
xxii. 28 . . 19
xxiv. 11 . . 20
xxvii. 8–11 . 36
DEUTERONOMY
v. 26 . . . 19
vi. 4 . . . 21
vii. 9 . . . 18
ix. 4 f. . . 69
x. 17 . . . 19
xiv. 28 f. . . 36
xix. 4–13, 15–21 . 36
xxi. 10 ff., 15–17 . 36
xxiv. 1 . . 36
xxviii. 12 . . 19
66 ff. . . 75
xxx. 3–4 . . 19
xxxii. 22 . . 34
JUDGES
iii. 9 . . . 19
xxi. 19 . . 7
RUTH
i. 21 . . . 20
1 SAMUEL
ii. 7 . . . 20
xi. 13 . . . 8
xxv. 26 . . 20
2 SAMUEL
vi. 6 ff. . . 18
vii. 18 . . 13
xii. 6 . . . 34
xxiv. 23 . . 20
1 KINGS
v. 13 . . . 12
viii. 30 ff. . . 19
xii. . . . 183
xxii. 21 . . 23
2 KINGS
xix. 22 . . 18
2 CHRONICLES
ix. 29 . . . 24
NEHEMIAH
x. 34 . . . 35
JOB
xix. 9 . . . 19
xxviii. 22 . . 34
xxxiv. 28 . . 19
xxxvi. 5 . . 19
PSALMS . 12, 24, 70
ii. 7 . . . 72
iii. 8 . . . 19
xviii. 26 . . 19
xix. 1 ff. . . 22
xxi. 3 . . . 20
xxii. 16–18 . . 79
xxiii. 4 . . 34
xxiv. 8 . . 19
xxx. 6. . . 76
xxxiii. 6 . . 75
xxxvi. 5 . 18, 19
xl. 2 . . . 34
17 . . . 19
xliv. 2. . . 20
xlv. 2–5 . . 71
xlvii. 9 . . 19
xlviii. 1–2 . . 71
xlix. 10 . . 20
l. 2–3 . . . 71
li. 15 . . . 19
lv. 24 . . . 34
lvi. 10 . . 75
lxii. 2 . . . 19
lxv. 20 . . 19
lxxii. 4 . . 19
lxxxviii. 6 . . 34
lxxxix. 1 . . 18
xciv. 8 and 9 . 19
xcv. 6 . . . 13
xcvii. 9 . . 19
cii. 26 . . 20
civ. 5 . . . 75
28 . . . 19
cvii. 3 . . 19
cx. 2 . . . 75
cxix. 89 . . 75
108 . . 20
ECCLESIASTES
ii. 8 . . . 12
ECCLESIASTES
ix. 7 . . . 20
xii. 1 . . . 19
CANTICLES
ii. 14 . . . 34
ISAIAH . . . 22
ii. 12 ff. . . 71
vi. 3 . . . 76
ix. 6 . . 19, 71
xxi. 1–14 . . 71
xxix. 11 . . 75
xl. 8 . . . 75
12–26 . . 22
28 . . . 19
xliii. 1. . . 19
xliv. 6. . . 20
9 and 20 . 21
xlvii. 3 . . 19
11 . . . 34
xlviii. 16 . . 76
xlix. 7. . . 18
l. 10–17 . . 18
liii. 5 . . . 79
liv. 7 . . . 19
lxi. 2 . . . 19
lxiii. 11 . . 20
lxv. 24 . . 19
lxvi. 18 . . 19
JEREMIAH . . 71
v. 9 . . . 19
ix. 9 . . . 19
x. 10 . . . 19
xi. 19 . . . 79
xiv. 10 . . 20
xxv. 17–38 . . 27
xxix. 13 . . 7
xxxi. 32–34 . . 81
31 f. . . 18
28 . . . 20
xxxii. 18, 37 . 19
LAMENTATIONS .
i. 5 . . . 20
iii. 4, 30 . . 79
EZEKIEL . . 71
vii. 26 . . 34
viii. 5–18 . . 21
xvi. 37 . . 34
xx. 40–41 . . 20
28 . . . 35
xxii. 19–20 . . 19
xxxi. 15 . . 20
xxxiii. 22 . . 19
xxxviii.–xxxix . 34
xl. 43 . . . 35
xliii. 27 . . 20

Daniel . . . 71
ii. 21 . . . 19
iv. 37 . . . 21
vi. 20, 26 . . 19
ix. 14 . . . 20
26 . . . 79
x. 21 . . . 26
Hosea . . . 71
vii. 16 . . 19
ix. 1 . . . 19
Joel
ii. 28–30 . . 81
iii. 2 . . . 19
Amos . . . 22
v. 6–11 . . 18
Micah . . . 71
ii. 12 . . . 19
Habakkuk . . 71
i. 12–13 . . 18
iii. 3 . . . 75
viii. . . . 27
Zephaniah . . 71
iii. 17 . . . 19
Haggai .
i. 10–11 . . 27
ii. 17 . . . 27

Zechariah . . 71
i. 12 . . . 23
xiii. 7 . . . 79
xiv. 12–19 . . 27
St. Matthew . 48, 81
iii. 7 . . . 34
v. 28 f. . . 40
vi. 26 ff. . . 22
vii. 39 . . 32
xviii. 9 . . 40
xix. 17 . . 74
29 . . 34
xxviii. 19 . . 75
St. Mark . . 81
vii. 11 . . 35
23. . . 36
xii. 29. . . 21
xiii. 32 . . 34
St. Luke . 13, 81
iv. 1 . . . 32
xvi. 24–25 . . 12
St. John . 12, 48, 81
i. 1, 4 . . . 75
v. 28 . . . 34
vi. 34 f. . . 13
41 . . . 13

St. John
vii. 39 . . . 32
ix. 31 . . . 40
x. 11 . . . 74
xiv. . . . 12
xiv. 1, 2, 11. . 13
16 . . 33
26 . . 32
xv. 26 . . 33
xvi. 13 . . 33
26 . . 33
xvii. 5. . . 75
xx. 17. . 32, 73
22. . . 33
The Acts
xix. 12 . . 36
1 Corinthians
ii. 9 . . . 37
viii. 4–6 . . 21
Galatians
iv. 22–26 . . 71
Hebrews
i. 1–2 . . . 24
xi. 3 . . . 22
1 John
ii. 1 . . . 33
Revelation . . 23

INDEX OF QURANIC PASSAGES

Sura II
27 34
32 23
33 23
35 19
37 7
46–49 . . . 11
48 ff. . . . 11
50 8
51 19
57 11
63 29
81 33
91 f. . . . 23
96 12
102 7
106 7
107 22
114, 124 . . . 8
125 7
126, 128 . . . 10
130 27
132 8
138 22
167, 175 . . . 36
181 8
226 36
228 f., 233 . . . 36
248 ff. . . . 11
249 21
250 12
256 19
257, 268 . . . 35
269 f. . . . 36
286 35
Sura III . . . 13
2 8
3, 6 . . . 19
9 7
25 20
28 22
30 10
30 ff. . . . 11
30–44 . . . 13
40 . . 13, 29, 33
42 29
43 . . . 13, 26
48 79
52 . . . 29, 68
60 10
73 7
86 36
89 . . . 8, 22
113 8
134 7
183 26
Sura IV
7 19
10 34
12 ff. . . . 36
20 19
24, 26 f. and 28 . 36
46 14
67 19
71 7
88 19
94 . . . 35, 36
112 35
129 19
152 11
156 . 8, 30, 33, 79
161 12
169 29, 31, 33, 65, 68
170 . . . 30, 33
Sura V . . . 12
8 14
8 f. . . . 36
19 33
23 ff. . . . 11
30–36 . . . 10
37 8
46 35
49 36
50 27
67, 68 . . . 35
73 ff. . . . 27
74 31
76 . . . 31, 33
79 . . 28, 30, 33
82 12
85 8
89 f. . . . 36
96 19
109 23
112 ff. . . . 12
114 13
116 . . . 32, 68
119 20
end 12
Sura VI
14 21
31 34
38 20
50 82
57–8 . . . 29
61 23
79 10
84 12
95 ff., 115 . . 22
138 ff. . . . 36
Sura VII
28 29
Sura VII
48 12
52 29
57 ff. . . . 10
101, 125 . . . 11
127–139 and 130 . 11
139 7
142 25
154, 160 . . . 11
Sura VIII
29, 42 . . . 8
Sura IX
5, 18 . . . 36
26 21
30 f. . 2, 31, 33, 59
36 26
40 21
40 ff. . . . 22
60, 104 . . . 36
105, 119 . . . 19
Sura X
3 . . . 22, 29
76–93 . . . 11
79 21
90 ff. . . . 11
Sura XI
5–8 26
42 10
43, 45, 69 . . 29
72 . . . 9, 10
78, 84 . . . 29
99–101 . . . 11
123 29
Sura XII . . . 10
67 11
102 21
107 33
Sura XIII
2 29
12 23
31 33
Sura XIV
48 19
Sura XV
44 34
Sura XVI
3 ff. . . . 22
35 29
48 f. . . . 22
104 23
124 10
Sura XVII
5 ff. . . . 27
33 35
46 34
57 12

SURA XVII
61 . . . 69
62 ff. . . 9
70 f. . . . 27
87 . . . 29
103 . . . 11
SURA XVIII
15 . . . 29
48 . . 23, 29
93–97 . . 34
SURA XIX
1–39 . . 13
14 . . . 21
17 . . . 76
29 . . . 11
34 . . . 79
36 . . 28, 31
38 . . . 27
56 . . . 29
57 f. . . . 10
94 . . . 30
SURA XX
8–82 . . 11
65 . . . 29
82 ff. . . 11
92 . . . 29
95 ff. . . 11
108 . . . 20
113 . . . 21
SURA XXI
48 . . . 21
49 . . . 8
78–81 and 78 f. . 12
91 . . . 76
98 . . . 22
104 . . . 34
SURA XXII
41 . . . 8
55 . . . 22
61 . . . 19
64 . . . 22
66 . . 26, 29
69 . . . 26
74 . . . 30
SURA XXIII
17 . . . 34
47–51 . . 11
52 . . . 13
54 f. . . . 29
88 . . . 34
90 . . . 21
SURA XXIV
10 . . . 19
35 . . . 60
35 f. . . . 2
SURA XXV
1 . . . 8
48, 60 . . 19
SURA XXVI
9-69 . . 11
SURA XXVII
13–15 . . 11
13–16, 15 f. and
20 ff. . . 12
76 . . . 26
SURA XXVIII
2–45 . . 11
7 . . . 35
76–85 . . 11
SURA XXIX
13 . . . 10
39 . . . 27
SURA XXXII
22 . . . 19
23–24 . . 29
SURA XXXIII
6 . . . 26
39 . . . 19
SURA XXXIV
10–12 . . 12
11 . . 12, 29
21 f., 25 . . 19
SURA XXXV
12 and 28 . . 26
SURA XXXVI
13 ff. . . 12
33 . . . 7
SURA XXXVII
21 . . . 33
99 . . . 10
SURA XXXVIII
6 . . . 8
8 . . . 19
16–29 and 35 . 12
71–79 . . 9
SURA XXXIX
47 . . 21, 22
67 . . . 19
69 . . . 7
SURA XL
12 . . . 19
24–49 . . 11
28 . . . 33
67 . . . 19
82 . . . 35
SURA XLI
8–11 . . 22
11 . . . 34
12 ff. . . 27
SURA XLII
2 . . . 19
3 . . . 23
9 . . . 21
17 . . . 34
26, 50 f. . . 19
SURA XLIII
45–55 . . 11
59 . . 28, 30
60 . . . 28
61 . . . 34
77 . . . 34
SURA XLV
16 . . . 29
36 . . . 21
SURA XLVI
19 . . . 12
SURA XLVII
2 . . . 35
SURA XLVIII
4, 18 and 26 . 21
29 . . . 15
SURA XLIX
12 . . . 19
SURA L
4 . . . 26
8 . . . 30
SURA LII
25–28 . . 19
SURA LIII
33 . . . 19
SURA LIV
46 . . . 34
SURA LV
27 . . . 20
SURA LVI
36 . . . 34
SURA LVII
3 . . . 20
7 . . . 36
9 . . . 22
12 ff. . . 12
18 . . . 7
27–29 . . 2
SURA LIX
15–16 . . 29
23 . . 18, 19, 21
24 . . . 19
SURA LXI
6 ff. . 27, 33
SURA LXII
1 . . 18, 21
5 . . . 8
SURA LXV
1 . . . 29
12 . . . 34
SURA LXVI
12 . . . 11
SURA LXVII
3 . . . 34
SURA LXVIII
17 ff. . . 35
SURA LXIX
9 . . . 35
17 . . . 23
SURA LXXI
14 . . 34
28 . . . 35
SURA LXXII . . 24
19 . . . 24
SURA LXXIII
1–4 and 20 ff. . 14

Sura LXXIV
1–7 . . . 34
30 f. . . . 24
Sura LXXVIII .
12 . . . 34
Sura LXXIX
15–29 . . 11
27 ff. . . 22
Sura LXXX
24 ff. . . 22
33 . . . 33
Sura LXXXII . 23
14 . . . 35
Sura LXXXV
5 ff. . . 1
10–13 . . 34
22 . . . 25
Sura LXXXVII
19 . . . 10
Sura LXXXVIII
16 ff. . . 22
Sura XCI
1 ff. . . 22
Sura XCII
2 . . . 7
Sura XCVI
3–5 . . . 4
Sura CI
6 . . . 34
Sura CX .
3 . . . 19
Sura CXII .
3 . . . 65
Sura CXIII . . 22

INDEX OF ARABIC AND PERSIAN WORDS AND PHRASES

A

abadī . . . 130
'abd . . . 30
adghāthu'l 'aḥlām . 177
'adhāb . . . 51
aḥadīya . . . 109
'ālam . . . 8
'ālam ṣaghīr . . 163
'amal . . . 113
'āmm wa khāṣṣ . 54 f.
amr or *amar* . . 29
amr Rabbī . . 29
amr Ullāh . . 60
'anāṣir (pl. of *'unṣur*) 121
anīya . . . 109
'anqā' . . . 121
'aql . . . 60
al 'aqlu'l fa''āl . 113
al 'aqlu'l mufāriq . 115
al asmāu' ḥusnā . 20
'arūb . . . 34
awhām (pl. of *wahm*) 95
āya . . . 7
'ayn . . . 64
azalī . . . 130

B

badīhī . . . 99
Barz ul Bārī . . 137
basa'iṭ . . . 121
bid'a . . . 57
bi'l fi'l . . . 102
bi'l quwwa . . 102
bi'ṭ ṭab' . . . 102
burhān mustaqīm . 112
burhān khilfī . . 112
buṭlān . . . 133

D

darasa . . . 7
darūrī . . . 99
dhabūl . . . 103
dhakka . . . 35
dīn . . . 7

F

fāḍil . . . 146
fā'il . . . 137
fājir . . . 35
fānī . . . 114
fasād . . . 103
fayd . . 113, 153
fi'l . . . 64
fi'līya . . . 126
fi'l khārij . . 121
fi'llāh . . . 37
Fiqh . . 35, 37
Firdaus . . . 34
furqān . . 8, 81

G

ghayr hayūlānī . 120
ghayr mursal . . 180

H

ḥādith . . . 130
Ḥajj . . . 7
ḥamd . . . 71
ḥāmil . . . 116
ḥanān . . . 21
ḥaqīqa . . . 60
hayūlānī . . 120, 126
hayūlī . . . 115
ḥulūl . . 61, 116
hūwīya . . . 109

I

ibdā' . . . 117
Iblīs . . . 24
iḍmiḥlāl . . . 103
iḍāfa . . . 64
idrāk . . . 101
iḥsās . . 101, 125
Ījād ush shay'i lā min shay'in . . 117
ilhām . . 51, 141
'Ilmu'l Kalām . . 51 f.
imām . . . 180
infi'āl . . 64, 125
inḥilāl . . . 117
inḥiṭāṭ . . 139, 155
injīl . . 24, 81
ishtimāl . . . 150
ishtirāk . . . 106
islām . . . 7
Isrā' . . . 40
istiḥāla . . . 103
istiqṣāt . . . 121
ithbātu'l Fā'il . . 51
ittiḥād . . . 61

J

jabbār . . . 19
jalsa . . . 15
jamād . . . 103
jawhar . . . 64
jihād . . . 69
jinn . . 23, 24
jism . . . 115
jummār . . . 160

K

kaffara . . . 35
kaif (*kayf*) . . 64
kalām . . 51 f., 64
kalima . . 29, 139
kam . . . 64
kawn . . . 103
kayfīya . . 103, 116
khabr . . 175, 177
khalīfa . . . 180
khaṭi'a . . . 35
kibriyā' . . . 21

L

Lāhūt . . . 39
lawḥ . . . 25

M

ma'anī . . . 181
ma'ārif . . . 183
madīna . . . 142
madrasa . . . 7
mafhūmāt kulliya . 120
maḥmūd . . . 71
ma'ida . . . 12
al majāzu qantaratu'l ḥaqīqa . . 48
malak . . . 23
malaka . . . 64
malakūt . . . 21
maqāmāt . . . 148

maqūlāt . . . 128
ma'qūl and *ma'qūlāt* 120, 127
masjid . . . 8
matā . . . 64
mat͟hal . . . 8
mawḍū' . . 128, 130
milla . . . 8
Mi'rāj . . . 40
mit͟hāl . . . 139
mizāj . . . 118
muḥaddat͟h . . 110
mu'jib . . . 109
mu'jib . . . 176
mu'jiza . . 51, 82
mujra . . . 176
mu'min . . . 18
munājāt . . . 180
muqarrabūn . . 29
muqawwimāt . . 131
mursal . . . 180
mushāhada . . 99
mushrikūn . . 65
muslim . . . 7
mutakawwan . . 110
mutakallimūn 51 f., 178
mutammim . . 103
mutanabbī . . 184
mut͟hul . . . 137

N

nabī . . . 24
nabuwwa . . 24, 51
nafs . . . 114
nafs nāṭiqa . . 133
namw . . . 103
Nāsūt . . . 39
naẓar . . 99, 113
nīya . . . 14

Q

qadīm . . . 130
qādir muk͟htār . . 109
qalam . . . 8
qibla (not the word). 14
qirā'a . . . 14
qissisūn . . . 8
qisṭ . . . 21
qiyām . . . 15
qiyāma . . . 34
quddūs . . . 18
qudus . . . 25
qurbān . . 17, 35
quwwa ḥaiwānīya . 95

R

Rabb . . 21, 31
rasūl . . . 30
riḍwān . . . 20
risāla . . . 163
riyāḍīya . . . 98
rūḥ . . 32, 163
rujz . . . 34
ru'ya . . . 51

S

sa'a . . . 34
sabab murakkab . 106
sabīl . . . 7
sajada . . . 7
sakīna . . . 21
ṣalaba . . . 8
ṣalāt . . . 14
ṣāliḥ . . . 146
ṣalla . . . 14
sam' . . . 175
ṣawāmi' . . . 8
ṣawm . . . 17
Sharī'a . 35, 51, 183
Shaiṭān, pl. *shayāṭīn* 24
shay' ma'qūl . . 127
shuhudā' . . . 7
ṣibg͟ha . . . 8
sifr (*sepher*) . . 8
sijda . . . 15
ṣubḥān . . . 14
ṣudūr . . . 113
suḥt . . . 35
sunna . . . 49
ṣūra . . . 115
ṣuwar hayūlānī . 116
ṣuwar d͟hihnīya . 121

T

ta'addud ul amt͟hāl . 109
ta'aqqul . . . 125
ta'at͟ht͟hur . . 169
ṭabī'a . . 102, 150
ṭab'īyāt . . . 95
tadbīr . . . 150
tag͟hayyur . . 136
ṭāg͟hūt . . . 35
tajalla . . . 7
takawwun . 110, 136
talqīḥ . . . 160
tamaddun . . 142
tanazzul . . . 155
taqīya . . . 54
taqlīd . . . 54
tarwīya . . . 7
tasalsul . . . 115
taṣbīḥ . . . 14
tas͟hbīh . . . 78
ta'ṭīl . . . 78
ta'wīl . . . 101
Tawrāt . . . 24
t͟hawāb . . . 51
ṭūfān . . . 10

U

'ulūm riyāḍīya . 98
ummu'l kitāb . . 25

W

wad' . . . 64
waḥī 51, 170, 180, 181
al Wāḥid . 106 f.
al wāḥid lā yaṣdiru 'anahu illa'l wāḥid 106
wahm . . . 121
Wājibu' l Wujūd . 105
wājib . . . 42
wuqūf . . . 7

Y

yawmu'd dīn . . 7
yawmu'l faṣl . . 33
yawmu'l ḥisāb . . 33

Z

Zabūr . . . 24
zajr . . . 179
zakā . . . 35
Zandaqa . . . 73

(See also List of Arabic Names for God.)

LIST OF LATIN WORDS AND PHRASES

argumentatio ex absurdo . . . 112
capita philosophica . 64
creatio ex nihilo & ex nihilo . . 87, 116
continuum . . 159
disciplina arcani . 55, *cf.* 49
ex necessitate naturæ 109
ex nihilo nihil fit . 116
in sensu eminentiori 113
phantasma . . 169
plenum . . 96, 129
predicamenta . 64, 128
primum mobile 137, 150
Primum Movens 106, 109, 110
solvitur ambulando . 56
subjectum . . 128
suppositum . 116, 130
tabula rasa . . 127
via negativa . . 111

Latin quotations as follows :—
from Jerome . 34
Cicero . 140
Porphyry . 136
John of Damascus 140

LIST OF HEBREW, ARAMAIC AND SYRIAC WORDS

Abaddon . . 34
'amidah . . . 15
b^e^er-shakhath . . 34
beshem Adonai eqra . 14
bōr-shā'ōn . . 34
^e^meth . . . 22
erets-teḥtīth . . 34
gibbor . . . 19
ḥēn . . . 21
ḥeṣed . . . 22
kawwana . . 14
KPR (root) . . 20
Lāhūt & nāsūt . . 39
memra . . . 29
midrash . . . 7
peraqlīt . . . 33
qeri'a . . . 14
rabban . . . 31
rabbi . . . 31
RTSH . . . 20
s^e^darim . . . 26
sepher . . . 8
sheol . . . 34
SHWB (root) . . 19
ṭīṭ-ha-yāwen . . 34
tsal-māweth . . 34
tsedeq . . . 22
TWB . . . 19
YSH' . . . 19

INDEX OF GREEK WORDS

ἀθάνατος, 137
ἀΐδιος, 137
αἰώνος, 137
ἁμαρτία, 35, 144
ἀμερής, 128
αὔξησις, 103
ἐγενέτο ἄνθρωπος οὐ συνήφθη ἀνθρώπῳ, 28
ἐξερρύη, 113
ἑταιριστάς, 65
ἔχειν, 64
ἐξ ἑνὸς νοῦ, 106
θεωρία, 113
καλαμος, 8
κεῖσθαι, 64
κόπτας, 65
νοερός, 151
νοῦς πα θητικός, 125
νοῦς ποιητικός, 113
οὐσία, 64
τὸ ὄν, 137
παράκλητος, 33
περικλυτός, 33
πάσχειν, 64
παρε κεφαλίς, 169
ποιεῖν, 64
ποιόν, 64
ποσόν, 64
ποτέ, 64
ποῦ, 64
πρᾶξις, 113
πρόοδος, 113
πρός τι, 64
Σάρρας κενούς, 65
σημεῖον, 7
σωματικός, 151
ὕλη, 115, 126
ὑπερερρύη, 113
ψυχικός, 151

Other common words appear in the Subject Index

ARABIC NAMES OF GOD

For convenience are included not only names which occur in the text, but those which are usually contained in list of the *Asmā u'l ḥusna*, the Ninety-nine most Beautiful Names of God with some additional which occur in the Qur'ān. The meanings given are common, but there is doubt in certain cases. Names marked * are discussed more fully in Vol. 2.

Allāh, the proper name of God.
al 'Afūw, the Pardoner.
al Ākhir, the Last.
al 'Alī, the Lofty, 19
al 'Adl, the Equity.
al 'Alīm, the Knower.
al Awwal, the First.
al 'Aẓīm, the Magnificent.
al 'Azīz, the Mighty.
al Badī', the Maker at the beginning.
al Bā'ith, the Sender.
al Bāqī, the Abiding, 20
al Bārī, the Creator, 19
al Barr, the Pure, 19
al Baṣīr, the Seeing.
al Basīṭ, the Spreader (sometimes the Simple), 19
al Bāṭin, the Inward or Intrinsic.
aḍ Dārr, the Hurter, 20
Dhi't Ṭawl, Long-suffering, He who waits a long time.
Dhu'l Jalāl wa'l Ikrām, Glorious and Benevolent.
al Fāṭir, the Creator, 21
al Fattāḥ, the Opener, 19
**al Ghaffār*, Great Forgiver, 20
**al Ghāfir*, the Forgiver.
**al Ghafūr*, Forgiving much.
**al Ghanī*, the Rich or Independent.
al Hādī, the Guide.
al Ḥafīẓ, the Watcher or Keeper.
al Ḥakam, the Judge.
al Ḥakīm, the Wise.
**al Ḥalīm*, the Mature or Clement.
al Ḥamīd, the Laudable.
**al Ḥaqq*, the Real.
al Ḥasīb, the Reckoner, 19
al Ḥayy, the Living, 19
al Jabbār, the Overcomer, 19
**al Jābir*, the Forcer.
al Jāmi', the Gatherer.
**al Kabīr*, the Great, 19
al Karīm, the Condescending.
al Khabīr, the Watchful, 20
al Khāfiḍ, the Abaser.
al Khāliq, the Creator.
al Laṭīf, the Subtle, Rare or Gracious.
al Mājid, the Noble.
al Majīd, the Glorious.
Mālik ul Mulk, the Master of the Kingdom.
al Malik, the King, 21
al Māni', the Hinderer, 20
al Matīn, the Firm.
**al Mu'akhkhir*, the Deferrer.

al Mubdī, the Beginner.
**al Muḍill*, the Misleader.
al Mudhill, the One who renders despicable.
al Mughnī, the Enricher.
al Muhaimin, the Protector, 21
al Muḥyī, Giver of Life.
al Muḥṣī, the Surrounder.
al Mu'īd, the One who sends back.
al Mu'izz, the Giver of Honour.
al Mujīb, the Acceptor.
al Mu'min, the One who keeps in peace ? 18
al Muntaqim, the Avenger, 19
al Mumīt, the One who causes to die.
al Muqaddim, the Preceder or the One who advances (another), 20
al Muqaddir, the Predestinator.
al Muqīt, the One who gives power.
al Muqsiṭ, the Equitable, 21
al Muqtadir, the Powerful.
al Murīd, the Purposer.
al Muṣawwir, the Former (Fashioner), 19
al Muta'ālī, the Self-exalted.
al Mutakabbir, the Haughty.
**al Mutakallim*, the Speaker.
an Nāfi', the Profiter or the One who confers benefit.
an Nūr, the Light.
al Qābiḍ, the Fastener, 19
**al Qadir*, the Powerful (sometimes *al Qādir ul Muṭlaq*, the absolutely powerful).
**al Qadīr*, the Powerful (intrinsically).
**al Qā'il*, the Sayer.
al Qahhār, the Violent, sometimes the Wrathful.
**Qābil ut tawb*, the Acceptor of Repentance.
**al Qarīb*, the Near.
al Qawī, the Powerful or Strong.
**al Qayyūm*, the Established or Self-subsistent, 21
al Quddūs, the Transcendentally Holy, 18
ar Rāḍī, the Propitious, 20
ar Rafi', the Uplifter, the One who raises on high.
**ar Raḥīm*, the Merciful.
**ar Raḥmān*, the Merciful (Proper Name ?), 21
ar Raqīb, the (jealous) Guardian.
ar Rashīd, the Right.
**ar Ra'ūf*, the Kind or Pitiful, 22
**ar Razzāq*, the Provider of daily provision, 21
**aṣ Ṣabūr*, the Patient 20 (note).
as Ṣalām, the Secure.
**aṣ Ṣamad*, the Eternal (?).
as Samī', the Hearer, 19
ash Shakūr, the One who renders the thankful their due (?).
**at Tamām*, the Complete.
**at Tawwāb*, the Great Repenter (Relenter), 19
al Wahhāb, the Great Giver, 19
**al Wāḥid*, the One, 106 f.
al Wājid, the Finder.
**Wājib ul Wujūd*, Necessary Existence, 105
**al Wakīl*, the Agent.
al Wāli, Patron.
al Walī, the Friend.
al Wārith, the Heir, or Rightful Owner.
al Wāsi', the Ample.
**al Wudūd*, the Lcving.
aẓ Ẓāhir, the Manifest or Extrinsic.

Printed in the United States
88138LV00004B/92/A

9 780227 171974